*The end of World War II* ~~struggle for power than t~~ ~~colorful figures in this int~~ *Patton and Hitler's deputy, Rudolph Hess.*

**General Patton was killed as a result of a dubious** accident, the mystery of which has never been solved and has been magnified by government refusal to declassify the file on the investigation of his death.

**Far more conspicuous and powerful was Rudolph Hess,** Deputy Fuhrer of Germany, who flew to England in 1941 as an envoy of peace and was imprisoned for life and suspiciously killed just before his imminent release.

**The current of intrigue and power which permeated these** two individuals and led to their downfall was the same current which led to a repatriazation of the U.S. Government and an undermining of a constitutional government that is run by and for the people.

**Patton and Hess wore different uniforms, but they both** shared common interests destined to link them in the strangest of ways. These included a strong hatred of communists and, more importantly, a strong interest in and belief in the occult. What is little known and completely unsuspected, however, is that both had within their grasp a force so powerful that, if properly harnessed, it might raise the ancient civilization of Atlantis itself. It was for this power that both were killed and so begins our mystery.

## COVER ART

✺

*A COLORFUL AND UNLIKELY CAST OF CHARACTERS
ARE BOUND BY THE SECRET HISTORY OF THE WORLD:
RUDOLPH HESS, DEPUTY FUHRER OF GERMANY;
GENERAL GEORGE S. PATTON, COMMANDER OF THE THIRD ARMY;
ALEISTER CROWLEY, MAGICIAN AND 33RD DEGREE FREEMASON;
NOBLE DREW ALI, FIRST MUSLIM PROPHET IN AMERICA*

# SPANDAU MYSTERY
## BY PETER MOON

*SkyBooks*
NEW YORK

**Spandau Mystery**
Copyright © 2007 by Peter Moon
First printing, February 2007

Cover art and illustration by Rick Smith
Typography by Creative Circle Inc.
Published by: Sky Books
                Box 769
                Westbury, New York 11590
                email: skybooks@yahoo.com
                website: www.skybooksusa.com

Printed and bound in the United States of America. All rights reserved. No part of this book may be reproduced in any form or by any electronic or mechanical means including information storage and retrieval systems without permission in writing from the publisher.

DISCLAIMER  Although partially based upon some historical characters who have actually lived, this book is a creative work of fiction. The viewpoints expressed by the characters in the book are not necessarily those of the author. If there is any question with regard to the actual history of the matters mentioned in this book, the reader should conduct his own examination by consulting historical texts and other avenues of investigation.

Library of Congress Cataloging-in-Publication Data

Moon, Peter
     Spandau Mystery
by Peter Moon
     360 pages
     ISBN 978-0-9678162-4-1 (13 digit)
     ISBN 0-9678162-4-6 (10 digit)
Fiction
Library of Congress Control Number  20069938667

*This book is dedicated to
Dr. Ellias Bey, aka Julius Coleman,
an Indigenous Great Seal Moor
who introduced me to the world of the Moors
and inspired the character of Ali Bey.
Ellias passed away during the writing of this book,
but his contribution will live on in these pages.*

# Acknowledgements

*I wish to give special thanks to the following people who have contributed to my knowledge of history and indigenous peoples. All of them have inspired and helped me in writing this book.*

*Hamza Sid Catlett-Bey*
*Dr. Ellias Bey*
*T. Buddha*
*Greg Castle*
*Artie "Red Medicine" Crippen*
*Cat Crippen*
*September Grey*
*Charlotte Henderson*
*Sharon "Winona Red Bird" Jackson*
*Dennis Marshall*
*Mary Ann Martini*
*Elihu Pleasant Bey*
*Sara Simmons*
*Tecumseh Brown-Eagle*
*Rick Smith*
*Mary Sutherland*
*Mike Zimmerman*

# CONTENTS

FOREWORD · 11

INTRODUCTION · 13

ONE · Message From Spandau  21

TWO · Briefing  27

THREE · Cairo 1903  33

FOUR · A Visitor  39

FIVE · The King's Chamber  45

SIX · The Picnic  49

SEVEN · The Vision  53

EIGHT · The Hanged Man  57

NINE · El Morocco  61

TEN · The Flea Bag  65

ELEVEN · A Seance, Circa 1908  77

TWELVE · The Advent  85

THIRTEEN · The Fabian Society  95

FOURTEEN · Intruders  99

FIFTEEN · Meadow Street  111

| SIXTEEN · Gretchen 115 |
| --- |
| SEVENTEEN · On the Run 121 |
| EIGHTEEN · The Christening 127 |
| NINETEEN · The Book 133 |
| TWENTY · Montauk 139 |
| TWENTY-ONE · Spying 151 |
| TWENTY-TWO · The Drive 153 |
| TWENTY-THREE · Amalantrah 167 |
| TWENTY-FOUR · Unbound 185 |
| TWENTY-FIVE · The Corporal 195 |
| TWENTY-SIX · A Suspicious Coincidence 201 |
| TWENTY-SEVEN · Fritz 203 |
| TWENTY-EIGHT · The Senator 207 |
| TWENTY-NINE · 7 Doris Place 211 |
| THIRTY · Pasewick 219 |
| THIRTY-ONE · Underground 225 |
| THIRTY-TWO · Lamps 235 |
| THIRTY-THREE · Resolution 241 |
| THIRTY-FOUR · Alone 245 |

THIRTY-FIVE • Little People 249

THIRTY-SIX • Lion's Paw Revisited 253

THIRTY-SEVEN • R.E.M. 261

THIRTY-EIGHT • Men-a-Tol 267

THIRTY-NINE • The Lion's Mouth 271

FORTY • August 12th 285

FORTY-ONE • The Time Machine 291

FORTY-TWO • Albrecht 301

FORTY-THREE • John Birch 303

FORTY-FOUR • Rendevous 311

FORTY-FIVE • Lam 317

FORTY-SIX • The Reckoning 325

FORTY-SEVEN • The Future 335

FORTY-EIGHT • Atlantis Rising 341

AUTHOR'S NOTE • 353

# Other titles from Sky Books

## by Preston Nichols and Peter Moon
*The Montauk Project: Experiments in Time*
*Montauk Revisited: Adventures in Synchronicity*
*Pyramids of Montauk: Explorations in Consciousness*
*Encounter in the Pleiades: An Inside Look at UFOs*
*The Music of Time*

## by Peter Moon
*The Black Sun: Montauk's Nazi-Tibetan Connection*
*Synchronicity and the Seventh Seal*
*The Montauk Book of the Dead*

## by Stewart Swerdlow
*Montauk: The Alien Connection*
*The Healer's Handbook: A Journey Into Hyperspace*

## by Alexandra Bruce
*The Philadelphia Experiment Murder:*
*Parallel Universes and the Physics of Insanity*

## by Wade Gordon
*The Brookhaven Connection*

## by Joseph Matheny with Peter Moon
*Ong's Hat: The Beginning*

BY PETER MOON

# FOREWORD

Although some people will disagree with this statement, the book you are about to read is my first work of fiction. In the past, I have been severely challenged as a writer because the topics I have chosen to write about have been deliberately obscured by various powers. While this has certainly not stopped me from finding out many interesting truths, there are key events in history that have been, so it would seem, irretrievably lost. This requires a new strategy.

"Stream of consciousness" is a common characteristic of both fiction and nonfiction. When you indulge in a stream of consciousness, you are no longer dealing with truth or fiction. You are dealing with a system or pattern of thoughts and ideas. In a sense, it enables one to transcend the polarizing thought processes of things being either right or wrong.

By taking on a subject that has been lost to history, one can still entertain the characters and surrounding circumstances to the best of one's knowledge. When one embraces what one does know and decides to write about actual characters, they begin to take on a life of their own. Sometimes they even "talk" to a certain extent. When they do not, the situation sometimes speaks for itself and answers questions that were either previously unknown or unsuspected. Ultimately, it becomes a creative process of discovery.

In writing this book, I have dealt with characters and circumstances that I have touched upon in my previous nonfiction writing. This book is, at least in part, an attempt to penetrate through the vehicle of creative writing what I could not necessarily achieve by examining historical accounts. What was most revealing in this process, however, was that writing deliberate fiction about various circumstances often resulted in me asking questions and consulting history books that gave me real answers. Sometimes the answers were not spelled out, but obvious and factual conclusions could still be easily drawn from what was available. So, while specific details of the truth might be inaccurate or even plain wrong in various parts of this work, the consciousness shed upon various events and circumstances cannot be denied. In any case, I hope it will help you to gain a better understanding or employ a more judicious approach when you consider or study the history of World War II and the other surrounding circumstances that have been described.

After reading this book, I invite all readers to examine the actual history of these matters for themselves. At the very least, you will gain a different perspective on how to look into such matters.

· · · · · · · · · BY PETER MOON · · · · · · · · ·

# INTRODUCTION

As one of the most decorated infantry soldiers of World War II, Hugh Oliver Wilson was better known for his fierceness and fearlessness in battle than for his medals. This was not, however, the only reason he came to be one of General Patton's favorites. The two men, somewhat mysteriously, were bound by the same family name.

Even before fighting for Patton's Seventh Army against Rommel's formidable Afrika Corp, Wilson came to the attention of the general by reason of his namesake alone. Patton's mother was also a Wilson, but she was much more than that. She was a potent clairvoyant who had fostered in her son an interest in and appreciation of the occult.

Besides having a strong psychic strain in their family tree, the Wilsons from which Patton descended were a wealthy and influential family who could trace their proud military roots back to the Revolutionary War. Patton's maternal grandfather, sometimes affectionately known as "Benito" Wilson, was the first mayor of Los Angeles and Mount Wilson, now occupied by the Jet Propulsion Laboratory, was named after him.

So it was that when General Patton learned of a young Hugh Wilson volunteering for the infantry, he went out of his way to get acquainted. Telling the young soldier that the Wilson line represents a long and splendid tradition of military excellence, he said that he expected nothing less.

Patton's self-styled pomposity and bravado were more of a self-willed creative show than they were inherent characteristics of his personality. As a general, he knew that the most effective means of getting troops to fight was through evocative demonstrations of theater that were designed to inspire. Although his methods were controversial and quick to be questioned, his success never was. George S. Patton was clearly the most effective field general known to modern warfare. This made him a formidable opponent, but it also sowed the seeds of his own destruction because the spoils of war he dutifully discovered and seized from the Nazis made him dangerous to those seeking power for themselves.

Patton's bravado may or may not have made Hugh Wilson a better soldier, but the initial personal contact and kindness Patton showed him made him an extremely loyal one. As the war ensued, Hugh Wilson surpassed all expectations, particularly when he single-handedly overtook and commandeered a Panzer tank and turned it back on the enemy. It is easy to like a hero, but Wilson never forgot the kindness and respect the general had shown him even before Wilson had distinguished himself in battle.

Often characterized as war mongers, generals often suffer the ill effects of war far more than civilians for they live and breathe it. They live through the carnage and, worse than any civilian, they make the decisions that send soldiers to their deaths. These decisions are never easy. It was this stark reality which had a tendency to bring out an extra dose of compassion and friendliness in George Patton, especially if he knew that a young man was risking his life. Such it was that Hugh Wilson came to be liked by Patton, but in battle, that affection turned to respect and deep admiration.

Despite his successes and remarkable competence in battle, Patton was eventually relieved of command of the Seventh Army due to a series of incidents. These included slapping two soldiers as well as behavior patterns that bordered on being insubordinate. When it came to the final invasion of German occupied Europe, however, it was of the utmost necessity that Patton was assigned to command of the Third Army. One of his first actions was to request a transfer of the recently promoted Sergeant Hugh Wilson.

As the war came to a close, most everyone expected that Patton's Third Army, undoubtedly the Army's finest, would be assigned to the final march on Berlin so that the Americans could beat the Russians to Hitler's lair in the bunker. Instead, and much to the surprise of all, the Third Army was ostensibly assigned to go after the German National Redoubt, sometimes colloquially known as the Werewolves. The press and public were fed a line that Otto Skorzeny was gathering the remains of the German army for a final last stand. It was further stated that they were protecting Hitler who had moved to a bunker in southern Germany. Historians have always questioned why Eisenhower sent his best general on such a lark when intelligence reports clearly indicated there

## INTRODUCTION

was no national redoubt that was of any threat to anybody. Actually, there was a redoubt of sorts, but it had little to do with the military.

The real mission of Patton's army was to go after the sizable fortresses where the Nazi's had developed avant garde weaponry and flying technology. This included the actual technology of the atom bomb that was later developed at Los Alamos for use against the Japanese.[*]

The bomb was the most forceful and useful of the technologies discovered in the German arsenal, but there was also a host of exotic craft and engineering designs. Many of these were not perfected yet, but some had reached a significant degree of evolution. These included flying wings and mysterious radar jamming weapons that are sometimes referred to as Foo Fighters. It also included the prototype of what later became known as flying saucers.

Patton's Third Army collected a vast array of technological information which was indeed the biggest prize of World War II. That is exactly why Eisenhower put Patton on the job. As the Third Army carried out its assignment, they also discovered key files from the German war department which had been strategically moved out of Berlin by the Nazis. Amongst the archives from the capital city came an equally unsuspected discovery. While it was not quite as exotic or sensational as the flying craft, it was potentially more powerful. This included the most comprehensive files on Freemasonry in Europe. Just as Jews, gypsies, and Slavs were vigorously purged under the Nazi regime so were the Freemasons. The Nazis even converted a Masonic temple in Berlin into a public museum designed to show the public the evil nature of Freemasonry.

The files found by the Third Army, however, were never on public display for they were far more sensitive. They included one of the most extensive network of financial dossiers ever collected and that included network charts of various bankers or financially influential Freemasons in different

---

[*] Several soldiers, including at least one German pilot, witnessesed a test bombing in Germany that featured an atomic mushroom cloud. This atom bomb, however, could not be delivered by the Germans because the Luftwaffe no longer had command of the skies nor did they have a plane that could successfully fly as far as America.

countries. These charts listed their names, affiliations and their rank or degree in Freemasonry. Although not exclusively so, an abundance of these names were Jewish. From a cursory inspection of the chart, it was plain to see that anyone who had access to it and also knew the secret communication codes used by Masons could access financial strings that reached from Tierra del Fuego to China and then back to anywhere else you might imagine.

After the capitulation of the Third Reich and the seizure of their resources, Patton became the virtual guardian of these assets. By reason of his military duties, he was not only the most knowledgeable, but stood in the center of the hidden political currents swirling around post war Europe. It was in the midst of these currents that he inherited the intelligence files of Reinhard Gehlen, the German chief of intelligence on Soviet matters.

Patton's first assignment in the postwar period was that of Military Governor of Bavaria where he obtained a dubious reputation for cavorting with and gaining the admiration of many top Nazis. He was soon relieved of his Bavarian command on the pretext that he not only cavorted with former Nazis but utilized them in key positions. Disgusted with the way German citizens were being treated after the war, Patton knew that hiring the old guard was absolutely crucial if he was going to bring water and electricity to the cities as well as maintain the other necessities of running a civilization.

What really tipped the scales against Patton, however, was when he arranged for a modest little Oktoberfest gathering that included many key Nazis. It all began as the officers became inebriated and both sides let their hair down with each other. It was then that one of the German generals presented a gift to Patton in appreciation of his hospitality and kindness to the German people. The gift consisted of a case of films.

The Third Army had already seized an extensive film library from the Nazis, but there had hardly been time to view them all. The German general who presented this gift to Patton readily acknowledged that these films might already be in the library Patton's army had confiscated (they were not), but he also made an offer that could hardly be refused. Telling Patton that these films would explain so much to him

## INTRODUCTION

about the history of the war, he suggested to show some of them that very evening. The German also offered to translate the films. It was here that Patton and Hugh Wilson discovered, for the first time, the important role that Rudolph Hess had played in the evolution of the Third Reich's technology.

To the utter astonishment of the Americans, these films began with Hess giving a presentation on the goals and overview of the Vril Society and the role they would play in developing a vast new array of flying craft. These lectures were either given to or sponsored by the Vril Society, a secret society which was really not so secret. Its purpose was to revive the ancient culture and ideals of Atlantis. This might easily have been dismissed as the ravings of a crackpot, but when the actual films of flying craft were shown and the German translators relayed Hess's meticulous instructions and detailed descriptions, it stunned the Americans.

The Germans that were present, however, were not surprised in the least. It was Hess, they said, who created and administered the Hitler Fund, a bottomless pit of capital that was contributed to by German industrialists. Sizable portions of this fund were dedicated to exotic projects that have remained largely secret to his day, only one of which was the Vril flying craft. As a leader and advocate of this society, it was the chosen role of Hess to establish superior air technology in the form of flying discs.

It did not take long for the wild events and discussions of what transpired that night to make their way back to the Allied Command. Eisenhower's reaction was swift and strategic. Based upon a pretense that Patton was enjoying too much fraternization with the Nazis, he was given a new assignment that required him to depend upon the Nazis even more than he had in his job as military governor of Bavaria. Patton was assigned to write the history of the war with particular regard to the German point of view. This required a full inspection of files and films but also involved discussions with the individual German generals.

So it was that General George S. Patton stumbled upon one of the greatest military secrets or the Twentieth Century. His camaraderie with the Nazis only made him more threatening to those who already feared him and wanted control of the incredible new technology that was discovered. Once

17

the full ramifications had been reviewed by the Allied Command, an accident was arranged for General Patton. While driving to a hunting site, his car was suddenly rammed by an army truck. It was a staged accident and not a very good one. The truck had to inconveniently turn into Patton's car in order to hit him. Patton did not die but was temporarily paralyzed. Making excellent strides towards recovery, his doctors listed him in good condition, but he was terminated by other means. The file on the investigation of his death has remained classified to this day. The story, however, does not end there.

For all of the controversy he created with his superiors, Patton also inspired a loyalty that could not be matched by his rivals. There were officers and soldiers, all intensely loyal to Patton, who were not fooled for a minute by what had happened to their leader that they loved and who had gotten them through the most harrowing period of their life. Wise in the ways of the military and the ridiculous culture it could foster, these loyal officers and servicemen created their own corps, a small group of patriots that swore to do everything in their power to avenge General Patton and, more importantly, to preserve and protect the Constitution of the United States against all foreign enemies. They no longer trusted their superiors, but knew the best course of action was to apply all they knew of military intelligence to be effective. Their first course of action was to remain silent, observe and be extremely careful not to manifest any disaffection with their superiors. While remaining silent to a large degree, they cached many of Patton's files and created their own intelligence files. As far as they were concerned, this was warfare and they were all proven warriors. This group, and the officers who manned it, became a secret and extended unit of G-2, Army Intelligence.

Eventually, this group gave rise to other groups that were launched into society for different purposes. The most conspicuous of these groups was the John Birch Society, a group which was eventually headed by General Patton's cousin, Congressman Larry Patton McDonald. McDonald, who inherited many of these files, utilized them as the head of a private intelligence agency called Western Goals. It did work that the CIA and FBI were not allowed to do by order of law.

## INTRODUCTION

Like his cousin, McDonald was assassinated when Korean Airlines Flight 007 was shot down over Russian air space in 1983. The actual black box was never found.

In the center of this maelstrom of events was Hugh Oliver Wilson, a young enlisted man who happened to be Patton's favorite soldier. Taken under the wings of certain Generals, Wilson was transferred to G-2 where his youth made him the hope of the future. Attending college part time on the GI bill, his new superiors saw to it that he was given a commision as an officer whereupon he moved quickly up the ranks.

Wilson found that staying "alive" in the intelligence corps was far more tricky than on the battlefield because your enemy was more hidden. It required a great deal of intuition and good judgment. Over the years, his most potent shield had been silence, but it was now over thirty-five years since Rudolph Hess had been captured. Most of Wilson's own mentors were now dead. The tide had changed, and it was time for the truth to be told.

## CHAPTER ONE

## MESSAGE FROM SPANDAU

After slamming down the phone, General Wilson threw his pen against the wall and slammed his open hand against his desk.

"God damn it!" he said. "Those god damn faggot Brits have sabotaged us once and for all."

Wilson's secretary, Heidi, jerked up her head as she heard her boss scream. In all the time she had known him, Heidi had never ever heard General Wilson lose his temper in such a manner. Running to the door of his office, she opened it.

"What on Earth is the matter?" asked Heidi.

"They've killed Hess — finally and absolutely. I think he was our last hope."

"You mean Rudolph Hess, the Nazi?" she asked.

"That's right. Rudolph fucking Hess, the Deputy Fuhrer!" cursed Wilson as he once more slammed his open hand against the desk.

The date was August 17, 1987 and reports were just beginning to surface on the news wires that Rudolph Hess, the last living member of the official Nazi hierarchy, had died of suicide in Berlin's Spandau Prison.

"Hugh," she said, "in all the time I've known you, I've never ever heard you use such language let alone lose control of your emotions. I think we'd better have a little talk."

"I'm sorry, Heidi. You have no idea how much I had riding on that man's life. Even so, had he lived, it was still a crap shoot and a big one at that."

"Sir," said Heidi, now addressing him formally, "I had no idea you had any operations with Hess. I never saw it in the papers or correspondence."

"Heidi," he said, "it *is* time we had a little talk. Just because you work in the SRU of Army Intelligence does not mean that you, or I for that matter, know everything that runs through this god damn slimy network."

SRU stands for Special Reconnaissance Unit, and it was not a formal designation. Rather, it was a coded designation for a unit that really was not recognized to exist. In fact, for anybody who did find out the real functions of the unit, there was very little reconnaissance going on at all. Their job was to locate and find victims, officially designated as targets. General Wilson, who had a reputation for being as tough as nails, was in charge of Army Intelligence Enforcement. In other words, he accomplished jobs that most did not have the stomach for. He was not, however, an indiscriminate killer. In fact, he did no killing at all but oversaw certain sensitive operations that sometimes included the elimination of approved military targets. Furthermore, he only engaged in military operations that were approved by the U.S. Congress. The only caveat to that, however, is that the general public does not realize that the U.S. Congress and military have their own rules, not necessarily illegal in terms of written law, that the public are not clued-in on. General Wilson, however, had a reputation for being a stickler when it came to following the law in his operations.

"Look it, Heidi," continued Wilson. "You've seen me in action for a long time. You've seen the Honduras bullshit and the operations in Afghanistan — all highly decorated, and all highly decorated bullshit as far as I'm concerned. It's not all I do, however. No good intelligence officer reveals everything he does, but it's time I shared more with you. Frankly, I'm at a loss, and I don't know what the hell to do."

"But," interrupted Heidi, "what about Hess?"

"No, Heidi, let me continue. It's finally time to talk. I've been lovers with you for over a year. I know I can trust you more than anyone."

Wilson then went over to a locked filing cabinet and opened it.

"Look," he said, pointing to a cabinet full of books and papers. All were on the subject of Nazis and most of the books featured the occult aspects of Nazism. Included were comics and old time copies of the *Police Gazette* which featured myths about Hitler escaping to Argentina.

"I never knew...." said Heidi.

"Just listen, Heidi. There's a lot to explain here. You remember the fellow you replaced on this job?"

"Thomas?" she said.

"Yes, that's right. Thomas," said Wilson, "but I want you to refer to him only as Agent T from now on. Through my connections, I was able to have him posted at Spandau Prison. He is my eyes and ears there and is trustworthy.

"But why did you post him at Spandau?" asked Heidi.

The phone then rang. Wilson picked it up without waiting for Heidi to screen it.

"Wilson!" he exclaimed into the phone before hearing the pleasant sound of a woman's voice that betrayed a slight German accent.

"Hello, General Wilson. I have a message from Tyler. He said not to worry. You will receive a package tomorrow at your home address," said the woman who promptly hung up.

Wilson now showed a slight bit of relief across his face. "At least there's some hope," he muttered.

"What?" asked Heidi in disbelief.

"Excuse me a second, Heidi. Could you get me some tea? Then we can talk."

The phone call calmed Wilson down. The news about Hess had made him feel both helpless and hopeless. So much that he had worked for and hung on in the Army for was about to go down the drain. For the first time in his entire army career, he was about to lose his marbles and even spill the beans to his beloved secretary. Maybe it was about time. At sixty-four, he was getting old. But now, this phone call couldn't have come at a more propitious time as far as helping him retain his normally calm composure.

The message from Tyler was not from anyone actually named "Tyler." It was from Agent T, a carefully placed agent in Spandau Prison whose secret function was to monitor Hess and all the different garrisons who guarded him. Agent T sent all of his messages under a fictitious name which was distinguished by using a first name that began with "T." This was in recognition that his actual name was Thomas.

The reference for Wilson to go to his "home address" was also meant to mislead. The term "home address" referred to a mail drop in Richmond. Agent T, in order to escape potential detection, used another agent to place his phone call to the general. In essence, he was tacitly letting Wilson know that he was on top of the scene with Hess's death and that more information would be forthcoming.

As Heidi returned to Wilson's office with tea on a tray, he decided firmly that he would now hedge his bet with her.

He did not have to tell her everything all at once. Instead, he could put her excellent mind to use so as to help him unlock the puzzle he had been trying to solve for years. Just a few minutes earlier, he was about to spill all the beans, mostly out of sheer frustration. Besides obvious security precautions, there was another reason not to tell her everything and that was her own safety. He did not want to endanger her. He would introduce her to the situation gradually.

"There you go, sir, just as you like it," she said as she handed the general a mug of tea with a dash of honey.

"Thank you, Heidi. Have yourself a seat and get comfortable for I have a few things to tell you and a little project, too. But first, tell me what you know about Rudolph Hess."

"Well, sir, I know that he was Hitler's deputy and that he flew his plane to Scotland and tried to make peace with England but was imprisoned. At Nuremburg, he was found guilty of war crimes, but I never understood that because he was against the war effort and tried to make peace. That is pretty much all I know off the top of my head."

"Heidi," said Wilson, "I'm a bit impressed. Your photographic memory has not failed you. I'd say you're pretty accurate. There is, of course, a whole lot more to the story. I've thought this over a bit. You know, that phone call calmed me down and gave me some time to think. I'm going to give you just a bit of background on Hess and then open up my files to you and see what you come up with. You know, I've never told you this, Heidi, but you're one of the best 'intelligence officers' I have; yet, by all appearances, you do only the work of a secretary."

"Thanks for the flattery, but tell me what it is you want me to do," she said.

"In a second. First, I want you to know that Rudolph Hess is a major key and is <u>the</u> central figure in an intelligence war that has gone on for half a century. You've known me for years, and you know my personality as well as most of my operations; but you don't really know key aspects of my history in the service. I'll share them with you, but I first have an assignment for you; and I don't want to prejudice it by saying too many things and making your head spin. Suffice it to say that Hess is key, but he is not key because he represents Nazis or dislikes Jews or any obvious reason that common people might think. If you do a little bit of reading, you'll soon see that there is a gigantic omission when it comes to books, articles and dissertations on Rudolph Hess. In so called "serious" discussions, there is almost no mention of his involvement in occultism. It is brushed away unless it is to portray him as being a fanatic nut. That is as far as common think goes, but there is a much deeper thread there."

"It would make sense that nobody would refer to it," said Heidi.

"And why is that?" asked Wilson, smiling inside because he loved to watch Heidi's mind work. It was neither as old or experienced as his, but it was a very bright mind.

"Because the word *occult* means 'hidden'," replied Heidi. In other words, it is out of sight. It is not meant to be seen."

"Yes, Heidi, good point, but if you've observed the Hess situation for as long as I have, there are too many pink elephants standing in the living room."

"And where do I start, general? What do you want me to do?"

"What I want you to do is to go through these books in my file and all the other papers and notes, too, and read up on everything you can find on Rudolph Hess and his association with occultism. Once you do that, we'll be on common ground. More importantly, I want to get your view, a fresh view, on a problem I've been dealing with for decades."

"And what is that problem?" asked Heidi.

"To find out what god damn secrets this man had inside of him. But that is another story, and I'm not gonna say anymore as I do not want to prejudice your own investigation. I've said enough for now."

"Fine, sir, but this problem seems to be at the heart of giving you a psychological crisis and, prior to today, I've never seen you budge psychologically."

"Suffice it to say, my dear, that what is at the crux of the Rudolph Hess mystery is as pivotal as the basic war between good and evil itself."

"If what you say it true, is it not odd that a man who is portrayed as the embodiment of evil, or at least the deputy to the embodiment of evil, should be so wrapped up in what might be termed 'certain conditions of goodness'?"

"What do you mean by that?" asked Wilson.

"Whatever negative things Hess made for himself and others, I always read that he was an easy mark for those Germans who had complaints of injustices. He corrected a lot of injustice and was even known to get certain Jews out of trouble during the purge against them."

"It's not really as odd as you think," said Wilson, "but I think you're catching on real fast. I'll be more forthcoming later, but for now I want you to start hitting those books. I'm gonna take the rest of the week off. I need a one week vacation to mull this over and just relax. You have full reign of the office for the next week. There are no vital operations going on and you'll be able to handle any stray calls. Notify me at home if there's anything urgent that might otherwise need my attention. I'll expect a verbal and written synopsis on your findings, specifically of what you find on Hess's occult connections. You might want to check some outside sources, too, like a library."

Finishing his tea, General Hugh Wilson rose from his chair, pecked Heidi on the cheek and headed for the door.

"I'm going to have some good old fashioned R&R!" he said as he began to walk out the door.

"Oh — I almost forgot something," said Wilson as he did an about face. "It's very important and will make your work a lot easier."

"What's that?" asked Heidi.

"There is a tape I have to fetch for you," said Wilson as he headed towards a vault in his office and began to unlock it. "It's a briefing that I gave to Thomas just before he left for what would be his eventual assignment as Spandau. I let him take notes, but there was no way I would let the tape go with him. It will give you an overview and also let you know some more things about myself. Of course, I completely trust you. Take what notes that you want, but do not make any copies. I want it back. In the meantime, keep it safe."

General Wilson kissed Heidi again and then walked out the door.

......... CHAPTER TWO .........

## THE BRIEFING

Wilson was gone, but Heidi still had a full day to put in at the office. She could have goofed off all day in between a few unimportant phone calls, but that was not in her character. Besides being efficient and businesslike, she was very interested in the assignment the general had given her.

Taking the microcassette, she placed it in a recorder and sat back on the office couch to listen. The tape began with no introduction or title. She just heard Wilson's voice as he started talking to Thomas, also known as Agent T.

"You're going to one of the strangest and most expensive operations in the so-called free world. Literally hundreds of millions of dollars a year are spent maintaining the facility to which you will be going: Spandau Prison in East Berlin. There are four garrisons of French, English, American and Russian soldiers who rotate duties once every month, each country serving a total of three months annually. The entire function of the countless personnel who work there, of which you will soon be one, is to watch only one prisoner: Rudolph Hess, the man who served as Deputy Fuhrer of the Third Reich.

"You are being chosen for this job for two reasons. First and foremost is your dedication to the Constitution and the patriot cause you have embraced. Second is your ability to speak French and German. I know you have made great strides in learning Russian. Keep working on that. You will soon be amongst them.

"Your assignment is to get as close as possible to the prisoner, find out his state of mind and find out as much about his history as you possibly can. It is therefore of the utmost importance that you understand the existing climate, political and otherwise, that you are going into.

"Gorbachev of the Soviet Union has indicated that the release of Hess is imminent. For years, different sources have appealed for his release on humanitarian grounds. As far as publicity is concerned, it is always the Russians who are blamed. There has always been, however, an undetected source behind the continued imprisonment of Hess and that

# THE BRIEFING . . . . . . . . . . . . . . . . . . . . .

is the British. Never forget for a minute that they were the ones who enticed him to their land in the first place — all on the pretext of peace — and then put him in the slammer. If you care to look deeper into the situation on your own, you will likely come to the conclusion that it was also the British who financed the overthrow of the Russian Czar and thereby established the Soviet Union.

"When Hess is released, and we believe it will be sometime in the near future, we want to have a line to him and also give him confidence in order that he might talk to us. Your job is to try and be his friend, and I mean that sincerely. Be aware, however, that the first commandant of Spandau Prison was a Knight of Malta. Besides being tied to the British, the Knights are also close to the Vatican and have always been involved in all sorts of international intrigue and bullshit. Do your homework on them separately, but realize they will be watching you and will not want any unauthorized access to Hess. You must therefore be very discreet. Just be his friend so that when he is on the outside he will trust us.

"One of the peculiarities about Hess is that there is very little known about his true background. Of course, there are plenty of biographical accounts of him, most of which are sketchy in the extreme. These tend to be misleading and inaccurate even when they cite certain facts about his life and association with Hitler.

"According to information I have, the best biographical sources on the history of Hess and all of his many associations was wiped out by Reinhard Heydrich, Himmler's top man. Whether this was by order of Himmler or not, I am not sure. Hess does, however, come from a line of nobility; and it is undetermined how this impacted his influence upon the rise of Nazism. It is something to consider. There is still a considerable amount of secrets that this man is in the middle of, particularly when it comes to the post war period and the resultant change of power.

"I first became interested in Hess when I served in Patton's Third Army at the end of the war. The German officers knew that I was a favorite of Patton's. One of them who spoke excellent English befriended me. After I had gained his trust, sometime around the German Oktoberfest, he told me he wanted to show me something. It was then that he showed me a film of Germany's secret flying craft and translated it as well. He said that I should show it to General Patton.

"The Third Army had already discovered the remnants of various flying craft, but this was a special film for it also featured the personage of Rudolph Hess. This German general insisted I call him by his first name, Fritz, and then emphasized that the Germans were not our true enemies. Those were the British who, he said, had executed the severest form of betrayal against Germany, all prior to America entering the war.

"Russia, he explained, was the real danger to the world. Japan knew that very well as they had run-ins with them before. The Germans felt the same way. A lot of the problems with Russia, he said, began when Russia's secret police, the Ouranka, had entered Tibet.

"Much of the British betrayal he referred to centered around a peace plan that had been arranged with Germany when they had enticed Hess to fly over to Scotland and meet the Duke of Hamilton. Hess, who had been one of the most powerful men in the Reich, suddenly became a tragic pawn in what would amount to a slow game of attrition against the German state, the Jews, and the whole continent of Europe. The moment that Hess was captured became the turning point for the war swinging against Germany.

"Hess, said Fritz, was not what he appeared to be. Fritz then proceeded to translate the film wherein Hess lectured on the flying craft as well as the purpose of what their new civilization was really all about.

"Although claiming the Germans had the best scientists and the best technical expertise in the world, Hess stressed that the impetus for these craft came from an innately spiritual source. Hedging on what he could reveal, Hess explained that the Germans had been chosen to revive an ancient culture that had once been prevalent on this earth. Buried in antiquity, this culture featured flying craft; but perhaps even more importantly, he stated that this craft, once perfected, could take us off of this planet and enable us to explore the stars and other worlds.

"To tell you the truth, Thomas, I don't know if what he said was more shocking then or would be more shocking in today's world. You begin to understand, nevertheless, that

# THE BRIEFING....................

my interest in Rudolph Hess became paramount. The tight security which would eventually wrap itself around these issues has made it extremely difficult to penetrate, to say the least. As you know very well, intelligence is a double-edged sword. It is a paramount that you stay alive. Keep this in mind when you are on your mission. You will be of minimal use if you are dead.

"There is more to the story, and every aspect cannot be indulged. It is, however, important for you to understand another aspect of the case with Hess. That has to do with his involvement in secret societies and occultism.

"Fritz told me that Hess came from a long line of aristocrats. Further, he stated that Reinhard Heydrich had literally stripped clear the archives of any biographical information about Hess. Only the most obvious points of his historical association of Hitler and his earlier life remained.

"There were many powerful struggles around Hitler, the most renown of which were the efforts of Goering and Himmler securing their status in the Reich. Hess was considered by many to have been reduced to a minor player. While there is a slight degree of truth in this, it often misses the point.

"What I want you to understand at this point, however, is that Hess was connected to occult societies. His mentor was Karl Haushofer. Haushofer's son, Albrecht, was part Jewish by reason of his mother and was "Aryanized" by Hess just prior to the latter's flight to Scotland.

"There is an odd convergence with Hess that in reality is perhaps not so odd at all. That is where occult societies meet the world of finance and industry. After all, these are the node points where world control and domination are accomplished. The most clever way to maintain domination is to let your subjects think they are being dominated by someone or something else. That way, they never perceive who is controlling them and have no cause to rebel against you.

"In the case of Hess, he was largely introduced into occult circles through his association with Karl Haushofer. That is at least the common thought, and it is true to a marked extent. It must be realized, however, that anyone of his lineage who grew up in Egypt — and he did — would likely have a connection to occult societies that are very old indeed.

"Where we take up the Hess case though is with the convergence of someone who played a very important role in Britain's naval intelligence. That is Ian Fleming, the same man who wrote the 007 stories of James Bond.

"Introduced into occult circles as a young man, Fleming was a protege of Aleister Crowley and went to college in Germany where he became a part of Karl Haushofer's fraternity. Crowley and Haushofer were members of the same circles.

"After working as a spy in Moscow, which was really at the behest of his occult connections, Fleming then worked in the City. Located within London, the City is an autonomous financial district which is basically a clearing house for international finance. It's primary agenda is to support global nationalism. In other words, the City ensures that countries have their own national identities, but these are identities chosen by committee and not by the indigenous people of the territories concerned. This is getting off the subject, but suffice it to say that Fleming was an international banker.

"At the outset of World War II, Fleming was handpicked by the British Admiralty to serve as one of the top intelligence officers for the war effort. He was key in getting Hess to come to Britain. To be frank, I am not completely sure that he was against Hess. He was playing a role and was not necessarily a decision maker in the process to incarcerate Hess. As a matter of fact, history tells us that he requested that Crowley be able to interview Hess but that he was denied. I have always been suspicious of that denial. After all, it was Fleming, Crowley and the Haushofers who precipitated Hess's flight to Scotland in the first place.

"Another thing I should also mention is that Crowley himself supervised an occult ritual in the Ashdown Forest that was designed with the express purpose of bringing Hess to London. The Haushofers, who were quite aware of English sentiments, were an intimate part of Hess's decision making process with regard to him taking this trip. Hess, however, was primarily encouraged by his English contacts that he could achieve peace between the two nations. Further, he and Hitler both knew that Germany could not survive a war on two fronts. Hitler had already briefed Hess that an attack from Russian was imminent. There was no choice but to seek a peace with England and an alliance that Churchill had

## THE BRIEFING . . . . . . . . . . . . . . . . . . .

already promised them. If you read the letters between the Haushofers and Hess, and there are copies in that box I have for you to read, you will clearly see that Hitler was well aware of Hess's maneuver and plan to bring peace. It was, however, Hess's idea. Hitler merely acquiesced. They both agreed that if it failed, Hitler would declare him insane.

"It is important that you peruse this box of books and files here, but I first wanted to give you this overview of the subject you are going to see and hopefully access. There are many secrets buried within that man, and the world may never know them. It is important, however, to realize that the secrets within him have long been in the possession of his custodians. That would apparently be the Allied Command at Spandau; but keep in mind that before the war ended, he was the exclusive prisoner of the British for over four years.

"Hess suffered more psychiatric examinations than any man in the history of the world. There is no telling what techniques were employed upon him to wrest out his secrets. The fact that he did not even remember Haushofer at the Nuremberg Trials is evidence of him having been extensively brainwashed. There is various literature and rumors suggesting that the Hess who was incarcerated was not the real Hess. This is clever disinformation to obscure the brainwashing and violation of the Geneva Convention. Don't put anything past the Brits and keep your eyes on the rest, too, including our American friends.

"Read what's in that box and we'll get you on a plane in no time."

The tape recorder clicked off. Heidi then closed her eyes and made mental notes of everything she had just heard.

........CHAPTER THREE.........

## CAIRO 1903

The early morning sun was stifling on the Nile River as Carl Hess[*] looked towards the shore and took in the scenery. The steamboat he was on was making its approach to port.

"Rudi," he called out to his excited nine-year-old son who was also taking in the scenery and was just a short distance away. "It's almost time to disembark. We need to get ready."

This year had been an excellent season of profits for Carl Hess, an international traveler and a master of languages who had finally made his fortune in Alexandria. He had just earned a handsome sum for arranging the import of modern farming equipment produced by the Mengele family. The Egyptians knew, as did most of the world, that no one made better farming tools than the Mengeles.

It was now late summer and, at the prodding of his son's tutor, he was going to spend some of his fortune taking Rudi on a cultural excursion to the Giza Plateau. As a result, Carl had already planned a tour of the Great Pyramid and the Sphinx. Rudi's tutor, who was just taking off on a holiday himself, said it would leave a lasting impression on the young boy and give him an awe inspiring grasp of this once great culture. The tutor had suggested he make arrangements with a tour guide named Aiwass, a very knowledgable and kindly man who often served as a tour guide for special parties. Aiwass was often sought out by wealthy tourists because of his immense knowledge of Egyptian history. He was often very well paid by the visitors.

As the vessel reached the dock and the mooring lines were secured, Carl looked out and could see a man in a red fez. That was Tariq, his contact. Carl knew Tariq from a previous transaction or two. In this case, Tariq would serve as the gateway to Aiwass who, locally, was known only as "the Moor." As Tariq approached, the two men exchanged

---

[*] I have found at least two versions of Rudolph Hess's father. One is recorded in a Welsh newspaper as Carl Hess whose first bride was British. The more common version known to historians is Fritz Hess. There is, however, no disagreement about him being a successful merchant in Egypt. In this book, I am using the more obscure "Carl" to portray his father.

greetings before Carl placed his luggage on Tariq's cart where it would be taken to their hotel. The Tanna Leaf Hotel was their accommodation of choice where they would be primarily surrounded by Germans and English on the outskirts of Cairo. The party then mounted three camels which Tariq had previously secured by negotiation with the throng of camel jockeys who always gathered to assist disembarking travelers.

Carl then introduced his young son.

"This is my son, Rudolph. We call him Rudi," said Carl.

"He will be in for a fine adventure today," said Tariq. "The Moor will see us around noon time. That will give us plenty of time to get to our destination and have lunch. You will then be handed over to the Moor, and I will see you back to your hotel when you are done."

The party of three then mounted the rented camels and headed towards the Giza Plateau.

It was a busy day for Aiwass the Moor, yet he could not help but think of a young man he had taken to the Great Pyramid just three days before. As part of a time-honored ritual initiation, the subject had been blindfolded and taken to the King's Chamber where he was purposefully deserted and left to die or find his way out. The Moor could not help but wonder where the boy was and how he had made out. He knew he was now scheduled to meet up with, by previous arrangement, a certain Carl Hess to whom he would give a tour and quick history of what had once been an ancient megalopolis. It might prove awkward if he ran across his old charge from three days before. Deciding to relieve his mind of the situation, he cast the fortune of the young man to fate and decided to take a rest in the shade where he waited for his friend Tariq to arrive.

When they arrived at the depot at the Giza Plateau, Carl and Rudi were both very impressed when they gazed into the deep blue eyes and leathery tanned skin of the man known as the Moor. After exchanging greetings and logistical talk, they all sat down in the shade for a quick lunch of dates and dried fruit which had been purchased and carried by Carl.

"Tell me," said the Moor, "what brings you to Giza?"

"My son is just of the age where he can appreciate such an ancient and magnificent culture. Besides, my son's tutor told us you could give us the best tour imaginable. He thinks very highly of you."

"But, what about you personally?" asked the Moor.

"I am here for my son mostly. Of course, I have a general interest in such in a place, but I am mostly a merchant by trade."

"Ah, yes, but I can see something in your eyes. There is another reason that brings you here. I can see it."

"What do you see?" said the bewildered Carl.

"I see many visitors. People have come here for centuries and centuries seeking answers to the mysteries of life. Some are just curious about these monuments, but you are seeking something. Perhaps I can help you find it."

As they finished, the party rose. As Tariq left, the Moor took his tourists towards the Great Pyramid where they would enter and walk about.

"The first thing you should know about the Egyptian civilization," said the Moor, "is that it is much older than anyone would think. Not only was it a great civilization but it unified the entire world as it once existed. This is not suspected by most historians, but it is pretty much true. More importantly, it is a microcosm of the heavens themselves. As you see this civilization now in ruins, so are the heavens. We live in a broken world but one that yearns to return to its fully glory. Written in the walls of the pyramids and of tombs and structures throughout Egypt are the secrets and call to immortality. In the dismal state of these ruins are the seeds of its recreation and all the knowledge by which to accomplish it."

"The engineering of this pyramid is magnificent," commented Carl. "What system did they use to move these ancient stones into place."

"That," replied the Moor, "is a great secret. It is known as the Vril."

At the sound of that word, young Rudi's ears perked up. The iteration of the word itself made him feel as if he were alive. It was a moment and a word he would never forget.

"And what is this mysterious secret?" asked Carl.

"If I could tell you the secret, it would no longer be a secret and would be quite commonplace," replied the Moor as they made their way into the pyramid itself. "But, the

Vril is a great mystery. It suggests a power and an energy, but it is more than that. More than anything, it has to do with the will or one's intention. But, it is not just intention. It is integrating one's will with the power to execute moving objects. That, however, is an imperfect description. Advancement in the Vril is not about moving objects, but these objects were moved through volition."

"Are you suggesting," asked Carl, "that this entire complex or pyramid was built via the mental energy of moving huge stones that may or may not have been crafted in a similar manner?"

"Not exactly. The entire proposition is very simple, but it is, at the same time, rather complex. You see, there was an overall intention to build a Great Pyramid. It required Vril to accomplish the feat. Tens of thousands of craftsmen and laborers had to be employed to execute this building. That in itself was a great accomplishment. The moving of the large stones followed suit. How did it follow suit? By execution of the original will to build this edifice in order to serve a specific purpose."

"I am not clear on what you say," responded Carl. "Are you suggesting that this was mental manipulation or not? Or, are you suggesting there was both?"

"You asked the key question. I am suggesting there was both. You, and most everyone else of course, is interested in where the physical labor stopped and the mental manipulation of gravity took over. Actually, there need be no mental energy to manipulate gravity, but that is a different topic. All anyone will ever be judged by is the final product or result they produce. How they get there is completely secondary and becomes of less and less consequence the more powerful you get. What I am trying to illustrate for you is that anyone's personal journey through life is a quest. It is a quest to execute one's will whether that will is just to survive, to amass a fortune, or to discover the truth of the universe. When supernatural phenomena assists the querent, it is often not unlike a sailing ship receiving an unexpected breeze from an unexpected direction. The destination, not the journey, is the object."

"That still doesn't tell me exactly how the stones were put into place," said Carl Hess.

"Well," said the Moor, "if I were to truly tell you exactly how that was done, could I not accomplish it myself? If I knew the secret of exactly how the entire Giza complex was built, I could do it again, and we would not be taking this trek and having this conversation."

"Yes," said Carl, "but you are deemed the most knowledgable, at least by my son's tutor."

"He is kind, and it is true I know more than most, but please keep in mind that those who are considered the greatest prophets of the world never built a masterpiece such as once existed here. It is therefore not such a great failing that I cannot rebuild what they did not even attempt."

"Is that because they lived in a realm of spirit as opposed to matter?"

"No," answered the Moor. "It has more to do with the fact that they fit into a pattern that was bigger than themselves, their disciples and all their detractors. If you study this pyramid and learn all the subtle meanings in its architecture and etchings, you will discover that it included the various prophets. It told their story before they even lived, or at least gives a microcosmic representation of it. These details, however, are too complex for what we are to accomplish today."

Carl Hess could not help but realize that he was in for much more than he had originally bargained for. What had begun as a tour and cultural excursion for his young son had caused him to look at the bigger picture.

"You know," said Carl, "I understand what you mean about obtaining an objective. In my business, I never know when customers will call on me. I do not always know what to buy or where or how to sell it. I could swear that people sometimes show up out of nowhere. I one time had a rare occasion to import a very fine cloth from the Orient. It was something I had never carried before nor likely ever would again. Out of nowhere, a wealthy woman came into my place of business and looked straight at me.

"'I heard you would have that cloth,' she said before promptly buying it at an enormous profit for myself. I had no idea that I could fetch that much and no idea of who I would sell it to. Most of all, I am absolutely certain that there is no way she could have known I had this cloth. I had no reputation for having it, and she was unfamiliar with my lines and means of import. It was like a dumb coincidence, but I felt it was like divine providence. The busier and bigger I get, the more this happens. It is like magic, but it is not magic."

"That is exactly my point," said the Moor. "It is like riding a bicycle. You just do it. If you ride over a hole that should have bumped you, you just continue. This is every man's quest on a personal note. When we are talking about this pyramid, however, we are talking about a much greater game, a game that embraces all."

## . . . . . . . . . CHAPTER FOUR . . . . . . . . .

## A VISITOR

After picking up his international Fedex package on Tuesday, August 18th, General Wilson made his way back to the office complex by taxi.  Entering the complex, he realized he had calculated correctly.  Heidi was at lunch.  Instead of entering his normal office, he used one of his keys to enter the door opposite his office.  To all appearances, this door was a utility closet with a high voltage sign on it.  It was, in fact, an auxiliary office, replete with spy equipment, arms and a somewhat indefinite supply of different foods.  It also contained comfortable sleeping quarters, a small kitchen and a television.  A place where General Wilson could virtually hide from everyone if needed, this office also featured a closed circuit television hookup whereby he could even spy on his own office if he needed to.

Wilson checked out Heidi several times before really trusting her.  He noticed her behavior when visitors came in, and she was always extremely professional and acted in a manner that was loyal to him.  There was never any casual chitchat with the various people who came in.  In fact, people were often trying to engage her in chitchat just to get something out of her about what was going on with General Wilson.  She never indulged.  This also made it safe for him to take her on as a part-time lover.

The current moment, however, was not a matter of trust about Heidi.  In the aftermath of Hess's death, which he considered to the intelligence coup of the decade, he wondered who might come by the office unannounced.  Furthermore, if he was not there, he wondered what they might try to get out of Heidi and who might ask about his whereabouts.

Turning on the closed-circuit TV and activating the taping unit, he made his way to his desk so he could decode whatever message he had received in the Fedex pack from Agent T.  Inside the package was a page of coded typing and a series of photographs, all blown up.  The letter was written in code.  The fifth letter of the fifth line was "d" and this told him to used his Code D translator.  After patiently and quickly

## A VISITOR

decoding the message, he read the following:

"Prisoner killed on American watch but left Spandau in British ambulance. Some say he was still alive when he left. As usual, I smell Brits. Inside prison, rumors abound that he hung himself but this is an impossible theory. Place here in chaos as no one will have a job here anymore. I acted quick and told our American commander that we should have photos to protect our own integrity whether we need them or not. Getting permission, I took requisitioned camera and took photos of entire area. Photos enclosed are not from requisitioned camera but from my hidden pen camera. Garden house where prisoner was taken from is a mess. See picture. What is most interesting and very strange is that I found three locations where occult tarot cards had been placed but prisoner is not known to have had such cards. They are all of a hung man and all are completely identical except for one in the garden house where he supposedly died. In his favorite garden spot, four cards were placed in a circle. One was left conspicuously on his bed in his cell and the different one in garden house. I got all this done within a couple hours of the incident. Place is now in a lock down mode with hardly anyone leaving or entering. I am on the outside now and will return and send you a follow up as soon as I can. This is all I know at this time."

Turning to the photographs, Wilson studied them intently. They appeared to be ordinary Waite-Ryder Tarot cards, all of the Hanged Man. The card in the garden house, however, was from a different deck known either as the Lady Freida Harris or Aleister Crowley deck. The implication was clear yet puzzling. Somebody on the inside, presumably the murderer, was making a bold statement to other insiders or those who might be on his trail: this murder was meant to symbolize the Hanged Man in the Tarot. Wilson was quite surprised. Who would flaunt murder in such a manner? This might be expected from a serial killer or a homicidal psychopath, but this occult message was deliberately orchestrated by someone who had access to some of the most sensitive areas of the military, either American and/or British. Further, why would they leave deliberate clues? What purpose would it serve?

Well aware that Hess had been deeply involved in the occult, Wilson realized that it was not unsuitable that his death might be accompanied by such trappings. In fact, he knew that Hess's penchant for the occult may have led to his demise. The British had covertly sent feigned astrological interpretations to Hess which indicated that a flight to Scotland would be successful in terms of bringing peace between Germany and England.

What disturbed Wilson the most was that the Hess situation had intrigued him for decades; but now, all of a sudden, it was as if the intrigue had expanded exponentially but, at the same time, was being handed to him on a platter. It was disturbing because such clues do not ordinarily appear unless one is being deliberately baited. Were they baiting him, someone else, or just making a bold and audacious statement to posterity?

Perhaps the whole situation boiled down to an occult ritual murder and leaving the cards was part of the ceremony. If so, the bait might just be a circumstantial condition of ritualized madness. If it was deliberate bait, he also realized that he could study and analyze the bait without necessarily biting at it. Either way, he realized that there was no turning back now. This was the ultimate challenge of all his years in Army Intel. He would apply himself fully to the task, win or lose in the attempt, even if it meant death. Wilson had never feared death.

Looking up to the closed-circuit TV, he noticed that Heidi had just returned to the office and sat at her desk. She was obviously studying the file of books and papers he gave her. Watching her, he noticed that her desk was immaculate. She seemed to study only what she needed at one time. He could also see that she was making extensive notes. Wilson then congratulated himself on his choice of enlisting her help. She would make some splendid observations.

Wilson then turned his eye to the morning paper which he had bought earlier but had hardly looked at. In the head-

## A VISITOR..........................

lines, it was mentioned that the ninety-three-year-old Hess had committed suicide by hanging himself in his jail cell with a lamp chord. "Bastards!" he thought to himself. It is hard enough to hang yourself when you're healthy and strong, and this was a person who could not even walk a significant distance without assistance. There was no way he had hung himself. Wilson then looked at the photo of the garden house and could even see a lamp chord that was still plugged in. Didn't even cover their tracks too good, he thought. He was keenly aware that the photos he had were highly sensitive and were not going to be secure in the hands of anyone else. Wilson then read the rest of the article before placing his palm over his forehead and burying himself deep in thought.

Lost in thought, Wilson heard a shuffling in the hall through the audio of the closed-circuit TV. Looking on the TV screen, he noticed a man approaching his regular office. "Who in the hell is that?" he thought to himself.

The man was large and carried a small briefcase. Wilson sized him up quickly and gauged him as being about 55 years old and 6'3" but very gawky. Wouldn't do too well in a tough fight, he thought. Might have some strength, but he could tell by the way the man walked that he would not be too hard to deal with. Knocking on the door, the man announced to Heidi that he was a professor who had a message for General Wilson. After discreetly placing her books in a closed drawer, Heidi let the man in.

"Hello. I am Dr. Frederich, and I was sent by the Joint Chiefs to announce that a new deadly flu virus has emerged in certain Pentagon staff. All military personnel in the general vicinity will have to be inoculated. General Wilson and the rest of the brass get the honor and advantage of receiving their's first."

"Oh, I'm sorry," said Heidi, "General Wilson will not be back until next week. You'll have to come back then."

"Oh?" said Dr. Frederich, who was genuinely surprised. "That is unfortunate. I'll have to come back."

Frederich turned to leave, but just as he reached the door, he suddenly stopped and turned around as if an idea had just occurred to him.

"Well, you know, I could administer your inoculation and we could get that out of the way right now."

"But," said Heidi, "I thought you said that the brass would receive this first. I am only a lieutenant."

Watching the closed-circuit television, Wilson then saw Frederich withdraw a syringe from his briefcase. This was too much. Wilson got up, grabbed a pistol and went to the door with the prospect of saving Heidi.

Frederich, holding the syringe as if he was about to inoculate, moved in her direction.

"Don't worry, my dear. It won't hurt you. Just relax."

Heidi stepped back quickly and scrambled for the drawer at the left of her desk. Inside was a pistol. As she grabbed it, the door opened. It was Wilson and he was brandishing his own pistol as well. He said nothing.

Frederich turned back. As he did, he saw Wilson and suddenly changed his tune.

"General Wilson, I have inoculation orders. I was just trying to assist the young lady here. Look here..."

Heidi now had her pistol pointed at Dr. Frederich who paid her no attention as he began to reach into his pocket, apparently to show his orders. The pocket, however, was bulging and revealed the contour of what appeared to be a gun.

"Shoot," barked Wilson, "that's an order!"

Without any hesitation, Heidi fired her pistol right into the heart of Dr. Frederich who slumped over, dead.

"Who in the hell is this?" he asked, assessing the damaged body without touching it.

"You sure came at the right time. He's some idiot who claimed you needed an inoculation and then me. He never showed any papers, but we should have a look at them."

"Just as I thought," said Wilson as he moved around the corpse, "the son-of-a-bitch had a gun."

"I saw that, too," said Heidi. "That is why I aimed straight for the heart. On second thought, perhaps we should have questioned him."

"Yes and no," said Wilson. "This sends a very strong message to whoever is bird-dogging me. Believe me, in this line of work, it is better to scare your opponent and put him on edge."

"Should we call the MPs now?" asked Heidi.

 "Yes," answered Wilson. Be careful not to touch him or his papers. Whatever he has on his person is relevant to our intelligence division, just by reason of the fact that he showed up here and threatened you. I've got him on videotape reaching into his pocket, a clear case of aggression. The gun is pretty incriminating.

"Why did you order me to shoot?" asked Heidi. "You could have done it."

"It looks all the better if it is a woman shooting an attacker and not a grizzled old soldier snuffing out a punk," answered Wilson.

"Or were you testing me to see how I would hold up under fire?" asked Heidi.

"Maybe a little bit of both," answered Wilson. "Once the MPs get here, I want a full inventory of everything in that ass hole's briefcase and on his person. We'll do a full report and then get the hell out of here for the night so we can regroup our efforts. Take your notes, too. We're gonna need 'em."

Heidi then picked up the phone so she could call the Military Police.

"A lame attempt," said Wilson, shaking his head, "a lame attempt indeed. They sent a limp fish to do a man's work."

"Who sent what and why?' she asked.

"I'm not exactly sure, but its pretty damn clear what quarter we're dealing with."

"Shrinks?" asked Heidi. "He looked like a shrink."

"No, Heidi. It's punks. We're dealing with pathetic punks."

## CHAPTER FIVE

## THE KING'S CHAMBER

As Aiwass the Moor led Carl Hess and his son into the King's Chamber of the Great Pyramid of Giza, he spoke.

"When you enter the King's Chamber, you are entering an area of high concentration. Whatever you think will be magnified."

As the party of three entered, Carl immediately heard a trace of a woman's voice, but he denied it. At about the same time, the younger Rudi's body suddenly twitched as if something had disturbed him.

"Did something bother you, Rudi? Are you all right?" asked Carl.

"It's just the peculiar energies of the pyramid," said the Moor. "Did you not hear the slight call of a voice as well?"

"You heard that, too?" asked Carl. "I do not know what that was exactly, but it reminded me of something you said earlier. I actually am on a quest of sorts, if that is possible...I mean to say, if it is possible, I would like to find out what happened to my beloved first wife. Her name was Elizabeth, and she died of pneumonia."

"And that was her voice?" asked the Moor.

"I have no idea, but I thought I should tell you that I do have a quest of sorts. I mean, it is background to taking my son on a cultural adventure, but I thought I should tell you."

"Perhaps you will get an answer. When I say that the pyramid is a concentration of energy, that also means an integration or unifying of energy. It brings things together and unites what might otherwise remain ununited."

"Like with the dead?" asked Carl.

"Yes, like the dead. This, of course, is the land of the dead. But it unites with much more than just the dead. The pyramid is a basic design of creation. It is the Great Mother and unites with all life. That means other worlds and all of creation. I will invite you to rest your mind and see what comes into it. Here, look at this coffer, sometimes erroneously thought to be a burial casket. This is a vehicle of rebirth by connecting to the essence of all that is."

## THE KING'S CHAMBER . . . . . . . . . . . . . . .

Pointing to Carl, he motioned him to get in the huge coffer and lie on his back."

"Empty your mind and just focus on an imaginary point between your eyes," said the Moor.

As Carl left his mind blank, he could suddenly see a picture of Elizabeth talking to him. He did not know if he was just hearing what he wanted to hear or if the voice was independent of him, but he listened anyway. The voice said that she missed him and loved him and that she was busy and would be doing things for him. Then she faded out and her voice was gone. He opened his eyes and saw the Moor and his young son still in concentration.

Getting out of the coffer, it was now young Rudolph's turn to lie in this ancient construct. As the young man relaxed, pictures came pouring in. His mind became filled with a beautiful and vibrant civilization that once existed where these abandoned pyramids now stood. His young imagination was rich and provocative as it built upon all he had heard from the Moor in the last hour. He thought of a great civilization uniting all of the people of the world. It was far more beautiful than anything he had ever imagined.

When Rudolph was finished, the Moor took a turn as well. He seldom missed an opportunity to focus while in the pyramid. In fact, he believed it was the pyramid which was responsible for his immense knowledge. He usually included the people he guided into his concentration exercise. As he sat there with his eyes closed, he could see the young boy he was now with portraying a great role in the future by trying to advance civilization back to what it might once have been in ancient times. He could see the young boy talking to a vast crowd. Then, his mind suddenly switched to something else. He saw the other young man he had taken to this very spot, the young man he had blindfolded and left in the King's Chamber. This young man, of dark skin color, was also speaking to a vast crowd, but this crowd was of a different skin color than what the other youngster spoke to. He then saw both of the two young people as men, talking and negotiating. They were making settlements of peace. The scene soon faded and he saw both of the young men in the King's Chamber itself while ghosts tried to get at them. The Moor, still in his vision, placed his hand over the air shaft to stop the ghosts

46

from entering, but they swarmed all around the pyramid, trying anyway they could to get at these two young characters. Aiwass then opened his eyes and said nothing.

Before leaving the King's Chamber, the Moor explained that the measurements of the pyramid and the hieroglyphics therein tell a story that correlates with the circumstances of man. Further, he stated that one could see a precise analogy of the events of the Holy Bible within the geometry and sacred writings, including the birth, death and resurrection of the Christ. He was quick to point out, however, that other great traditions of other civilizations could also be witnessed in this great construct. It was not exclusive to Christianity which, he said, is just one interpretation of events. The scheme of the pyramid included far more than could be imagined. If we are to believe the story of the pyramid, said the Moor, there will be great chaos followed by a great unification of universal truth and harmony. These were words the young Rudolph would never forget.

When they finally emerged from their guided tour of the pyramid, the Moor said he would show them a bit of the Sphinx before returning to find Tariq who could take them back to their hotel. As they made their way to the dusty ruin, the Moor explained that the Sphinx had always been considered a great riddle but that it was also a sign of great terror. The Sphinx was ready to consume the ignorant. Within that countenance of terror and apparent lack of sympathy, however, there was a great secret which could ignite boundless compassion.

"The Sphinx," said the Moor, "is a cleverly thought out monument that symbolizes the predicament of Mankind. It represents the elements, the juxtaposition of the stars and the potential enlightenment of mankind."

As they approached the area between the paws of the Sphinx, a dust devil suddenly whirled in their direction.

"Close your eyes," said the Moor, "it will soon pass."

When they opened their eyes and wiped any remaining sand away, they were all taken by surprise. Sitting in front of them, in a lotus position, was Timothy Drew, the same man that the Moor had blindfolded three days earlier.

"This," said the Moor, "is a cause for celebration."

**THE KING'S CHAMBER................**

## CHAPTER SIX

## THE PICNIC

As General Wilson and Heidi drove off after receiving what amounted to a rather routine interrogation by the military police, Heidi was the first to speak up.

"At least we can relax a bit," she said.

"Yes," but not much," he replied. "I knew the MPs wouldn't be much of a problem with the closed-circuit video of his assault. Just in case, I disabled the sound so they wouldn't hear my order to shoot. That might not have sounded too good."

"It wouldn't have mattered," she retorted. "They found a gun on him and false credentials as well. There's no way they would even think about bringing up any other angle than self-defense," she continued.

"Yes," he agreed, "but we've got much more business to conduct now. I haven't had a chance to speak with you freely until now."

Both of their minds were buzzing with thoughts.

"I have a question first," said Heidi. "By what miracle did you just happen to walk in the office at the moment he assaulted me?"

"It wasn't a miracle at all. I was staking out the office from across the hall. The high voltage closet is actually an entrance to an auxiliary office for me. I was not taking any chances and was waiting to see who might visit me after the Hess affair. With the closed-circuit hookup, I could see you were in danger, but you handled yourself pretty well."

"Why did you order me to shoot?"

"I knew it would look better for the MPs. I could've gotten away with it, but it just looks much better. Would you have shot him anyway?"

"I didn't think about it, but when I heard your order, I just aimed straight for the heart."

"Good shot you were, too. That pistol training paid off very well. Now, back to business. First, I knew the Hess affair was and is highly charged, but I had no idea that the opposition would either be so fast to act or be so suspicious of

# THE PICNIC..................

me and my inklings to get to the bottom of the mystery. I was not even sure they knew of my interest. I mean, I've kept it a well-guarded secret or what I thought was a well-guarded secret. I'm still not sure how much they know of me. I've been leaking somewhere."

"Where are we gonna go?" Heidi asked.

"We can't go home; not to your house or to mine. That is too risky. Any major hotel is suspect, even if I use an alternative identity. The best bet is to check into a flea bag and pay cash. Once there, we can regroup. We need to eat first though. The weather's nice and I prefer to eat outdoors. Besides, no one can eavesdrop on us if we are outside."

Stopping at a deli, they picked up picnic food and walked to a nearby park. It was the dinner hour of a beautiful Virginia evening. After a few bites, General Wilson looked around, somewhat suspiciously, to make sure he was not being listened too. He then spoke to Heidi.

"As I told you the other day, I have more to tell you, much more. First though, I want to know how far you made it with the Hess materials. What did you learn? Just tell me."

"I got into it pretty deeply in a rather short time. I even went to the library last night to see what I could find from the newspapers of May 1941. As you know, I'm a speed reader."

"Did you see today's paper?" Wilson asked.

"Yes."

"Let's hear your analysis thus far."

"First," said Heidi," Hess did not die by hanging, at least by his own hands. That is virtually impossible to pull off for a feeble man of ninety-three.

"Next," continued Heidi, "that he died at the age of ninety-three is suggestive of an occult message."

"What do you mean by that?" asked Wilson.

"In the materials you gave me, an occult reference boldly stated that ninety-three is the symbol of thelema."

"God — that's right! I forgot about that. Do you know what thelema means, Heidi?"

"I didn't until I looked at those books you gave me. Thelema is the numerological equivalent to the Greek words for *will* and *agape*, the latter meaning the higher aspect of love."

"If," asked Wilson, "his murder was deliberately accomplished at the age of ninety-three, do you think it is symbolic of him dying at the hands of a willful murder grace for a miserable old man who was suffering Hess was?"

"It would be all of the above, plus any other you might not have said," she fired back.

"How do you know that?" asked Wilson, surprised by her self-confident answer.

"Because you have to include all potentialities. The event is always going to reach beyond the will of the murderer. Even if the murderer did not kill him with the age of ninety-three in mind, the coincidence cannot be dismissed in a thorough investigation. It may have no relevance in a civic trial; but, when you are dealing with occult matters, and the tarot cards at the murder scene tell us that we are, all aspects must be fully entertained."

"OK," said Wilson, seemingly satisfied for now, "continue."

"The number ninety-three is only a clue that suggests an occult connection, either deliberately or by happenstance. Hess was deeply involved in such matters so an occult murder should not surprise anyone. His known associates in occultism were Karl and Albrecht Haushofer. Karl was the occult mentor of Hess and some people say Hitler as well. Albrecht, his son, was one-quarter Jewish by reason of his mother. Besides being a clairvoyant and well versed in the religions of Tibet and Japan, Karl Haushofer was involved in the Green Dragon Society, the most politically powerful organization in the Orient.

"Although Haushofer was known to be a practicing occultist who was deeply involved with the Thule Society and the Vril Society, there appears to be an absence of information when it comes to the exact occult connections between Hess and the Haushofers. Hess apparently became enamored of Haushofer in Munich where the latter was a professor who lectured on geopolitics," said Heidi as she paused for breath.

"You're doing pretty good, Heidi, but I'm not too surprised. Did you read the Haushofer letters?"

"I read what was in a book, not the originals. They were a series of letters between both of the Haushofers and Hess, all about six months prior to his flight. It is very clear from those letters that Hitler knew about Hess's flight to Scotland as an envoy of peace," said Heidi.

PICNIC . . . . . . . . . . . . . . . . . . . .

"You're damn right he did," said Wilson. "Now, I'd better give you a chance to eat your dinner before we carry on. As you eat your dinner, I'll elaborate a little on that last theme in hopes of bringing out any loose ends that you might have picked up."

"Hitler," said Wilson, "did not want England in the war, but Hess was even more adamant about it. Once France, Holland and Belgium fell, it would have been an ideal situation for Germany if England agreed to peace. Haushofer realized that with the fall of these countries, Germany now had more than enough living space. Both he and Hess, even better than Hitler, knew that a fight with Russia could be devastating. A war on two fronts was extremely risky."

"Yes," Heidi stepped in, "but Hess was being baited in an occult fashion but also by political entreaties. He took all the risk and ended up strung out like a...like a...."

"You mean like a hanged man?" asked the General.

"Ahhhh!" Heidi gasped in surprise, almost screaming.

Wilson became suddenly concerned, fearing that she might have downed something dangerous while she was eating. After all, his faculties were still on high security alert.

"Are you all right, Heidi?" asked Wilson.

"No, no, I'm fine. It was just that you said 'hanged man.'"

"Yes, I did say 'hanged man.' What of it?"

"I had a quickie card reading just the other day," said Heidi. "You know — where a gypsy pulls one card out of a tarot deck and gives you a quick reading on a question. I asked her about my relationship with you, and she pulled a single card out of her deck. It was the Hanged Man! I can't believe you said that!"

"I can see how that would unnerve you, Heidi, "said Wilson, "but please don't scream out if you can help it. I don't want to attract any attention, and you might find the rest of what I have to say to be just as unbelievable."

## CHAPTER SEVEN

## THE VISION

Having been escorted to the King's Chamber of the Great Pyramid by Aiwass the Moor, Aleister Crowley and his new bride made themselves as comfortable as possible and began what was to be a momentous ritual of love. After staking out a circle and placing four elements around it, thus designating the four cardinal points of a cross, Crowley consecrated the circle and began a long series of chanting incantations that would have sounded like a complete jumble to anyone who was not familiar with his brand of speech. There was a sonorous rhythm in his voice that ranged from the extremely pleasant to an onerous depth that suggested the denizens of someplace sinister.

As his bride listened to him, she heard him begin to chant in a voice she had not heard him use before.

"I haven't heard that before, have I?" said Rose Kelly as he murmured none too softly.

On the outside, it appeared that Crowley ignored her. In fact, he was oblivious to what she said. Prior to this endeavour, he had consumed a considerable amount of hashish. When he had finally finished his incantations, he led Rose to the coffer where they would engage in what Crowley would term magical sex.

Crowley, who possessed an abnormally large pineal gland, was not a normal man. Having suffered at an early age from sadistic school masters and clergymen, Crowley became an avowed enemy of anything "civilized Christianity" stood for. Consequently, he developed his own philosophy that he called Magick and sought in his own way to overturn all that "civilized Christianity" stood for. In his mind, Christianity was hypocrisy, cruelty, browbeating, subjugation of the weak, and an entirety of other descriptions that might well portray any powerful institution of Mankind. His mission, so he thought, was to advance Mankind by enabling him to access hitherto unforeseen dimensions of the mind and spirit. By putting man in touch with this and allowing everyone to uncover their true will, he foresaw a new era of enlightenment.

# THE VISION

This new era is what astrologers commonly refer to as the Age of Aquarius.

In light of the above, it should not surprise anyone that, instead of nullifying the sexual urge, Crowley saw this urge as the hallmark and crowning glory of his own belief system. The will, combined with the sexual urge, was viewed as the most powerful expression of the holy spirit. The will, when aligned with the orgasmic function, was sublime and at its most potent. It was therefore in this place of great concentration that he sought to make his greatest magical act: an invoked state of ecstacy and a supplication to the gods to change the world once and for all and reverse the tyranny of Mankind's spiritually feeble institutions.

After finally being consumed by a certain amount of physical exhaustion from travel, the aroma of hashish, intense mental exertion, and a round of strenuous physical sex within the confines of the coffer in the King's Chamber, Aleister Crowley went out like a light. Whether it was sleep or a trance is best left to debate.

Whatever happened, he was seeing the world without any reference to his physical body or what could be termed ordinary perceptions. He was virtually viewing the entire world in such a manner that he was simulating the position of a god. He had no body, no arms, no legs but only eyes. Perhaps he could hear but there were no sounds. He was completely unrestricted and could see the Sphinx and pyramids below. It was beautiful, but that was not something he could appreciate. He was no longer in a state of mind that could be termed human. For the most part, it was a state of mind he would not remember very well at all.

There was a feeling that he was outside the realm of creation. If God was a single viewpoint or consciousness, this must be what it is like, he thought. If his perceptions approached what might be termed a perfect state, however, it was only perfect in terms of perception and only from the perception of the observer. The possibilities, however, were quite limitless. The proposition he faced was that each and every creature possessed the same potential.

This experience of great ecstasy, however, comes with a significant caveat. No matter how perfect one might be, there is no easy escape from the convoluted introversion that takes place when a spirit returns to the physical plane by going through a birthing canal and struggling to survive. The birthing process, amidst many other evolutionary nightmares and perils, distorts and reduces the capacity for perfection that is achieved in a remote state of god consciousness. In other words, being detached and godlike is not so hard when one has no attachments or survival considerations to attend to. The spiritual state and the incarnated state are two very different worlds. In Crowley's case, his enlarged pineal gland made the distortion and conduit to this "god consciousness" all the more exaggerated.

As Crowley looked over the Great Pyramid and Sphinx from his extended state of consciousness, he began to see their mathematical underpinnings. All of a sudden, the entire landscape looked more like a draftsman's board with equations and measurements. More and more details appeared until it looked like a three dimensional holographic version of a drafting board that eventually folded into nonlinear space. In other words, the immediate geography of Earth folded into another continuum or dimension. It then came back into three dimensions. He watched it fold and unfold several times until he got the point.

When the math lesson was over, the space above the pyramids was black. He witnessed seventy-two figures who appeared in white. They looked like the jinn, he thought. They were then met by an additional seventy-two counterparts appearing in black. He knew they were of a similar consciousness to what he had experienced in his godlike state, but he also knew they were different. They represented keys to the physical dominion that lay before him.

As Crowley watched, he saw the black and white figures spawn into a myriad of multiple figures that struggled against each other in a contest. It was white versus the black and vice versa. The different figures formed into energy spirals and a myriad of other forms. Sometimes the black would overtake the white and sometimes it was the other way around. It represented the endless struggle of the forces between light and dark. Countless renditions and dramatizations of history were acted out until he came to the realization that virtually any historical event was only an iteration of infinity. That realization resulted in the cessation of the dramatizations.

# THE VISION.....................

Lying in the coffer, Crowley was now alone, his wife having climbed out. Now fully conscious of being in his body, he looked up. When he closed his eyes, he could see the figures of energy once again, but now all of these forces were dive-bombing towards his body. All were rushing in to make their claim. From the outside, he looked as if he was in a state of shock. Soon after, he fell asleep.

As he dreamed, Crowley saw the black and white spirits again. They dramatized the death of Osiris and then the birth of Horus. They went into him and then out of him. Some wanted to do good things and others bad. In all, each sought him out as an entry way to the physical world. For Crowley, it was not an envious position to be in. He would never be the same for he had become a magnet for forces that were outside the boundaries of time.

........CHAPTER EIGHT.........

## THE HANGED MAN

"Heidi," said Wilson in response to Heidi's shock over the fortune teller having picked the Hanged Man card, "I'm not sure what this gypsy card reader was getting at, but she was right about you and I being involved with the Hanged Man."

"What do you mean?" said Heidi, almost recovered from her shock.

"Read this report," he said.

Heidi then read the report from Agent T which explained the mysterious Hanged Man cards found in Spandau. When she finished, her eyes opened a little wider.

"Oh my, God!" she said. "What the hell does this all mean?"

"I'm not sure," said Wilson, "except that someone is acting with a great deal of deliberation and audacity as well as trying to send a message. I only received this after I put you onto the case."

"Well," she said, "the first thing I want to do is study what the Hanged Man means."

"I've been working on that," replied Wilson.

"What can you tell me?" she asked.

"The Hanged Man" said Wilson, "is the most mysterious card in the Tarot. It contradicts itself in countless ways because it represents the paradoxical nature of life. A paradox is a contradiction, yet it is true. It cannot be denied. In the case of the Hanged Man, it presents certain truths but the meaning is hidden in the apparent opposites of those truths. Have I said a mouthful already?"

"Yes, but there is more," replied Heidi.

"In a traditional reading," continued Wilson, "the Hanged Man tells the aspirant to 'let go' and not push a matter. In Chinese philosophy or Taoism, this is *wu wei*, the action of causing by not causing. In other words, one moves forward to advantage by standing still and not stressing. One sacrifices action or pomposity of oneself in order to emerge as the victor. It is a card of spiritual victory by letting go of the physical."

"What else?" she persisted.

## THE HANGED MAN..................

"The hung man on the card is the Fool of the Tarot. He is on a spiritual journey. Finding a tree, not unlike the Buddha, he remains under it for nine days. Why the number nine I am not sure."

"In numerology," said Heidi, "nine means coming to an end."

"Okay," replied Wilson. "Everything passes by him for nine days: people, animals, rain, weather, the sun, the moon but he remains under the tree, nonplused. With no reason why, he climbs the tree and dangles from a branch, completely giving up. He cares about nothing, including his identity. When the coins in his pocket fall to the ground, he sees them only as round pieces of metal. His perspective completely changes as he now hangs between the physical world and the spiritual world. He can see both very clearly. For the first time, the mysteries of the universe are revealed to him. He is connected to the deepest mystery of life itself. It is an awakening."

"I feel," said Heidi, "like I have just been injected with adrenaline. It is all too much too fast."

"We are immersed into it beyond our knees and waist. Up to our neck, I'd say," replied Wilson. "There is no turning back. But I must tell you, I have faced far more harrowing situations on the battlefield."

"OK," said Heidi, "I don't even want to address why or how the psychic came up with the Hanged Man as far as me and you — not just yet. It's obvious we are immersed in this case. I want to know why it shows itself with Hess. What do you think for starters?"

"It's ill advised to think too much. We can think, but primarily we have to just connect the dots. Hess," said Wilson, "was the last living symbol of the Third Reich. The card plays off a murder but suggests victory."

"Victory for who?"' asked Heidi.

"It depends on your perspective. If you look at it one way, it is as if the card suddenly presented itself on our path, especially with the psychic reading you had. That would mean that we will find victory through standing still."

"You mean I shouldn't have shot Frederich and just taken his hypodermic like a limp fish?"

Wilson laughed. "God no. That would have been his victory. It's important not to take this stuff too literally.

Above all, one has to carry out the duty of one's life. Remember, this is a complex card and the truth is found in the apparent opposite."

"Exactly!" exclaimed Heidi.

"Now," continued Wilson, "there's another aspect here and that has to do with Hess himself. The cards suggest that Hess has achieved victory through his own self-sacrifice."

"Someone pushed the envelope however and had him killed," said Heidi.

"Yes," said Wilson, "it's complex. Did Hess himself achieve victory or did the person killing Hess achieve victory? That is the question."

"It wasn't the death card they chose. Someone is proclaiming victory but victory of what?" asked Heidi.

"Hess led a magical life, an occult life, but most of that was wiped out after he was captured, at least as far as I can tell. That he died in his ninety-third year suggests that it is in alignment with his will or someone else's will."

"Yes," said Heidi, "but why are they leaving clues behind? Are they talking to you deliberately? I mean, they came after you with Frederich."

"Whether they are talking to me exclusively or not, they are talking to me. I mean, me…and you too now…are being talked to — stalked actually. We are just not exactly sure who is doing the talking, but it doesn't matter. You just listen and treat it as an invisible voice. The battlefield is like that. You don't think and ask questions or ask for someone's serial number. You shoot and kill. If you do not, you'll be dead. After a while, you develop something of a sixth sense or intuition. That is your ticket to life on the battlefield."

"So, what are the cards saying?" asked Heidi.

"If I back up and look at the whole picture, the leaving of the cards at the crime scene is an invitation."

"An invitation to what? How are you sure it is not bait?" she asked.

"Well, it is both. The Hanged Man is an invitation to pursue the mystery of all mysteries. It symbolizes self-sacrifice with a transformation from a materialistic consciousness to a spiritual consciousness."

"Yes," she stated, "and extended to you by a willful murder. It would appear our initiation into these mysteries, whether by the specific murder of Hess or the bigger picture, is being conducted by a murderer."

"So it would appear," agreed Wilson, "but remember, appearances are not what they seem, particularly when you are dealing with this particular card. Remember, the Hanged Man presents certain truths but the meaning is hidden in the apparent opposites of those truths. There is one other possibility though."

"And what is that?" asked Heidi.

"Agent T. He has become a variable in this equation. Because of all the intense ramifications that have ensued, we have to consider that he has either been compromised or plays another role than just reporting on Hess. In this business, one always has to take the double agent factor into account."

"He did say we'd be hearing more," said Heidi.

"Yes, but for now, we'd better get going. It is quite likely that both our homes will be monitored. We're going to check into a flea bag motel. That way we won't be monitored."

Gathering up the remains of their picnic dinner, they placed it in a nearby garbage can and headed for the car.

## CHAPTER NINE

### EL MOROCCO

When Carl Hess and his son strolled into the El Morocco Cafe, it was mid-morning. They were going to have a late morning meal and enjoy themselves before visiting the Cairo Museum later that day. As they got situated, they noticed a strange man in the corner. He had a deck of cards and was spreading them on the table. A lady sat in front of him, but she was quiet. The man was so intent on the cards in front of him, he seemed impervious to all that was around him.

Suddenly and unexpectedly, the man looked up from his cards and stared directly at Carl's eyes.

"What do you want?" said the strange man in English.

"As a matter of fact," said Carl, speaking impeccable English, "I do have a question. I was taking a tour of the Great Pyramid yesterday, and the fellow who guided me, a Moor...."

"You mean that man?" said the strange man as he pointed to Aiwass the Moor who had just entered the cafe from a rear door. Aiwass was accompanied by quite an entourage that included the young man they had found between the paws of the Sphinx just the day before.

"Why, yes, as a matter of fact," said Carl. "He had suggested I was on a quest. In fact, I was just showing my son here the sites of antiquity. Actually, I do have a spiritual question. Perhaps you could..."

Carl Hess was interrupted when he felt a friendly hand grasp him on the shoulder. It was the Moor, his tour guide from yesterday.

"I can't say I expected to see all of my patrons from the last few days. Come, all of you, and join us. We have cause for celebration! You are most welcome, too," said the Moor to the strange man and the lady. The strange man was Aleister Crowley.

Crowley, who had been able to successfully overcome the interruption of his own card-induced meditation, now found himself having to recover from the shock of having been interrupted twice. His eyes looked disoriented. The Moor, sensing his discomfort, spoke again.

# EL MOROCCO . . . . . . . . . . . . . . . . . . . . .

"Yes, do come. As a matter of fact, that man in the colorful cap insisted I invite all of you over."

The Moor then pointed to an oriental man who was wearing a rainbow-colored cap which made him stand out amongst the others. He was also wearing a white saffron robe.

Crowley looked up at the Tibetan as if he recognized him. He gestured to Rose, and the entire party made their way to the table of the Moor's entourage. Although not a word was spoken, this was a very special gathering of a brotherhood that traced its roots back to the ancient Magi of antiquity. They were a sacred brotherhood of wisdom that reached across continents. On this morning they had gathered to celebrate the initiation of young Timothy Drew, a man who was just about to begin his education in the brotherhood.

Just days before, the Moor, at the direction of his brethren, had taken a blindfolded Timothy to the King's Chamber whereupon he was to either find his way out or perish. It was an ancient rite of initiation into adeptship, but it was not offered to just anyone. Timothy Drew was a man of special abilities who had found his way from America to the delta of the Nile. From there, it did not take him long to get to Cairo.

When he finally arrived, the brethren was already waiting for him. In fact, he was expected; not because he had sent a letter or was summoned by normal human means but because it was foreseen. Now that he had passed his initial test of initiation, he would undergo a ten year training program before returning to America to teach that land the truth of its ancient heritage and what had been forgotten.

On this morning, however, the brethren was celebrating. The Tibetan, the man with the rainbow headdress, invited the others to come and join them. He spoke a somewhat broken English but seemed to understand much. Although from diverse backgrounds, everyone of the brethren spoke English. In fact, all had a background in linguistics and spoke different languages.

The Hesses and the Crowleys were invited to sit at the center of the table, right across from the Moor, the Tibetan and Timothy Drew.

Addressing the Moor, Carl Hess was the first to speak. "I was just saying to this man...excuse me, sir, I did not even ask your name. I apologize."

"Crowley. Edward Alexander Crowley. My friends call me Aleister, and this is my wife, Rose."

"I am Carl Hess, and this is my son, Rudolph."

Crowley's eyes darted immediately at the young boy.

"Well, as I was saying," continued Hess, "this man right here had suggested I was on a quest. To make a long story short, my first wife died almost ten years ago. As I walked into the land of the dead, I became curious to find out how Elizabeth might be. When I saw you were gifted in the art of reading cards, I thought maybe you might be able to give a clue. Is that possible. I could pay you, of course."

"Payment is not necessary. Be silent. I will focus and choose a card," said Crowley.

Crowley then went back into his trancelike state. He focused hard on the deck and seemed to be making supplications to an other worldly contact. Suddenly breaking the focus, he reached into the middle of the deck and pulled out a card. It was the Hanged Man.

"*This*," said Crowley with emphasis, "is the card, but it is not for you. It is for your boy. Here, take it. It is for you."

Crowley then gave the boy the card. The whole affair had caught everyone at the table by surprise, but they were all taking in every word as if it were a great sideshow.

"Excuse me," said Timothy Drew. "If I may offer it, I have an answer. The woman named Elizabeth has come to me. She is well and sends her love to Carl, but she wishes to notify you that she is also with us today on a mission. It is not an accident that we have come here today. Elizabeth says that the young boy here, Rudolph, has a big role to play in his future life. He will be a very important man. She wants you both to know that she will attend to him throughout his life. There may be difficult periods, and she will be there to see him through. Once again, she sends her love."

As murmurs could be heard all across the table, two Caucasian men at the end of the table, one rather short, began a rather animated discussion. Aiwass the Moor then stood up and addressed the group.

"Our new initiate has indeed shown his worthiness. Perhaps he would like to treat our new friends to a demonstration of what I discussed with Carl yesterday?"

"You mean the power of the Vril?" asked Carl Hess.

The Moor nodded and all suddenly became quiet. The Tibetan with the rainbow hat then produced a piece of parchment. "Use this," said the Tibetan, "it will make the job easier."

The Moor was about to test the new initiate's abilities. He did not know, but readily suspected, that the young Timothy Drew could move this leather parchment without touching it. Placing the parchment in front of Timothy Drew, he cleared off the rest of the table. Everyone was silent once again.

Timothy concentrated but did not waste any time. Before anyone could think skeptical thoughts, he had, either through pure will alone or by a stage magician's trick, lifted the parchment off of the table without touching it. It then began to move, ostensibly at the will of Timothy Drew, in the direction of the young Hess. As it moved towards the young man, however, the direction of the flow was interrupted. Instead, it began to shift towards Aleister Crowley as if it were being influenced by another force. The parchment then appeared to tug itself back in the direction of the young Hess as if there was a war of two wills. Finally, the parchment moved unfettered and stood right in front of Rudolph.

"Grab it!" said the Tibetan, and the young boy did.

"Well, there you have it!" said the Moor to Carl Hess. "What I told you yesterday about the pyramids is backed up by more than a simple theory. You have now experienced the force of will, also known as the Vril. Remember, the power of the Vril is the power of the pyramid and that is the power of Allah. And, that is what we are all here to discuss. I must now ask our new friends to leave us to our work."

Nodding to the Crowleys and the Hesses, it was clear the Moor wanted to continue their discussion alone.

"Excuse me," said Aleister Crowley. "Would it be all right if first you introduced me to the two white men at the end of the table?"

"Of course," said the Moor who then walked around the table and escorted Aleister Crowley to meet Karl Haushofer and George Ivanovitch Gurdjieff.

........... CHAPTER TEN ..........

## THE FLEA BAG

After checking in at an inconspicuous motel, General Wilson and Heidi sat down on the their respective beds. Both were ready and eager to talk about the momentous events of the last few days.

"Where did we leave off?" asked Heidi.

"Agent T," answered Wilson.

"Yes, and the prospect that he either might not be what he seems to be or what we would like him to be."

"Exactly, but we can't evaluate that until we hear whatever else it is he has to tell us," said Wilson.

"Unless," said Heidi, "he was part of the setup for Frederich."

"No," responded Wilson. "Agent T is not that lame. Dr. Frederich was one lame son-of-a-bitch. Agent T wouldn't be inclined to involve himself with such a group of imbeciles. Not likely at all."

"You might call Frederich lame, and I think you're right, but whoever sent him represents a powerful force," said Heidi.

"Oh?" said Wilson betraying inquisitiveness. "Exactly what power are you referring to?"

"They are the ones making us sweat bullets now," said Heidi.

"Listen, I've been on the battlefield. Even though it's been a long time, you never forget the lessons learned there. You're right — there are powerful people behind Frederich, but what they did is like the Baltimore Orioles sending out a bunch of little leaguers to play their first inning. They're gonna have to do a lot better than that."

"Then," said Heidi, "why are you going to all this extra attention to avoid scrutiny?"

"Because," answered Wilson, "you are right. We <u>are</u> dealing with a force that is potentially very powerful."

"Unless," said Heidi, "we are being deliberately baited by someone who wants us to make a move and show our hand."

"Our opponent has already shown that he has tremendous resources or at least tremendous access to key institutions. My

## THE FLEA BAG . . . . . . . . . . . . . . . . . . .

first guess would tell me that they are far more abundant with resources than with intelligence. We have to consider all sides of the equation though. You are right.

"Now, let's get back to Agent T," continued Wilson, "His only possible involvement with Frederich is if he was part of a trap for us and I doubt that. I picked him because I trusted him and also had a beat on his profile. He's a good man."

"OK, General. You know Agent T, and I don't. We'll discount him for now, but how about you fill me in on some of the missing pieces of how you got involved in this whole thing in the first place. If I'm going to be of any help, I'll need to know."

"True," said Wilson. "Up to now, you've just been taking orders. You did a damn good job, too. I guess you could say you've passed your initiation."

"By shooting a man?" asked Heidi betraying her disdain. "I'm not sure I want to be part of anything that requires killing someone like a sacrifice."

"I didn't mean it like that, Heidi. In fact, I wasn't even looking at it like that. We've both been through a lot today. I meant to convey that you've been through one hell of a series of events and you're now proven and battle tested. I'm impressed, but as I said, I'm really not too surprised."

"OK, Hugh," said Heidi, now addressing him in the familiar, "how about filling me in on where you got involved in this whole mess."

"It goes back to the African campaign in World War II. I was still in my twenties and was serving in General Patton's Seventh Army in Africa. I performed quite well in battle. There was no fear in me, but that was only because my intuition took over in the heat of battle chaos. If you take charge when everyone is running about in confusion, your odds of survival actually increase, but you have to keep on taking positive and energetic action. You don't wait for lulls or look for lulls. It's kind of like creating a force field around you. I learned that and used it to the hilt."

"Is that why you're taking this all so seriously even though they made such a lame attempt upon us?" asked Heidi.

"Exactly," answered Wilson. "No waiting for lulls. What I experienced on the battlefield was just survival and it came quite naturally to me. In the meantime, I didn't realize that it was going to make a virtual hero out of me, particularly in Patton's eyes. He not only heard about what I did, but he saw it, too. When he found out my last name was Wilson, he took a personal liking to me, too."

"Why is that?"

"His mother was a Wilson. He later told me that she taught him about reincarnation and that he used that in his battle strategies. She taught him other occult stuff, too. Patton was a unique character, but his troops loved him.

"To make a long story short," he continued, "Patton was very disappointed as the war played itself out, particularly when it ended. Ever see the movie?"

"Sure, I saw it. How much of it is true?" asked Heidi.

"Enough," said Wilson. "That part about slapping the soldier..."

"You mean," she interrupted, "when he got in trouble for slapping a shell-shocked soldier and called him a coward?"

"Exactly! That was true as hell. Actually, he slapped two. Eisenhower gave him some public upbraids, but he was Patton's friend and was not about to have him shipped home. He was too valuable and that later proved out. In the movie, Bradley told him that slapping that soldier probably did more to win the war than any other act. It did rally his troops behind him."

"Wasn't Patton put out to pasture soon after that?" asked Heidi.

"Damn right he was," replied Wilson. "At least for the most part. It was that one act of slapping the soldier, however, that changed his whole strategy."

"What do you mean?" asked Heidi. "And, by the way, you must've known him pretty well."

"Far better than anyone would believe. He trusted me, too. He liked my battle-savvy, and besides, we were both Wilsons. Now, let me explain.

"For the last part of his life, Patton was forced to lay low, but he didn't always. After the war, he realized that the Russians would be a problem. He was not fooled for a minute. Personally and privately, he was outraged that the world stage was being set for what he called an old-fashioned Mexican standoff (with the Russians). To be more accurate, he called it pussyfooting.

THE FLEA BAG. . . . . . . . . . . . . . . . . . . .

"You see, in the old days — from the Old West to the days of the Vikings — men used to fight like men. Modern warfare, he said, mixed with diplomacy, had created a dangerous tendency. The whole setup predisposes one to fight like a fucking coward. In other words, when cultured men get involved in "civilized" fighting, they begin to employ rules which take away from unabashed aggression and domination. It sets up a passive-aggressive situation that eventually makes your opponent appear quite covert and complex. In fact, he said, it's like fighting the invisible man. With modern diplomacy, your enemy is no longer visible."

"In other words," asked Heidi, "the more 'civilized' war gets, the more opportunity there is for complexity and manipulation?"

"Exactly. It gets to the point where the enemy is not the fucking soldiers trying to kill your ass. Its the fucking politicians and people behind them that put everybody out there in the first place! Worse yet, your worst enemy might be the assholes sending you into battle! That incident with the soldier really ticked him off because it symbolized the whole essence of what he had noticed for years. Soldiers were covertly being told that it was acceptable to conduct themselves like fucking cowards. Can you imagine Caesar, Ghengis Khan or Alexander putting up with that?"

"Yes, I see your point, but Patton didn't allow that, did he?" asked Heidi.

"No, not at all, but that's not the point. What I'm saying is that the slapping incident dramatically symbolized to the outside world what was already going on inside of the Army. Like an attack bulldog, Patton wanted to go out and win the war. The so called "gents" wouldn't let him. McArthur went through the same damn thing in Korea. They wouldn't let him win the war, and he ended up being double-crossed.

"Even before the war was over," Wilson continued, "Patton knew something had to be done. The movie shows him 'taking it on the chin' and 'being a good soldier.' No, no no. Patton was not that resigned nor was he that stupid. Knowing full well that his ideas about the war and the near future were correct but were not about to be accepted, he made a bold and stunning counter-maneuver. He contacted other top brass and soldiers sympathetic to him, and he formed his own secret group."

"A secret society?" asked Heidi.

"No, he had no time for that bullshit — no brick-a-brack or secret oaths. He chose only people he could trust."

"That sounds like, technically speaking, he was flirting with treason," said Heidi, "at least as his superiors would have viewed it."

"No, not at all," said Wilson. "Hear me out. First, you have to understand how he identified and approached the problem. The problem, as he saw it and defined it, was pure and simple: cowardice — cowardice in human affairs. I mean... there is always going to be cowardice in human affairs. That is part of what makes human drama. But he was talking about cowardice ruling the roost or being the fulcrum when it came to power maneuvers in war or even in espionage."

"You mean," said Heidi, "that a culture of cowards was being created?"

"Exactly," answered Wilson. "You see, when people think of Patton, they think of someone who is war mad and not too rationale. The man had the spirit of a warrior, arguably too much, but he was not devoid of intelligence. He was a West Point graduate. There, he was taught to use models of warfare from the past.

"After he was censured for slapping the soldier, he was upset, but he soon got over that and went about constructing his model. He patiently and steadfastly identified all of the factors that made his own generalship or earlier career either difficult or impossible. In his final analysis, it all came down to two things. First and most obvious, it came down to the inability of bureaucrats and politicians to properly assess or perceive an actual need. This was, of course, exacerbated by their inability to see or follow logical or rational conclusions to a series of events. Most bureaucrats and politicians are just trying to do the irreducible minimum of what they consider "their job." They evaluate most duties with reference to fear of losing their office or job. This, in turn, goes hand in hand with the second factor in his analysis and that is cowardice."

"Yes," agreed Heidi, "but it is also quite clear from reading my field manual that headquarters or bureaucrats most often hamper an operation because they have not been in a similar position themselves and do not have commensurate experience with what they are dealing with."

"Of course," agreed Wilson, "you are right. That can explain bureaucrats and politicians to some degree. We can't expect them all to have basic military training, but his analysis was blatantly clear that it extended to military personnel as well. But, let me make it clear. I'm not necessarily talking about cowardice in the sense of being afraid to punch someone or take action. That is a big part of it, but there is a different type of cowardice that can worm its way into the military. It usually follows the pattern of either saying "yes" or using protocol to the detriment of an operation. People look at the rules before they look at the object.

"As he continued his analysis, Patton began to categorize all the exact events in his career where he had failed as a result of this type of behavior by others. It's kind of funny actually, and this is where his analysis finally broke away from what might be termed sobriety. In his own vernacular, he blamed all his misfortunes on 'god damn fucking queers.' "

Heidi laughed.

"It's funny, sure, but his analysis was not so funny. He traced every instance of either supply failure, backbiting, or deliberate sabotage. He named names and traced back their connections and then started making simple inquiries. Uniformly, except for the cases where the situations were too old to be completely verified, he found what he called a 'faggot in the woodpile.' "

"Was he saying that homosexuals are all bad?"

"No — he never said that, at least in relation to his analysis. He might've believed that or said something disparaging out of anger, but his analysis was unbiased. What he said was that all of his misfortunes were either directly or indirectly caused by an act of cowardice, expanded to mean what was referred to previously. In every instance, this was aggravated and/or caused by a person who had the symptoms of an effeminate coward."

"Today they would call him homophobic, no?"

"Yes, and a lot worse. But he was not really attacking the sexual part. He was funny. In fact, when he explained it to me, he said, in that most humorous vein he could display, 'I don't care if these guys fuck each other up the ass or in the ears. I just don't want to see any of these fucking faggots sabotaging my operations or getting our brave soldiers killed.' "

"So," asked Heidi, "he declared all gays as fair game?"

"No, that's not quite accurate. He was targeting cowardice. It just so happened that it was his informed conclusion that cowardice in his life was accompanied by men with effeminate characteristics. That is really the whole point. Women never fell into the equation as they seldom crossed him. It is not a condemnation of gender but of what he termed a 'lack of male element.' This often included backbiting or whispering campaigns as opposed to direct confrontation."

"Women can be spies, too. Remember Mata Hari."

"Yes, Heidi, but remember, we are dealing with Patton's analysis of his own experiences. He did not have a Mata Hari. He also said that it was important to target only the characteristics of a coward, not the person himself. He said that you could salvage a soldier by getting rid of his cowardice and making a man out of him. You then had a real soldier."

"Too often," said Heidi, "the effeminate man and the coward go hand-in-hand."

"The real problem was not homosexuals," continued Wilson. "The real problem was the erosion of the U.S. Constitution and the fabric of America. The original construct of America was being deconstructed through various means such as the Thirteenth Amendment never being legally ratified and when FDR took us off the gold standard. This was a covert subversion of America."

"Are you saying FDR and Woodrow Wilson were effeminate, too?" asked Heidi.

"Not exactly, Heidi. They did not come up in Patton's analysis, but you could make a case for FDR being a coward with the way he handled Pearl Harbor and the manipulation of data with our ambassador in Poland.

"What piqued Patton," continued Wilson, "was the manipulation that was going on behind the scenes. He could see that a pattern was being set to excuse the real war criminals: the European industrialists. What was worse than that, however, was that he could see the stage was being set to create what we now call the Cold War. This would create plentiful opportunities for profiteering by the same industrialists who made money off the first two world wars.

"What really set him off, however, was when the Russians, instead of returning a bunch of our own POWs, simply

## THE FLEA BAG . . . . . . . . . . . . . . . . . . . . .

liquidated them. They coldly killed our troops and they were supposed to be our allies. As a soldier, this was something he could not fathom. The Russians had shown their true colors. This, not the slapping of the soldier, was what caused him and Ike to suffer an irreversible falling out. You see, he and Ike had been good friends prior to the war. But, he saw more and more that Ike was cowering and appeasing to whatever he was being directed to do. Ike would not avenge the Russian atrocity."

"You mean he saw Ike as a coward, too?" asked Heidi.

"He said the man had no backbone, and that he was taking on the same characteristics of what he called "the new faggot rule. Ike sold out his country and his soldiers when he let the Russians get away with that atrocity."

"Patton," said Heidi, "could not politically exist today. He would be labelled, not inaccurately, homophobic."

"He would attribute that to the homos themselves," said Wilson, "and with at least some reason behind it."

"How do you figure that?" asked Heidi.

"From Patton's perspective, it is all quite simple and he wouldn't give a damn what anyone would think, especially on this issue. The homosexual fifth column has created the whole circumstances by which you cannot attack someone like a man. The way of the coward and the spy is in vogue. You see, what the Russians did was cowardly and the ultimate betrayal of trust, not unlike a jilted or vengeful lover."

"Or from someone who is very insecure," said Heidi.

"There you have it," said Wilson, "a classic homosexual who is having an identity crisis. The Russians still have one hell of an identity crisis.

"Patton had his prejudices, "continued Wilson, "but he was not as prejudiced as everyone thinks. His opinions were based on experience but also careful study. He had his staff study the whole history of homosexuality.

"One of the most glaring facts he learned was that when the Communist Party conquered Russia, one of the first laws they passed was to protect homosexuals."

"You're kidding?" said Heidi.

"No, I am not," replied Wilson, "and the fact that the Russian Revolution was a Jewish revolution did not help their cause in his eyes either. But what galled Patton more than anything was that Ike was tolerating the assassination of his own soldiers in deference to a country that patted homosexuals on the back. He considered them all back-stabbers."

"I find it ironic," said Heidi, "that Ike was the same one to reprimand him for slapping the soldier, someone Patton considered a coward."

"Believe me," said Wilson, "that irony was not lost on Patton. Ike capitulated to cowardice and that, frankly, is what makes a typical politician. Ike was his old friend, and a friend who was not only compromising him but the U.S. Army and the entire country. That's how Patton saw it, but he had no time to be bitter. He was a soldier and a general who had been to school on warfare. He studied the situation."

"What else did Patton learn in his studies?" asked Heidi.

"The Greeks advocated homosexuality extensively, even in war, but Patton saw it as the downfall of that civilization. Ultimately, he said it was an affront to the gods."

"What else?" asked Heidi.

"The word *faggot* itself arose in the boarding schools of England," continued Wilson. "In those environments, kids had no access to their parents or other protectors, and it was a haven for domineering school masters who would exploit the vulnerability of young boys. In the cold months, all the boys had to gather wood for fires. The older and tougher boys would have the weaker boys do their chores for them and have them fetch the faggots which are, by definition, sticks. Over time, the faggot sticks became synonymous with the weaker, often effeminate boys. This is just one example, but a prime one in our Western culture, of how homosexuals became an oppressed minority.

"Oppression is a very important aspect of understanding the homosexual. In primitive tribes, homosexuals and people that were unusual were often held in high esteem and sometimes recognized to be in divine communion with the gods. Sometimes there was ample justification to support this principle. Homosexuals were sometimes referred to as the Third Sex and in a manner that was not uncomplimentary. Their psychic abilities, however, could lead to further oppression or witch hunting when they were really accurate."

"Boy," said Heidi, "I know many gay people are sensitive and even intuitive, but I had no idea they were recognized for such in ancient cultures. Patton knew all this?"

## THE FLEA BAG..................

"When it came to warfare and history," answered Wilson, "Patton was not really prejudiced. He had his personal opinions and predisposed prejudices, but he did not let these interfere in his assessment of culture or war. It was a very clear window to him. Besides, he was psychic himself, but he didn't know everything."

"What do you mean?" asked Heidi.

"He died before he was able to study the full low-down on those he considered his enemy. The Germans did their own research on this topic under the tutelage of Dr. Mengele, but we're getting off topic to what I'm talking about."

"You're talking about Mengele, right?" asked Heidi. "You are saying that Mengele did his own research on homosexuals?"

"That's right, Heidi, he did," said Wilson. "In his research on twins, he studied the psychic potentials of homosexuality, but that is getting off topic. The psychic aspect of homosexuals, however, made them a threat to any body politic."

"In modern culture, where all non-Christian or racial minorities were subject to oppression, homosexuals became some of the most oppressed. Black people and uneducated minorities were viewed more as victims of circumstance. Homosexuals, however, were viewed as those who deliberately chose to sin against God. This made their plight subject to vindictiveness; thus, greater oppression.

"As I said earlier, the Soviet Union was the first country in modern history to proclaim homosexuals noncriminals. Lenin's party abolished all legal discrimination against homosexuals. The October Revolution, however, was not considered a victory for just homosexuals. It was considered a victory for the proletariat, the working class, as well as those groups who had been oppressed by the exploitation of capitalists.

"All of this, of course, became a rallying cry for oppressed peoples everywhere. You see, homosexuals become very dangerous to a body politic because they are one of the first to occupy and proliferate a fifth column. By fifth column, I am referring to a clandestine and subversive group dedicated to overthrowing a nationality. As homosexuals have always been a minority, they have, throughout history, found themselves to be in the center of the action when it came to rallying oppressed minorities. After all, they were usually more oppressed than anyone else — and this includes the Jews.

"About four years after Patton died, Harry Hay, a member of the Communist Party, began the first organization which would advocate what we now know as gay rights. Harry Hay was a homosexual who became a communist because they were the only group that advocated homosexuals as a result of the October Revolution of 1917. Stalin, however, changed the entire equation. As a result, Harry Hay eventually dropped away from the communists and formed his own group. What he did do, however, was study and use the same methodology that the Bolsheviks used in their overthrow. He took on oppressed minorities like the blacks and instigated the civil rights movement. Knowing that the blacks had a much more publicly acceptable cause than homosexuals, he rode the tail of that movement and finally made tremendous progress. Until 1975, it was a crime to hire a gay in government. So, you can see that homosexuals have always represented a threat to any body politic. It is not whether they are right or wrong, it is that they are oppressed."

"If they are not oppressed, however, then there is no problem, right?" interjected Heidi.

"There is no cause for a fight you mean?" asked Wilson.

"So it would seem," replied Heidi.

"We won't know until we live in a world with no oppression or one that is completely fair."

"This is all very interesting, Hugh," said Heidi, "but I'm not sure what it has to do with how you got into this Rudolph Hess business. Was he a homosexual?"

"There are many who like to think that, but gay people have a tendency to want to make every celebrated person gay. It adds to their cause. Hess had a wife and a kid. That doesn't mean he was clean, but it doesn't matter. The most interesting part about Hess has nothing to do with homosexuality."

"Yes," said Heidi, "but he was undermined by them, right?"

"If you mean the British aristocracy, you are quite right," replied Wilson. "They wheedled their way into China and Russia and then set their sights on Germany. There is nothing more undermining than the self-hating homosexuals that comprise the true elite of the British aristocracy."

"Do you think," asked Heidi, "that repressed and self-hating homosexuals are directly behind this mysterious attack by the doctor?"

"Funny, but I hadn't thought of it," said Wilson.

"I don't think you've had time," said Heidi.

"No, I haven't," said Wilson, "but there is one other angle I should mention with regard to of all this."

"What is that?" asked Heidi.

"Patton had a cousin, Larry Patton McDonald. He was the Congressman who the Russians shot down over Korea."

"Yes! I remember," said Heidi.

"He was at first an extension of our core group and then became a very loose canon. I could no longer trust him because he took on too many double agents and sort of ended up being something of one himself. He acquired many of the files of Reinhard Gehlen, the Nazi who set up the CIA, and ended up creating Western Goals Foundation, an outfit which fronted for the FBI and CIA. They could collect information on citizens without the Government breaking the law. He fed his information to the Government. In the end, he attracted too much power and had to be eliminated."

"By the Russians or his own government?" asked Heidi.

"Good question. I am not sure," said Wilson. "But you might begin to get an idea if you recognize where his files ended up."

"Where?" asked Heidi.

"With Roy Cohen, a leading player in the so-called Velvet Mafia. He ended up 'inheriting' Western Goals from McDonald. Cohen also ended up owning Studio 54. That was an Army Intel op of sorts. One of the original owners, who had served in Army Intel, was a homosexual. That's how Cohen fit in. Cohen was one of Hoover's boys. There's your *real* fifth column — and a fifth column that created the FBI!"

"Interesting," said Heidi. "and not too long after the Russian Revolution either. I want to hear more about the fifth column homos and we need to look at all that, but let us get back to what I originally asked you. How did you get into this Hess business?"

"I've been doing a lot of talking. Let me rest my voice a bit and get a drink," said Wilson.

He then walked out the door of the motel to find himself a vending machine.

·········CHAPTER ELEVEN·········

## A SEANCE, CIRCA 1908

If Aleister Crowley was not the most notorious homosexual of his times, he was most certainly high in the running. As an appellation, however, homosexual is not exactly accurate. More aptly described as a bisexual, Crowley's spouses are said to have suffered horrible fates, but his marriages were not shams. His life with Rose Kelly was actually quite promising; but when her first child eventually died, she turned to alcohol and never recovered. Crowley felt helpless to assist her, and she ended up in an asylum. Perhaps that experience contributed to his future patterns.

Crowley's honeymoon with Rose in the Great Pyramid eventually led to a return trip in 1904 whereupon he, as a result of her surprising and unexpected psychic direction, led him to dictating his most pivotal work, *The Book of the Law*. This work espoused the ideas of *Do What Thou Wilt* and *Love is the Law, Love under Will*. For several years, Crowley did not understand this work and it had no particular meaning to him. After all, it was dictated to him by intelligences that were exterior to his own "human" mind. Eventually, he would become possessed by this work to the point where he considered it his life's work. It ran his life.

The intelligence behind *The Book of the Law* was well represented in the visions he experienced in 1903 while in the Great Pyramid. These represented the universal forces of dark and light that are the guardians of expression in this domain: inhuman intelligences that march to their own tune and do not equate themselves to good or bad from a human perspective. In their expression, however, these forces could easily represent human tragedy or even joy as they play themselves out in the multifold drama of life.

It was thus that Crowley, a 33rd degree initiate of Freemasonry, found himself walking from the Masonic Lodge in London, a locale where he had either enjoyed or suffered the acquaintances of different people. Tonight, however, he was en route to an even more secret enclave to be held at the home of H.G. Wells. Subsequently known by a host of

## A SEANCE, CIRCA 1908............

different colloquial names, including the Oxford Group, these merry old gentlemen liked to refer to themselves by their own private name: the Dee Group. They also referred to themselves as the Privy Council, but that term was usually reserved for important matters of state.

The Dee Group represented the intellectual elite of England and consisted primarily of scholars from Oxford and Cambridge. They were, in fact, the best minds behind the ruling aristocracy and took their namesake from the man considered to be the most important figure in the establishment of the British Empire: Dr. John Dee. Although it was a closely guarded secret (but a secret that was quite out in the open for anyone who wanted to ask some simple questions), Dr. Dee laid the foundation for virtually all of Western science. Although he did not discover the science, it was through his pen that these foundations found their way into Western universities.

What made John Dee equally exciting to the Dee Group was that he was also a remarkable conjuror whose magic was so potent that he was even arrested once for being a sorcerer. It was Dee who used astrology to advise the Crown and conceived the idea of *Rule Britannia*, a motto Britain would use in becoming the largest empire on Earth. Above and beyond that, however, John Dee played another key role. Through his mystical writings, he served as translator to the realm previously referred to as the forces of dark and light. His Welsh name derived from *du* which means "black."

As Crowley walked into the home of H.G. Wells, he was greeted by a familiar and deep voice.

"How are you, old man?" asked Wells.

Crowley nodded. "May I inquire as to what order of madness you have in store for me tonight?"

Wells laughed. "You might say it is a formulation of a hypothesis for the future."

"You mean you wish to ensure that the Eloi keep the Morlocks at bay?" replied Crowley who was sarcastically referring to Wells' novel *The Time Machine* which espoused the class division between a ruling elite (known as the Eloi) and a lower class relegated to subterranean slave labor (Morlocks).

As Crowley was escorted to the parlor, he saw an eclectic group of intellectuals, all considered to be very important in terms of politics. He knew most of them about as well as he wanted to know them. After a short period of shaking hands and exchanging greetings, Wells made an announcement.

"Now that our guest of honor is here," he said, referring to Crowley, "we may begin!"

The group now moved into Wells' library where a large circular table had been brought in so that Crowley, an adept medium, could conduct a seance on behalf of this elite group.

Anticipation could now be felt in the extreme. Nobody knew what was going to happen, but all knew that Aleister Crowley was a potent medium. *Something*, whatever it might be, was going to happen.

After everyone was seated, Crowley asked for a moment of silence before chanting in the ancient language known as Enochian. He then circled the room and sprinkled small amounts of sulphur dust which he had brought for the occasion. A typical occult trick is to spread salt to chase away negative spirits, but Crowley was using sulphur to draw them in. He felt a certain contempt for these people and their well being was not his concern. If they wanted a show, the sulphur would only help their cause.

After finishing the circle and chanting some more in Enochian, Crowley bowed his head and rested his head in his hands as he leaned forward.

"For what purpose have I come to you?" he asked the group.

"For humankind," replied Wells. "We seek the answers for the plight of human kind and to seek the transformation into what the Christians would call saviorship but the evolutionists might term an enlightened consciousness and consequent utopia — an answer to the human dilemma."

Crowley then continued in concentration until he experienced a sudden jolt. He had now been taken over and spoke for a different entity. His voice was different but dramatically authentic.

"Sit not on what you have thought," said the voice. "Do what is wrong to your nature but right by the world. Indulge in war. War! War! War! War is the salvation of this planet. War! War! War! Drive the enemy down! Drive the enemy to annihilation. Pitiful weak souls — destroy them!"

"And by what rationale should we proceed?" asked Wells.

## A SEANCE, CIRCA 1908 . . . . . . . . . . . .

"By the reason that if you wanted to win at cricket, you would have a team composed of skilled and effective men, not weaklings. Kill and destroy the weak!"

A voice from the other side of the table from Wells now asked a question.

"But what of karma and what of the meek in the Bible?"

"If you want to win, you play to win," continued the entity. "The spoils will accrue to the winner."

"But, what of Taoism and using inaction as a higher but more subtle principle?" asked the same voice.

"Then you will have everything. Because I said to destroy the weak, you should first destroy the weakness in yourselves. On the outside, those who appear weak may not be the truly weak. If you are going to build a bridge, you must first have the components to build with.

"War is the enemy of peace," continued the entity through Crowley, "and peace is the enemy of war. Your class and your rulers have long ago enslaved the working class. If they never rebel, they will always be slaves. If you let them free, they will ruin you. They are unthinking masses and cannot lead themselves. They need to be led. Would you free a cow only to have it be slaughtered?"

"Only if I was not a vegetarian!" quipped Wells. "But tell me, there is something in my consciousness which tells me that everyone should be included in this transformation."

"That is like having all the nations in the world decide on what is best. It is impractical and will not work. You must lead and lead you will."

"And thus," asked Wells, "we must relegate the masses to being part of the food chain, not unlike cattle?"

"If you want the souls of people to transmigrate to a higher form, you must lead them but not at the expense of sacrificing your leadership. It is no different from the many societies you all belong to. People do not advance by being herded but only be awakening and noticing the drum. You owe everything to your position. From your position you then have the power to do work."

"But what of the herds?" asked Wells.

"The herds seek a lower form of life. They seek safety and security by way of rules and regulations. The rules are for the weak. Those who are strong live life by their own idea of right and wrong. They make their own rules and also the rules for the weak. Do not seek to be the herd. The herd is there to support the strong."

"OK," said Wells. "Might I ask what is the relevance of emotions in this equation? Being strong and squashing your enemies has a point, but what of the emotions of all living beings, including those on the lower end of the food chain?"

"Life is pre-date...predatory. The early forms of biological life are predatory for survival. If you do not eat your neighbor, you do not live in the jungle. Balance occurs only after survival is achieved."

"And is the purpose of this life to evolve or transmute energy that will bring all life higher?" asked Wells.

"The high cannot exist without the low. Concern yourself with where you are, not only on the food chain but in the politics of experience. If you lead with superior intelligence and ability, only then can you expand your horizons."

"What of Christ in this equation?" asked Wells. "Not only the Christ in the Bible but the Christ of other traditions. I mean, can we possibly reconcile with the source of the universe?"

The entity laughed through Crowley. The laughter was quite uncontrollable. Every time Crowley's body would start to calm down, it would begin laughing again, uncontrollably. When the laughter finally finished, the entity spoke again.

"There is no Christ!"

"But," said Wells, "how can you nullify an idea if it is only nothing more than an idea? An idea has its own existence whether historical or not."

"True," said the entity, "but if you consider the historical concept of Christ to be valid, you have to realize that, at best, it occurred only for a short time. It was not a permanent frequency or arrangement that could propagate itself. The best it could do was create a legend and one that could be easily twisted to suit those of you in power. Yes, you can use religion to herd and steer the masses. That is what it is for."

"I am talking about," said Wells, "the arrangement or vehicle by which souls can release themselves from suffering. Whether it is called nirvana, heaven, or eternal bliss, can this arrangement be made?"

"Suffering...," laughed the entity. "Do you not realize that suffering is a commodity just like the food chain I have

## A SEANCE, CIRCA 1908............

spoken of? Your suffering feeds what you would call the ghastly state of affairs in your world. If it was not useful, it would disappear, just like a commercial product that is outdated. To be useful, suffering must serve the leaders, the powerful. Only induce suffering to bolster your position. It has no use beyond that. And remember, fear of suffering is a more useful tool than suffering itself."

"Let me ask about what you said earlier," said Wells. "If there is a frequency or arrangement by which the Christ could propagate itself and continue to vibrate into the world, what would it be? How could it be maintained?"

"435 Megahertz," said the entity.

"What do you mean by that?" asked Wells.

"These are questions which are better not asked."

"Why?"

"Because if I told you, I would have to kill you."

"Can you explain better?" asked Wells.

"The universe is consciousness, all of which emanates via a fundamental or underlying frequency. All of the particles within matter have a constituent common denominator. There is also a frequency that can change these particles. It is the Lion Frequency. It can change particles."

"Why is it called the Lion Frequency?" asked Wells.

"Because it is the king of all frequencies. With it, you can change reality."

"Is it 435 Megahertz?" asked Wells.

"No, but it is close."

"Can you tell us more?" asked Wells.

"No, I have already said too much," said the entity. "It is not yet time for you to know these things. You would only destroy yourselves."

"Then, may I ask, how can we move into a position where we might learn these things?" asked Wells.

"It is not by following or preaching dogma. In the Bible, the Jews are blamed with killing Christ. Follow that idea."

At this point, everyone's ears perked up. There was great interest on the subject of Jews, especially on the potential to portray them in a negative light.

"The killing of Christ," said Wells, "at least in the story, is necessary to bring about the higher importance: the resurrection. That precipitates the salvation of Mankind."

"Yes, but where is the resurrection?" asked the entity. "You have nothing, only an idea or legend that is to be distorted. You are all still relegated to this world. The resurrection was short lived and demonstrated an idea that you are without, no matter how much lip service is paid."

"But why should we focus on the Jews being blamed?"

"It will bring you much power. That is why. And, you are suited to lead, all of you. But the Jews killing Christ is symbolic. They have all the wisdom and knowledge that Christ fulfilled and was here to serve. That is what he represented. The Jews have not used their tools. They claim to hold a monopoly to God, but it is not something they can back up other than to subject others to their mental and financial superiority. In this regard they are leaders, like you. Use them! You are all leaders."

"This logic is all so circular," replied Wells.

"It is circular," said the entity, "because you are travelling on a treadmill that goes round and round. Humanity keeps repeating the same mistakes and dramatizations."

"Can you then teach us this Lion Frequency so that we will not make the same mistakes?" asked Wells.

"As I said, you are not ready. If you pursue what you refer to as redemption, you will have to pursue these things but they can destroy you. That which gives birth gives death. That which heals destroys."

"Until we are ready, how might we proceed so as to have the best advantage in understanding these things?"

"The Jews had this frequency in the Ark, but they did not use it and have now lost its secrets. Do not make the same mistakes they made."

"Are you saying we are the same as Jews?" asked Wells.

"As the leaders of society, you have inherited the mantle of the Jew, the greatest Jew: Christ! You must sacrifice everything!"

At this bewildering and astonishing statement, Crowley shook violently. The entity departed and Crowley sat there motionless, his head and arms falling down on the table.

A SEANCE, CIRCA 1908............

......... CHAPTER TWELVE.........

## THE ADVENT

By the time Wilson had returned to the room with a can of soda, Heidi was in her night clothes and inside the covers.

"That feels better," he said. "It is relaxing just to go outside and look at the stars."

"Yes, it is. I wish I would've joined you."

"You know," said Wilson, "this whole experience is so damn surreal. I'm confident we're not under surveillance right now. It's like the whole world has stopped for a moment. I haven't seen action for a long time, but I tell you, this experience is not unlike a lull in the battlefield."

"It's exciting all right," agreed Heidi. "Now, are you going to tell me about how you, Hugh Wilson, got so wrapped up into this whole affair with Hess?"

"The story really begins in my own childhood," said General Wilson. "My father came from a Protestant family but was not religious. My mother, however, was a Catholic and she wanted me to attend Catholic school with catechism and the whole works. Things went pretty well for me in so much as many students were given corporal punishment — they had their knuckles wrapped with rulers or worse — but I was left alone. I tended to mind my own business and was a decent student.

"One day, however, when I was about thirteen, we had this priest who was a nasty son-of-a-bitch. He wore horn-rimmed glasses and had a reputation for going after kids. He'd often wrap their knuckles and even draw blood. In the past, I'd had him for a few classes, but again, he never bothered me. By this time in my life, however, I was pretty burly. I played football. In fact, I was so good at age thirteen that I even gave varsity players a hard time. For some insane reason, professor horn-rim took it upon himself to single me out and teach me a lesson one day.

"We had been studying the Protestant Reformation, and I asked a rhetorical question about Martin Luther revolutionizing history by bringing the Bible to the common man. Well, professor horn-rim did not like that at all. On my part, it was an innocent question and fairly intellectual for that age, but he would have none of it. There was no discussion or anything. He grabbed his pointer and hit me across the left shoulder.

"To this day, I still don't know who the hell he thought he was. I grabbed him and stopped him, but he kept trying to hit me. He should have realized early on that he was no match for me. Instead, he kept trying to hit me harder and harder as if that would subdue me, like he had some sort of divine right to make me submit. After he struck me about five times, I began punching him. I bloodied his nose real good. In fact, after all was said and done, I heard I even broke it."

"What happened to you?" asked Heidi. "Did they kick you out of school?"

"They couldn't," Wilson laughed. "I quit. I just left and headed straight for my father's office. He was a lawyer and boy was he pissed — not at me but at them. He had little patience for religion as it was, but this was the last straw as far as he was concerned. My father had taught me to be honest, and he always knew that I was. There was no history of trouble in my life prior to that. In no uncertain terms, he told both me and my mother that I was, under no circumstances, to return to Catholic school or church. That was it. Under the circumstances, my mother did not complain."

"What happened to the priest?" asked Heidi.

"Well, my father called in some of the other kids, those who were my friends. He interrogated them and got a very good legal picture of this man. Then, he instituted a law suit against the priest. He did some further investigating, and I didn't find this out until later in life, but the priest was a pedophile. The upshot of it all is that the priest was found dead, an alleged suicide. Now, I'm not so sure if it was a suicide. Maybe someone killed him."

"That somewhat explains your track on homosexuals," said Heidi, "but not Hess. How'd you get onto him?"

"As I grew older, that experience told me that things were not right in the world. Things were not what they seemed to be. I mean, I could never trust the Church after that.

"In Africa, Patton took me under his wing because I was a good soldier and because I was a Wilson, just like him. He told me that fags and communists went together and they were the real enemies, not the Nazis. He said the Nazis were bad, but the Germans were excellent soldiers. Most of the trouble, he said, had to do with politics and bad leadership. He said the bankers fucked things up, too.

"Besides all that, he never understood why Hess's peace proposal was never considered. Hess wanted to protect Germany against communism. According to Patton and many others, Churchill had reneged on an earlier agreement with the Third Reich — but, back to the bankers. One of the things Patton pointed out to me about Hess, and certainly not the only thing, was that the man was in charge of all administration for the Nazi Party. In other words, he was a signatory on all financial accounts for the party.

"British Intelligence had always run clandestine operations into Germany. I mean, if an Englishman can speak fluent German, you can't tell him apart from a Kraut. As the tide turned in the war, more and more operations were being run into Germany. One of these operations was for the express purpose of tracing German money. For example, when the Nazis would conquer a country, they would loot the treasury. Besides the art and hard loot, they would steal accounts and transfer such funds to their own accounts. This sort of financial crime was far more prevalent than what Holocaust survivors cry about. Besides the treasuries of various countries, this financial looting extended to many others, particularly organizations and businesses in various countries.

"The Brits very cleverly traced the funds and eventually discovered what banks they were being deposited in. As one might guess, the trail eventually led to Switzerland. When this was found out, Ian Fleming visited his old banking contacts. Prior to the war, Fleming had been an international banker and he knew the ropes in Switzerland. Using the full authority of the Crown, he was able to either threaten or brow beat the Swiss into giving him the scoop on who controlled these Nazi funds. Towards the end of the war, it all came down to one man: Martin Bormann."

"He was the man who replaced Hess as the administrative head of the Nazi Party," said Heidi.

"Exactly, and he was the signatory on all of their accounts. After all, you didn't expect Hitler to be signing checks and doing bank drafts, did you?  Well, when Fleming and Morton found out about Bormann, it became imperative to do something.  The war was rapidly coming to a close.  Finances were a big issue yet you never ever hear much about it in the press.  War is always about money in the end."

"You just said Morton?" said Heidi.  "Who was he?"

"Desmond Morton, the head of special intelligence under Churchill.  He was Fleming's boss."

"Oh," said Heidi.  "I've heard about Bormann, of course.  I have read stories that he lived, but I would assume that he escaped on the Nazi rat-line and ended up in South America.  I think it was Brazil."

"No, Heidi.  That's what the British disinformation agents would like you to believe.  They got to Bormann and literally escorted him out of the bunker at high speed, right after Hitler's demise.  Von Ribbentrop, the Nazi Foreign Minister, had been negotiating with the British for his own escape, and he set up the contact between Fleming and Bormann.  The British, however, didn't care about von Ribbentrop.  He was small potatoes.  Bormann had the money.  Basically, they saved his ass in return for the money."

"So, are you saying the money ended up in the hands of British Intelligence, the Crown or who?"

"All we really know," continued Wilson, "is that it ended up out of the hands of the Nazis.  To the best of Patton's knowledge and to those he extended his legacy of information to, the signatories on the accounts passed from Bormann to both Desmond Morton of British Intelligence and to William Donovan of the O.S.S.  The assumption, however, is that these funds all went to what might be called "their due and proper place."  In other words, Churchill would have been in the loop more than likely.  Roosevelt was dead, and it is hard to say what Truman did and did not know.  In any event, there is no accountable tracing of the enormous sums accumulated by the Nazi Party under Bormann's name."

"How does Hess fit in here?  Was he a signatory, too?  He must've been at some point," asked Heidi.

"I'll get to that in just a minute.  There is one other point I want to make with regard to Desmond Morton and William Donovan.  They were both devout Roman Catholics and were extremely loyal to the Vatican."

"So, you're suggesting that all the loot ended up in the hands of the Vatican?" inquired Heidi.

"There is that distinct possibility," answered Wilson, but it is not that simple. "You see, this was a pure intelligence operation. In fact, the extraction of Bormann was known as Operation James Bond. Bond was the name that Ian Fleming used as his alias. It might sound funny today, but he was introduced to Bormann and the other Germans as James Bond. That is why he picked the name for his novels.

"But," continued Wilson, "in an intelligence operation, there is no true or complete accountability. Sure, Ike and Churchill would've been given reports. Donovan and Morton, however, just between the two of them, would've been the only ones with a complete accounting of what Bormann did and did not have to offer. They could have turned it over to the Vatican or funneled it to any other source they were plugged into. In any event, it is an unknown variable. Such things are never made easy to trace. It is a part of the puzzle."

"The puzzle of Hess?" questioned Heidi.

"Well, yes, a part. You are also quite right to suggest that Hess was a signatory. Beginning as Hitler's secretary in the Nazi Party, Hess gained more and more power. Because Himmler controlled the S.S. and Goering was head of the Air Force, Hess was often overlooked. It has been inaccurately suggested that he was overshadowed or on the outs with Hitler. This was never the case. In fact, historians don't focus on him at all other than the blatantly obvious. His youth and early years are almost as mysterious as the missing years of Jesus."

Heidi laughed at this last statement.

"He was born in Egypt, correct?" she asked.

"Indeed," answered Wilson. "His whole history, which is filled with the Egyptian connection and secret societies, is still quite a mystery. Reinhard Heydrich, the head of the Gestapo, went to the trouble of having Hess's biography and almost any trace memory of him stripped from the archives of history. All we are left with is the standard stuff about him being put into prison with Hitler, helping him with *Meinkampf* and being tutored by Karl Haushofer. The missing years of Jesus indeed!"

Heidi laughed again before Wilson continued.

# THE ADVENT

"Hess was not only the Deputy Fuhrer of the Nazi Party prior to Hitler assuming the role of Chancellor in 1933, but he also conducted the negotiations that secured Hitler his position. Through his connections with Haushofer and the Thule Society, he had access to anyone who was important. I guarantee you that if there was no Rudolph Hess, Hitler would never have made it to the post of Chancellor. There would have been no Nazi Germany, no Nuremburg rallies..."

"And no holocaust," interjected Heidi.

"Oh yes," answered Wilson, "there would've been a holocaust. It would've just drummed to a different tune."

"How so?"

"Well, neither Hitler nor Hess composed the laws which enforced sterilization and justified eliminating certain members of the population. They both endorsed them, but that was one of the conditions of them assuming the mantle of power.

"Anyway," continued Wilson, "when Hitler assumed complete control, Hess was assigned the title of 'Minister Without Portfolio.' This meant that he was a cabinet level member of the German government and that he also had the authority to cancel and make up new laws. While Himmler and Goering had military force behind them, neither had the power to change or make laws. For Hess, this job was in addition to his role as Deputy Fuhrer of the Nazi Party.

"Hess was quite prolific when it came to legislation. One of the first orders of business was for him to legally construct the German state so that the Nazi Party literally <u>was</u> the German state. In other words, the party was no longer just a party. It was the government. This meant that he was Deputy Fuhrer of Germany, just as Hitler was the Fuhrer of Germany."

"So," asked Heidi, "when he flew to England to seek peace, he was completely authorized in being recognized as a peace envoy of the German nation, right?"

"Completely. He was the German nation and answered only to Hitler. Unfortunately for Hess and Germany, the British double-crossed him and used him as a political and psychological pawn."

"Well," said Heidi, "after what you have told me, it looks like they were using him as a financial pawn, too."

"This brings us to another interesting point," said Wilson. "Hess was in charge of financing the Nazi Party. He created something called the Hitler Fund. At least once a year, all the major German industrialists within Germany and abroad contributed heavily to the Hitler Fund. This money was completely at his disposal. How it was spent and what unnumbered Swiss accounts it went into is anybody's guess."

"Except for the Brits," interjected Heidi. "They must have debriefed him on all that once they caught him."

"Exactly. The Brits had Hess completely at their disposal. They could do with him whatever they wanted."

"From what I have read thus far, it seems unlikely that he would've turned everything over to Bormann," commented Heidi.

"Excellent point," said Wilson. "Bormann took over the Hitler Fund after Hess was captured. Hitler also granted Bormann carte blanche over the party's finances, but he never elevated him to the status of Deputy Fuhrer. In his will, Hitler stated that Bormann was his most loyal party member. He was named the head of the Nazi Party but, prior to that, he was never accorded quite the same status as Hess."

"Well," said Heidi, "with Bormann officially listed as dead or missing, that definitely would have created problems of successorship for the British. Hess was formally in charge of the German government. It might have been unpopular, but it seems that all the actions he took to make himself such were, in fact, legal."

"Yes," said Wilson, "but the Allies declared an unconditional surrender and basically outlawed the Nazi Party."

"But they couldn't change his status as head of state unless Hitler cancelled his status," said Heidi.

"That still left a problem for the Brits," said Wilson. You and I know that Hitler only declared Hess insane by prior agreement in the event that the peace mission was a failure. As Deputy Fuhrer, however, Hess had full authority to act as an envoy. The argument of an illegal capture and the British violating international law would change matters entirely. As untenable as it might seem, Hess had a legal argument against the Brits, and a rather substantial one as well."

"What about the finances he controlled?" asked Heidi.

"That is something we don't know. It's just one of the

# THE ADVENT . . . . . . . . . . . . . . . . . . . . . . .

reasons I wanted to get to Hess. Even a few clues would have been priceless. He might have had numbered Swiss accounts that no one ever found out about. Further, he would have had a signatory claim on at least some of the accounts that Bormann turned over to Morton and Donovan."

"Well," said Heidi, "I'm beginning to get the idea of why they wanted Hess dead. It's about as complex as the Kennedy assassination."

"Don't get me started on that one," said Wilson. "The bottom line is that the Brits did an excellent job of looking after their own interests. Hess twisted in the wind for the remainder of his life. There is another aspect here, too."

"What's that?" asked Heidi.

"Mind control," said Wilson. "Hess is on record as having been subjected to more psychiatric treatment than anyone in the history of Mankind."

"That in itself says a lot," said Heidi.

"Yes. They claimed they were trying to figure him out. I think they did a pretty good job. There's no telling of what they downloaded from him. It's entirely possible they might have, through brainwashing and the like, acquired his numbered accounts and taken large sums of money. This is just one of the reasons I wanted to get a crack at him."

"Out of curiosity or what? Why exactly are you on this trail?" asked Heidi.

"It goes back to Patton. Remember, he was in charge of putting Germany back on its feet. I mean, we had to pick up the pieces. He has been characterized as being war crazy. It is true that he wanted to fight the Russians, but he was much more than a crazed soldier.

"He had collected a load of intelligence files from the Germans, particularly on the Russians. Those of us who knew about it were few and we were also extremely loyal to him. Patton was bringing up all sort of issues that were uncomfortable to the OSS which, by the way, was in the grip of the Brits. People forget that Ian Fleming had drafted the setup for the OSS and Donovan gave him a gift pistol in return. You see, the Brits set up our intelligence service, not us. I am talking about the OSS and CIA here, not military intelligence. We already had plenty of experienced people in military intel and didn't need the Brits. It was the idea of the Brits to set up an intelligence division that they would either influence or control. This put our military out of the loop and Roosevelt bought into it. The CIA is still under British influence.

"Patton became increasingly irritated at the duplicity and dubious nature of what was going on within our own administration. He was not only taking too much initiative, he was asking too many questions about the Brits and questioning their whole role. He didn't care for them.

"In September of 1945, Patton had me transferred to his office in Bavaria to assist him. When I arrived, he told me of the dire world situation he perceived. He said that we were being set up, not only to lose Germany but to lose a war against Russia. At that time, he did not know that it would be a politically contrived Cold War, but he had already boldly stated that we were in a time when true warriors and generals were no longer relevant. He referred to it as "faggot warfare" where the soldiers would be used as fodder, dancing on the marionette strings of cowardly politicians. It was no longer a man's world, he said. The very nature of honor and integrity were undergoing a profound change. He also alluded to the fact that he was not long for this world. Patton knew that his type of warrior belonged to a different time.

"As a result, he gathered a small number of brass he could trust. I was not brass at that point, but he trusted and included me. Eventually, those connections set me up so that I could make it to general. Essentially, we formed our own small group of men who dedicated ourselves to upholding the Constitution. Patton insisted that we would only trust people who played football or wrestled. Additionally, these would be the only members of our small party. The reason for this, he said, was to minimize the possibility of any effeminate influence. This was not a perfect marker, he said, but it would at least make a useful demarcation. He didn't want paper pushers or accountant types per se.

"Patton died almost as soon as we got started. This only molded our commitment to serve his dream. There was initially a circle of six of us. Eventually, we would meet annually and pool our data. Our purpose was to serve as an unknown and unseen watchdog for the U.S. Constitution. As time went on, we expanded our group to about twenty. The larger group would meet every summer while our inner core of

# THE ADVENT...................

six would meet once every winter. If other meetings would be necessary, they would be called as well.

"Our primary focus was to just blend in with the existing status quo, rub elbows with the seats of power, and do what we could to maintain the constitutionality of America. As you might imagine, politicians are our biggest enemy. But if I keep talking here, I'm going to go too far off topic. I just wanted to give you a bit of background so that you will know the context in which you and I are now operating. And by the way, neither you nor I are doing anything illegal here. It is, however, extracurricular activity, but I know I can trust you to keep your mouth shut."

"Definitely," said Heidi. "How about we get some sleep? I want to ask you some more about Hess in the morning, but I feel we both need a good night's sleep right now. My intuition tells me the next few days could be rather hectic."

. . . . . . . . CHAPTER THIRTEEN . . . . . . . .

## THE FABIAN SOCIETY

As Crowley sat in a slumbering stupor, H.G. Wells put his head down and whispered to his secretary, Virginia Wilson. Sitting next to him, she had been dutifully transcribing Crowley's transmission into stenographic notes.

"Fix this up in a readable form and bring it over to me at the Fabian Society later tonight, in about an hour. I'm going to present it to an audience," said Wells.

"OK, will do," answered Virginia. "If you don't mind, I'd also like to alert my brothers to the notes. They'll be very interested in anything Aleister came up with."

"As a matter of fact," said Wells, "your brothers were planning to be here tonight. I don't know what happened to them. You can use the typewriter in my office if you like. I've got to get down to the Fabian Society. Be there as soon as you can. Actually, I won't need the notes themselves for about an hour and a half."

Wells immediately stood up and scooted out the front door. Except for Virginia, everyone else left the house save for Crowley. He remained there, neglected, and in a twilight state of consciousness.

Virginia's brothers were Preston and Marcus Wilson, twin brothers who manufactured scientific instruments but who also had a passion for occult subjects. The Wilsons had an early dependency on Crowley's family for funding their operation. Together, with Crowley's father, they had formed an electronics company. Crowley, who received his father's shares upon the latter's death, was their business partner.

A quick and efficient secretary, Virginia finished the typing within twenty-five minutes. Making her way to the door, she could not help but notice that Crowley was still slumbering at the table. She was well aware that his information was valued, but nobody seemed to care about him. Thinking she should do something to comfort him and bring him to, she was suddenly interrupted by a knock at the door. Before any of the servants could get to the door, she opened it and saw her twin brothers poised to enter.

## THE FABIAN SOCIETY............

"You're late," she said, "you just missed it. George just went down to the Fabian Society where he will give a summary. As a matter of fact, I've just typed up the notes right here. You can look over them very quickly if you like."

"You didn't miss a damn thing!" said Crowley, awakening from his slumber. "Come on in and have some tea, won't you?"

As the Wilson brothers entered the house and came to Crowley, Virginia put a carbon copy of the notes on the table.

"You can have those," she said to Aleister. "I made a copy for you, one for George and one for my files. I'll put some tea on the stove and then I have to go."

Despite having been out-cold a minute earlier, Crowley showed no signs of sluggishness and woke up fully and unexpectedly at the very moment the Wilsons appeared.

"How's business?" asked Crowley. "I trust that Zeppelin has not been giving you any troubles."

"We have made great strides, most of it far afield from the executives of industry," said Preston Wilson.

"Excellent; just as it should be," replied Crowley.

Crowley was referring to their German client that manufactured dirigibles. The Wilsons, who supplied specialized barometers to airships, were also brought over as consultants to Zeppelin on a highly secret project.

"Vacuum tubes are not vacuum tubes," said Marcus Wilson, interjecting into the conversation.

"How do you mean?" asked Crowley.

"Under certain conditions, particularly at high altitudes, I can affect them by thought alone," replied Marcus.

"You mean that you can by will and will alone, change what is going on electronically inside the vacuum tube?" asked Crowley.

"That's because a vacuum tube isn't a true vacuum. It only seals out air," said Preston.

"Well, it depends what's in it," said Crowley. "Neon gases create some interesting effects. What about the vault?"

"It's proved interesting, but it is relatively unstable. Zeppelin is mostly interested in the financial end of things at this time."

"As with John Fleming, you don't need to worry about the finances. Just teach them the technology," replied Crowley.

"Now, please tell me" said Crowley, "what in hell's name did I do here?"

"We don't know," said Preston, "we just arrived ourselves. We can look at these notes and see what happened. We were supposed to sit in on the session, but we arrived late."

"It's probably just a bunch of drivel," said Crowley. "I hope George doesn't take it too seriously. He usually does, you know."

"I don't know what he has in mind with that Fabian Society," said Preston.

"What you boys are dealing with," said Crowley, "is technology; and since the beginning of time, technology has been the best friend of war. All of these characters in British intelligence and in the military are interested in getting one leg up on their rivals and you boys are the best asset they could ever want. That's why I keep you as a secret."

"That might explain why you don't want us to have a high profile, right?" asked Preston.

"Essentially," said Crowley, "your job has been to illustrate and convey technology to these characters so that they can run with it. Whether that was a good idea or not could certainly be debated, but these people will want to use technology for war or profit."

"Our hands are clean," said Preston.

"So far!" said Marcus.

"What we did with the airships years back certainly created a minor stir," said Crowley, "but no one realized a thing. It only took a few years for Zeppelin to release that technology in a manner that would ostensibly be useful to the public at large."

"These boys in the Fabian and Dee Society are all about world domination. They are a pretty perverse bunch, I'd say," said Preston.

"You have no idea!" said Crowley. "But, I plan to dominate them."

"Why is that?" asked Marcus.

"Because if I don't, nobody else will! I may be mad myself, but I'm not as mad as all of them, especially all together."

"The notes..." said Marcus. "We were going to review the notes just before you referred to them as drivel. We got here late."

"Frankly, I don't give a damn about those notes. I'm going to a christening tomorrow. I've got to get some sleep. Perhaps you'd like to come along. It's for one of the Fleming children."

"Fleming?" asked Preston. "You mean John (Ambrose) Fleming? The one we taught vacuum tube theory to?"

"Close," said Crowley. "It's for Robert Fleming's grandson. John Fleming is a cousin of Robert and he's planning to be there, too. I did want to ask him some questions about vacuum tubes. Perhaps you can both come along."

"Perhaps we can all make it over to the Fabian Society right now," said Marcus. "I'd like to hear George's rendition of your notes."

"Not me," said Crowley. "I'm going to retire for the evening. Come to the christening tomorrow. Then you can let me know if I said anything significant."

# CHAPTER FOURTEEN

## INTRUDERS

General Wilson and Heidi made a quick exit as they checked out from their motel in the morning. Grabbing a quick bagel, they made their way back to the base. As they drove, Heidi reflected on what she had learned the previous night. The implications that Rudolph Hess presented to the Allies was quite fascinating with regards to world politics; but the intensity of how it interrelated to the adventure at hand left her with a foreboding and a feeling that danger was about to happen to them.

"At least, I have Hugh with me," she thought to herself. "He's been through far worse than this many times before."

"We were smart not to return to our homes last night," said Wilson.

"True," said Heidi, "but they are going to be very sensitive to the fact that we know they are looking for us."

"It's turned into a real chess match," said Wilson.

"What do you expect next?" asked Heidi.

"Well, I would expect to be surprised. If I expect surprise, then I might not be too surprised," answered Wilson.

"Do you mean that you might expect them to be waiting for us in your office?" she asked.

"Exactly!" said Wilson, "Or, I might be called in to see my superior only to discover that he is at their beck and call."

"From what I understand about the military and your superiors," said Heidi, "that is not too likely to happen."

"If you consider protocol," replied Wilson, "it's pretty near impossible. Nevertheless, I have to be prepared for anything."

"Well, here we are," said Heidi as they came to the base.

"Let's give it a go," said Wilson as they passed by the gate and went to the parking lot.

Wilson and Heidi walked to the office and passed another security check point. When they got to the door of their office, Heidi spoke up.

"Sir, just for the record, what exactly would you do if they were waiting in our office?"

"Well, I guess I had better enter first, with a gun." said Wilson. "If someone is in there, I'll shoot. If I holler, that means you can come in and start shooting, too."

"Agreed," she said.

With his gun drawn, Wilson entered first. The lights were off, and there was no one in the reception room.

"Well, everything seems fine," he said.

Going into his office and seeing that it was also empty, he returned to the door and beckoned Heidi to come in.

"OK," said Heidi as she came inside, "nobody's here. What do we do now? How do we start the day?"

"I'm going to continue your briefing on Hess. As we do that, we're going to have to wait for something to develop. I believe we are due to get a follow-up report from Agent T as well."

"You made the case that Hess had both a legal and a financial connection to the Third Reich that could open a hornet's nest; however, politics would never have given him much of a leg to stand on," said Heidi.

"True, but those matters should never be discounted. There are a lot of inherent technical issues as to who and what Hess represented in terms of legalities. There are, however, other intriguing issues concerning him which do not bode well for those in power and might even carry more weight in themselves. These include his role in hidden adventures by the Germans."

"What hidden adventures are you talking about?" asked Heidi.

"They were doing all sorts of strange things, but their most ambitious goal was the resurrection of Atlantis."

"Based upon the books you gave me, I thought you were going to tell me about their expeditions and interest in Tibet and the Antarctic," said Heidi.

"You're not far off. But you should be asking me what they have to do with Atlantis; and, more importantly, what they have to do with Hess.

"Hess is always overlooked in popular literature, but he was in charge of the Auslands Organization and this particular authority was never revoked. The purpose of this organization was to promote German colonization and this included the Nazi's colony and military base in New Schwabenland."

"You mean the one in Antarctica?" asked Heidi.

"Exactly. They built quite an extensive colony there after the war."

"I have read that they have a UFO base in the area. Is that true?" she asked.

"You're missing a bit of information there," replied Wilson. "You heard the briefing I gave to Agent T, right?"

"Yes, but it would be good to hear it from you directly, at least the key points as it relates to Hess and our predicament."

"Fine," said Wilson. "It goes back to General Patton once again. It concerns his final days. As the war came to a close, it was assumed by many that Patton would make the final run on Berlin and not only capture the capital city but the Fuhrer himself. Many important people were perplexed at Eisenhower's decision to leave Hitler and Berlin to the Russians. After all, those targets seemed to offer the most prestige. There was, however, a much bigger and more interesting prize and that is what Eisenhower wanted. That is why he sent Patton to the south."

"And what was that prize?" asked Heidi.

"All of the alternate flying technology that the scientists of the Third Reich had worked so hard on. This included flying wings, the Hanebu flying craft, the Vril space craft and all sorts of other avant garde projects. This was Patton's terrain and legacy. Officially, he was pursuing the Nazi Redoubt as it had been reported that Otto Skorzeny and his Werewolves were going to make a last stand in Bavaria. Those who made the report, however, knew it was complete rubbish. There was no Nazi Redoubt. There was, however, a mad scramble by both the Americans and the Germans to safeguard as much as possible of this technology.

"The proof in the pudding of all this concerns General Hans Kammler who was put in charge of the entire technology redoubt before the end of the war. Hitler trusted him implicitly and not even Himmler could counter him. He was in control of all technical development of flying craft, but he mysteriously disappeared after the war.

"About a year before the bunker incident with Hitler, Martin Bormann called a meeting of all major industrialists and organized the real German Redoubt which was really a plan to secretly infiltrate other countries with hard assets.

They also used millions and millions of counterfeit currency. These countries included Argentina, Chile, Paraguay, Bolivia, Brazil and Mexico."

"Where did General Kammler go?" asked Heidi.

"No one knows for sure. There are theories, the most logical of which would place him at a German industrial plant in Antarctica."

"Making UFOs?" asked Heidi.

"Something like that, but let me get back to Patton. As he began to learn so much about the Nazi operations, he developed an even deeper appreciation of German military technology and its potential. As it was, he already greatly admired the Germans as soldiers. The flying technology only improved his admiration for them as a people.

"In point of fact, he was rapidly becoming the most knowledgeable American on the scene. In this regard alone, Patton was a flagrant danger to those interests who would want to seize that power for their very own."

"Where does Eisenhower fit in in these matters?" asked Heidi. "Was he a good guy or a bad guy?"

"A good yes man," answered Wilson. "He basically did what he was told and did not rock the boat. By following orders and being a good soldier, he was eventually rewarded with the presidency. Patton, who was not so subordinate, was not so lucky."

"He died in an automobile accident, right?" asked Heidi.

"Well, that's the official history, but I know that he was killed. If you doubt it, try and get the files on his death. They are still classified to this day. There was an OSS agent, Doug Bazata, who took out a contract on him."

"So," asked Heidi, "how did all of this impact upon you? You were around then, weren't you?"

"Yes, Heidi, I was. This created the impetus for our little grouping that I told you about. We were all more than a little upset over what happened to the general. But, an interesting point of fact is that Patton was found to be too chummy with the Germans. With the pretense of "fraternizing," he was taken off his job as military governor of Bavaria, but it was never really about that. He was both harnessing and accessing the true power of the German Reich in a way that was making his military superiors very uncomfortable.

"His next assignment was to round up the history of the war. Historians often think that he was simply assigned the boring job of putting together the military history of what happened in the European theater. While this was true, it was a two-tiered project. I know because I assisted with it. This project was chronicling vast portions of the secret Nazi flying craft and this included its eventual transfer to New Schwabenland. In effect, Command wanted to know everything he knew."

"And by getting him to write up the history, they would be sure to have at least a part of it!" said Heidi.

"It's all quite simple and can be found in common history books if one knows what to look for and how to read between the lines a bit. As a matter of fact, there's a booklet I'd like to give you. I think you'll find it most interesting. It's in my secret office across the hall. I'm gonna run and get it."

"OK," said Heidi. "Don't get into any trouble!"

As Wilson made his way to his secret office, he pulled his keys out of his pocket. All of a sudden, it occurred to him that Heidi's last statement just might be pertinent. What if there was somebody waiting for him in his secret office? In the interest of safety and his motto of never being surprised, he could not afford to overlook that possibility.

Wilson then sized-up the door and noticed a piece of broken tape which had connected the door to the frame. He then turned around and went back towards Heidi.

"Heidi, I want you to be ready. A piece of tape I placed on the door has been broken. Somebody opened that door."

"Somebody's in your secret office?" she asked.

"Either that or they went in and left. Here, take this semiautomatic. If you hear me blow this whistle, it means I have hit the ground and you are to come in spraying bullets. If I give it two short blows in succession, that means to come in and be ready to shoot."

"OK," said Heidi. "I'm ready to back you up."

Wilson took out his keys and unlocked the door. If there was anybody on the other side, they would have heard the movement and would be prepared for him. Wilson then made his way through the short ante chamber and went into his office. Stepping softly inside, he saw three men, two of which were tall in stature. All were dressed in professional business suits and none of them looked imposing despite their rather large physical size. They all wore glasses.

"Shrinks!" Wilson thought to himself. "No doubt about it — shrinks!"

Instinctively, Wilson noticed that one of the psychiatrists was holding a dart gun in his hand and that it was going to be directed at him immediately. Before he could even think about blowing the whistle, Wilson fired his pistol and hit the shrink right in the hand. The dart gun fell to the floor. Wilson then gave a short blow on the whistle two times. Heidi came in immediately and held her gun on the three psychiatrists.

"Not a bad shot, especially after all of these years," Wilson said to himself, actually gloating that he could make such a direct hit as if he were a gunslinger from the old west.

Directing Heidi to keep the other two at bay with her gun, he approached the injured man in order to get a closer look. The right hand was bleeding, and it appeared that the man had lost motor control of it.

"I need medical attention — quick!" said the injured psychiatrist.

"How's this?" asked Wilson as he slapped the psychiatrist across the head with his free hand.

"Looks to me like you've got all the medical help you could need right in this room — you fucking ass hole!"

"General Wilson," said one of the other two psychiatrists, "you are overreacting. This does not have to be such a big problem."

"Oh really?" asked Wilson who then took a large paper weight off his desk and flung it at the psychiatrist who had spoken to him. It landed on the man's torso, partially deflected by his hand. It hurt him.

"You fucking bastards!" said Wilson. "You'll speak when spoken to and not until then — if you do not want to get hurt further. Now, you fucking bastards, take off all of your clothes."

When one of the psychiatrists started to protest, Wilson went over and kicked him. Before long, they all complied with his directive. Wilson then took each one and tied them up so they were helpless.

The psychiatrist who had been shot groaned in agony. It was evident that he was in considerable pain and was not faking. After Wilson finished restraining all of them, he then went over to a medical dispensary and gave him a pain killer.

"This will calm you down, at least for a while," said Wilson to the psychiatrist.

Having them all naked and tied up, he spoke to Heidi.

"You can relax now, Heidi," said Wilson. A pretty pathetic lot, no?"

"You can say that again! I've never seen such small penises on such big men," she said in a deliberate and calculated attempt to humiliate these unwelcome intruders.

Wilson then went to the psychiatrist who had tried to originate a conversation.

"Look it, you son of a bitch," he said. "I want to know who sent you, and if I don't like your answer, I'm gonna get some more answers. You hear that?"

Wilson's questioning style was rough, tough and uncompromising. He knew how to deal with these characters whom he considered the bottom of the barrel when it came to humanity. Wilson was ordinarily a congenial and somewhat charming individual in his day-to-day activities, but these men were a direct threat to his person and everything he believed and stood for. His commando style from his earlier days was in full force.

"I'll talk to you. Don't worry. Just give me a chance," pleaded the psychiatrist.

Feigning to strike him once again, Wilson spoke.

"That is your first mistake," said Wilson. "Do not speak in a consoling tone of voice to me. I want answers or nothing, and I want them in a matter of fact tone. Who sent you?"

"It doesn't work that way. You see, we were doing a study," said the psychiatrist.

Wilson slapped the man across the face, just hard enough to mean business.

"You damned bastard. Don't tell me it doesn't work that way. Tell me who the fuck sent you. I just want name, rank and serial number. If I want details, I'll ask for them."

Now horribly frightened, the psychiatrist began to cry.

"You seething sack of shit!" yelled Wilson, "Answer me!"

"Hans Krieger," said the man, somehow barely pronouncing it. "Dr. Hans Krieger. He has a boss, too, but I'm not sure who that is."

"Very good," said Wilson, "you're finally starting to fucking learn something. Maybe one of your nitwit colleagues here knows who Krieger's boss is. Wilson walked over in a threatening manner to the other two. The only man who had not been injured by Wilson nodded and spoke up.

"Yes, I know Krieger's boss. It's Dr. Karl Konrad. Both have offices on Meadow Street."

"In D.C.?"

The man nodded.

"OK, you sons of bitches. Maybe we're not getting off to such a bad start after all, but I guarantee you one thing. If I find your information is a red herring, I'm going to have your nuts," said Wilson.

"It's true, it's true," pleaded the man.

"OK. We'll check it out. Heidi, call Colonel Mack. We've got to report these criminals to the MPs. Check that. You keep an eye on them, and I'll go in the next room and call Colonel Mack."

Wilson went to an adjoining room where he could not be heard and picked up the phone and dialed Colonel Mack who was in charge of the Military Police on the base.

"Don't tell me they struck you again general," asked Mack when he heard the general's familiar voice on the phone.

"Damn right they did. Get down here right away and bring a squad with you."

"Right away," said Mack before hanging up the phone.

"Heidi, come in hear. I want to talk to you out of ear shot of those bastards. They're not going anywhere in their current condition, and tell them not to even think about it. Bring their clothes here."

Heidi entered the room and gave the clothes to Wilson. He threw them contemptuously in the corner.

"Yes, sir," she said, reporting for duty.

"It's not easy to think with all this crap in my face. I move a lot on instinct as you can see. Two heads are better than one though, and I want to consult you. Just tell me now — what are your thoughts?"

"The most disturbing thing is that they knew about your secret office," said Heidi.

"Yeah, but they were already stalking me. They could have a connection with the architect for all I know. Funny, the secret office was my saving grace with the first episode. It is as if they were somehow able to read my mind, but that is impossible."

"Remember not to be surprised by anything," she reminded him.

"True," he agreed, "but my intuition is that they have a low grade spy in the maintenance department and someone who fiddles around with locks. Nobody knew about that office outside of you and a couple of contractors. Look for the maintenance man. He has access to this hallway and has locksmithing skills. There's the connection."

"Are we going to have any trouble with the MPs?" asked Heidi. "I mean, we are starting to look suspicious with all these attacks."

"No, not at all. Colonel Mack is one of us."

"Then why didn't you call him in yesterday? He could've gotten us off the hook even faster."

"It's not always good to call in your favors right away. I wanted to follow standard procedure and document everything clearly. We did not do anything wrong. This whole mess, however, is getting deeper."

In almost no time at all, Colonel Mack and the MPs arrived. Hearing them out in the hall, Wilson emerged.

Colonel Mack stood just above six feet and had a strong but not imposing build. His manner, which was gentle but firm, was not overly intimidating.

"Where are the culprits?" asked the Colonel.

"Right in there, all tied up and ready to sing," asked Wilson. "I suggest you send your squad in to keep guard while we discuss what happened."

"Fair enough," said Colonel Mack as he addressed two of his MPs. "Morton and Sanders, keep an eye on the prisoners until we have a little discussion."

Accompanied by Heidi, Colonel Mack and General Wilson went back into Wilson's original office where Heidi made some coffee. For the first time all day, a feeling of normalcy and relaxation was present. Even though it was only 11:00 a.m., it seemed like they had been at this all day.

"Who are these sons of bitches?" asked Mack.

"Three psychiatrists. Well, I haven't seen their credentials yet, but I can tell. They're just like that son of a bitch from yesterday. These guys can't even hide the most obvious fact about them. You check their credentials and tell me if I'm wrong."

"Well, if they keep sending button-down shrinks to go after a commando, even a gray-haired one, I'd say that your opposition is pretty lame," said Colonel Mack.

"They're weak when it comes to physical force. They have no experience in military. Their strengths are going to be elsewhere," said Wilson.

"Don't sound too bright to me period," laughed Mack.

"What I see thus far," said Wilson, "is that they have persistence, plenty of men to waste, and powers of observation that cannot be overestimated. I'm sure they have more strings to pull, but I'm not sure what they are."

"Well," said Mack, "they've just blundered big time. They're not only invading military property, they have entered a top secret area — your office. They can easily be classified as spies. Civilian justice is not something they have recourse to. This is a pure and simple military matter of the highest order. Just tell me, general, what do you want me to do with these bastards? But first, give me a clue as to why they are after you. I'm a little bit in the dark."

"It's the Hess affair. We were ready to crack that open. He was about to be released. Then, at the last minute, the Brits or their agents got to him and killed him. Someone got wind of Agent T and now I'm a target. What would seem to be an overreaction tells us that we were just too close to finding out some of the major secrets now buried with Hess."

Mack nodded. "What a damn crazy world we live in. What do you want to do with the prisoners?"

"I want to interrogate them, and I want to use sodium pentothal. You know, truth serum. They offered a bit so far, but I doubt that they even know what the hell it is that they really represent."

"No problem," said Colonel Mack. "Let me know what you need."

"First," replied Wilson, "I must alert you that there could be a slight problem. When we killed their first agent, the shrink who broke into my office yesterday, they took no time with their follow-up reprisal. They strengthened their numbers, too. I'm sure they sent some sort of hit squad to our houses as well. Whoever this is, they mean business, and if we can rely on their past pattern of doing business, they're going to strike again in the same place but with a heavier amount of force."

"Could be," said Mack confidently, "but not likely. This is a military base. They've weaseled their way onto it twice and have lost both times. I can simply shut it down until further notice. Besides, this is a crime scene. I can give you a good while."

"Is it possible," asked Heidi, "that we could be interfered with through ordinary command channels?"

"That would surprise me very much. But, in keeping with what we said about surprises, I'll be ready for anything," said Wilson.

"No," said Colonel Mack. "This is a crime scene and espionage has been committed. Any senior officer trying to counter that will be named as aiding and abetting such. You're on safe ground as long as I can maintain this as a crime scene."

"Excellent," said Wilson. "Now, Colonel, if it's all right with you, I'd like to have a couple of your MPs escort Heidi down to the address these guys gave for a Dr. Karl Konrad. It was on Meadow Street in D.C. They can go down to Meadow and see if either Dr. Konrad or a Dr. Krieger even exist."

"No problem," said Colonel Mack. "That will not only tells us whether the shrink is lying, it will give us further leads to investigate. The MPs can escort Heidi immediately."

"Thank you very much, Colonel Mack. Now, let's see what we can do about drumming up some sodium-pentothal. I'd be happy to begin the investigation process right away."

"Fair enough," said Mack, "but I think we might get a lot more mileage if you can interview Konrad."

"Yes," agreed Wilson, "but we'll have to see if he's real first."

"OK," said Mack. "Heidi, you come with me and I'll have a couple of my best men escort you. General, I'll be back in a matter of minutes."

As Wilson stood guard over the prisoners, Heidi and Colonel Mack walked out the door.

**INTRUDERS....................**

......... CHAPTER FIFTEEN .........

## MEADOW STREET

    Escorted by two members of the Military Police, Heidi descended upon 321 Meadow Street in Washington, D.C. A decent walk from the Watergate Hotel, Meadow Street could not really be considered a "nice" area of town but rather on the cusp of what some people might consider a dangerous neighborhood. It was a rather simple and nondescript address sandwiched in between other shops. On one side was a book store and on the other side was an old but seedy-looking Orange Julius concession. There was a large painting of a red devil on the window which looked like it must have been twenty years old or more.

    Heidi and the MPs made their way into the office at 321 Meadow Street and went to the second floor office of Dr. Konrad. At the outset, she could readily see that she had already accomplished her primary mission which was to establish that 321 was not only a real address but that the name Karl Konrad was displayed prominently on the door. There was, however, no sign or any evidence of a Dr. Krieger.

    Heidi then opened the door to find a waiting room that was on the verge of being seedy itself. She immediately cast her eyes in the direction of an unusual looking man of swarthy complexion who wore a red fcz with a black tassel on the top. Much to Heidi's surprise, she then directed her eyes to another corner of the room wear she recognized a woman, the only other person in the waiting room besides the unusual man with the fez. It was the fortune teller who had done her tarot card reading the previous day and had picked the Hanged Man card. The "gypsy" however was looking straight ahead as if in a trance. She did not see or recognize Heidi at all. Further, her appearance bordered on the outlandish. The woman wore a black gown that was so open in the front as to be considered socially inappropriate.

    Heidi immediately noticed that the gypsy neither turned towards her nor seemed to recognize her. Taking advantage of this circumstance, Heidi turned to make a quick exit, fully realizing that she might spoil something if she did not.

"Looks like I've entered the wrong room by mistake," she said as she looked toward the man in the red fez.

Heidi then walked straight out of the office and returned to the MPs who had patiently waited outside.

"OK," she said to them. "We've done what we needed to do here. We can return now."

When they reached the sidewalk outside of the office, one of the MPs looked at Heidi and spoke.

"I'm thirsty. Anybody mind if I go into the Orange Julius and get a drink?"

"No," said the other MP. "We'll wait right here for you and enjoy the fresh air."

It was a particularly nice day as Heidi and the MP remained standing on the sidewalk and watched various people walk by.

"I'm going to have one last look," said Heidi. "He's taking a long time getting that drink."

Heidi then went back into the building. As soon as she climbed the stairs to the second floor, she was surprised to encounter her second coincidence in the period of a few minutes when recognized an older man with white hair and a moustache who had emerged from Dr. Konrad's office. He looked confused and puzzled. Quickly turning around before the man noticed her, Heidi rapidly went down the stairs and returned to the sidewalk.

Before she could wonder too much about why she just might seem to know two people who seemed to be Dr. Konrad's patients, Heidi remembered this man as an old friend of her uncle. He was a physics professor and his name was Nathaniel Simon.

"Something else happened," said Heidi as she rejoined the MP. "I just saw an old professor in Konrad's office. He's probably going to come out any minute, but he didn't see me inside. I want to have a few words with him. Just play along."

"Sure," said the MP.

A few seconds later, Dr. Nathaniel Simon walked out of the building where Konrad's office was located.

"Dr. Simon! Hi there! It's Heidi. Do you remember me?"

The man still looked puzzled and disoriented but looked into her eyes. It had been a long time since the two had seen each other.

"Heidi! Of course I remember you. And your uncle — how is he? It's been too long."

"I'm afraid my uncle passed away a couple of years ago," answered Heidi, "but it is certainly nice to see you. Tell me, what on earth are you doing here at this particular time on this particular day?"

"I was just upstairs visiting a Dr. Konrad. He called upon me to consult my expertise on the understanding of time. He is trying to wrestle with the psychology of time, but I'm afraid that is a bit too far removed from my field. I am far more familiar with the physics of time than the psychology of it."

"Time?" asked Heidi. "That is interesting, but I don't understand why a professor of psychiatry would be so interested in time."

"Time it seems, according to the doctor, is the primary source of psychological dysfunction. He feels that if you can straighten out a person's problems with time, you can then straighten out the problems with the psychology of the individual. I don't know if he's right, but that's the angle of question he was pursuing."

"Well, professor, I would be most interested if you could give me your card. Perhaps we should get together and reminisce about old times with my uncle. Do you have a card?"

"Certainly," said Professor Simon in a friendly fashion. He extended her a card and said, "Do call, Heidi. It is wonderful to see you. You look as beautiful as ever."

"Thank you so much professor. I'll look forward to seeing you again."

Just as Heidi finished her conversation with the professor, the other MP returned with his Orange Julius. Having successfully completed their assignment, they proceeded back to their car so they could return to the base and make a report.

# MEADOW STREET . . . . . . . . . . . . . . . . .

## CHAPTER SIXTEEN

## GRETCHEN

When Heidi arrived back at the base, it seemed as if there was a welcoming committee to greet her and the MPs. Colonel Mack and General Wilson sat in the latter's office, and there were other MPs there, too. Much to Heidi's surprise, however, there was also a new lady on the scene, but she was dressed in civilian clothes.

"Heidi," said Wilson, "I'd like you to meet Gretchen, a friend of Agent T's. She just flew in from Europe."

Colonel Mack made a motion and the MPs left the office but Gretchen remained. As soon as they left, Wilson spoke again.

"Heidi, I've got to brief you on a few things."

"Sir," replied Heidi, "I've got to brief *you* on a few things, too."

"Did the address check out?" asked Wilson.

"Sure did," replied Heidi, "but there were some other interesting points of fact I must relay."

"Later, Heidi," said Wilson. "I don't want to be rude to our visitor. She just arrived, and we both need to hear what's up from her."

"OK," said Heidi, "but I can't believe how this investigation has blown so wide open and is now being viewed by everyone. Also, what happened to the prisoners?"

"They're in a holding tank on the base right now and are under armed guard," said Colonel Mack. "This investigation is now wide open and is a matter of military record. It is still, however, top secret. Only those with proper clearance will find out about it. Remember, I'm on your side, but we don't need to play up the Hess angle."

"Now, let's hear from Gretchen," said Wilson. "Would anybody like any coffee?"

As Wilson prepared coffee for everyone, Gretchen began to speak.

"Agent T insisted that I come here directly and tell you what happened. He didn't even want it written down in case I was compromised on the way here.

## GRETCHEN . . . . . . . . . . . . . . . . . . . . . . .

"When he had the photos from the Hess death scene processed, Agent T returned to his car and became very upset at what he found. In his car, prominently placed on the dashboard, he saw three more tarot cards of the Hanged Man, and they were all the same card and all from the Aleister Crowley deck. Somehow, somebody had entered his locked car and placed the three cards in there. As you Americans might say, he "freaked out." He told me that he was being targeted and that I should take great care myself. Agent T made the Fedex package for you, included the photos, and then told me to make arrangements to go to Switzerland and send it from there. He then told me to make clandestine travel arrangements and fly to you immediately. In other words, I had to take extra precautions to be sure I was not being tailed. As for Agent T, he is hiding out."

"Just in case this room is bugged," said Wilson, "do not say or suggest where Agent T might be."

"Well, I can certainly tell you that he is no longer in Berlin. He sought safe harbor and said you would know where that is. He did not tell me where he was going."

"This is certainly the strangest case I have ever been involved in," said Colonel Mack.

"Yes," said Wilson, "it doesn't make any apparent sense. I could certainly see political reasons for killing Hess. That doesn't surprise me in the least. What is so odd is that the apparent killer is exhibiting the behavior pattern of something on the order of a serial killer. He's advertising his crime, but more importantly, he's leading us with an occult message of the Hanged Man."

"Yes," said Colonel Mack, "he's certainly waving it in your face."

"Let's be a little more specific," said Heidi, "none of this would be of significance if it were not for Agent T taking the pictures and acting on them. The fact that the tarot cards were placed in his car means that it was personally directed at him. Somebody was tailing him and was keenly aware of his interest in the cards at the scene of the crime. It is somewhat presumptive to assume that the man leaving the cards is the guilty party with regard to the murder, but it is quite likely that the party who left the cards at the scene of the crime is the same one who arranged for the cards to be left in Agent T's car. Also, consider that not too many people have that many copies of tarot cards. We're talking about several decks or someone who has a tie to the publisher of the card decks and has an ample supply.

"He's giving you something to think about," continued Heidi. "In Berlin, Agent T is being baited, but then it is relayed to you. Then, you are staked out by these strange psychiatrists who seem to come out of a funny farm themselves. The shrinks and the placer of the cards are obviously in league together."

"Ordinarily," said Wilson, "I wouldn't put psychiatry and occultism together. Carl Jung might be the exception, but these two factors do not normally synchronize, at least not in my brain."

"Remember," said Heidi, "do not be surprised by anything!"

"It was only in Berlin that the cards were left as bait." said Wilson. "We have yet to see any cards appear in the States."

"Except for the tarot reading I had," said Heidi. "There's more mystery here than you know about as you have not yet heard my briefing."

"Do you mean to tell me that you saw cards at the address of Dr. Konrad?" asked Wilson.

"No, not exactly," said Heidi. "But, I did see the lady who had pulled the Hanged Man card in the reading for me. In fact, she looked most bizarre."

"Bizarre?" asked Wilson. "How so?"

"For starters, she had the blankest stare I've ever seen. She looked so blank that I swear she did not even see me, let alone recognize me. I've had different readings from her so she should have easily recognized me had she seen or paid attention to me. I do not know her well, but she seemed to have a psychic line into me just by doing the various readings she had done for me. In fact, she certainly hit a strong chord when she pulled out the Hanged Man for me."

"What was she doing in the office?" asked Wilson.

"I don't know," said Heidi. "I didn't want to upset the apple cart and got out of there as fast as I could without being recognized. I was only there to confirm that the address belonged to Dr. Konrad. There was another thing though. She was dressed in a manner that attracted a lot of attention.

She was wearing a black gown. In fact, she would've looked quite at home in a witch's coven with that dress. It was also open down the front in a manner that was going to attract attention. I have never seen her dress that way before. It was out-of-character and something was very odd with her."

"That is all interesting in itself," said Wilson, "but we still don't have a solid link to your tarot reading and the cards that appeared in Berlin."

"It is a psychic link," said Heidi. "I know it is not a material link, but remember your motto: 'Do not be surprised by anything!' We cannot dismiss it."

"She's right," said Colonel Mack. "But it *is* a material link. At least it manifested in the material realm when Heidi got her reading. The Hanged Man card that this witch lady pulled IS connected to the cards laid out at the crime scene. It's the same god damned card. Now she turns up at the shrink who is supposed to have sent these shrinks to get you."

"What you are suggesting," said Wilson, "is that we are going to have to factor in the psychic or metaphysical aspect here. The lady is somehow connected to the murder."

"I don't see any way around it from a logical standpoint," said Mack. "That does not mean we have abandoned conventional detective work, but we have to factor this connection in."

"But perhaps more to the point," said Heidi, "we also have to consider the possibility that whoever left those cards was aware of Agent T all along and that he was baiting you through Agent T."

"If that is true," replied Wilson, "we also have to consider the prospect that I was somehow being baited by Heidi's card reading through the vehicle of the witch lady."

"Yes," said Mack, "but we have to take stock of the fact that if you were being baited, the baiter would've known all along that Agent T was going to make a report to you. Do not be so sure that you were not the one being baited all along."

"Yes," said Heidi, "and whoever is doing the baiting is psychically linked, deliberately or otherwise, to the tarot reader."

"Whether or not I am being baited," said Wilson, "I am certainly being targeted. These shrinks wanted to either take me out or bleed me of whatever information I might possess. Heidi, what does your intuition tell you?"

"My intuition tells me that Agent T's boss at Spandau, the one who allowed him to take the photographs, was either in on the murder of Hess or was privy to it. Further, he had some sort of a beat on Agent T's connection to you. Apparently, they consider you to be a bigger fish than Agent T. In fact, it is obvious they consider you very important or they would never have put so many people on you."

"I guess they considered I was too old to fight back. After all, I am in my sixties, but what they sent after me was really pathetic. It looks like an operation of shrinks who have no military experience."

"Well," said Colonel Mack, "if Heidi's right, there was a military man in on it. I would not expect him to be so inept. Then again, you can never tell about military brass."

"It's clear they know more about me than I ever suspected," said Wilson. "As a matter of fact, Colonel, we're going to have to track down who it was that let them into my secret office. There should be a clear clue there as to the nature of that security leak."

"Agreed," said Mack.

"Besides that," said Wilson, "we've also got the truth serum to consider on our arrested candidates. But, I'm very interested in the fact that this address for Konrad checked out as genuine. Maybe these guys can give an honest debrief about their masters."

"Do you want to pursue that angle as our next course of action?" asked the Colonel.

"No," said Wilson, "it's probably better to butter them up at this point and reward them for telling the truth. They gave us some information already, and we might want to try a little bit of kindness and sympathy. At least we can see if that tactic works. Right now, I'm of a mind to go over to that office on Meadow Street and find out who this Dr. Konrad is."

"Well," said Mack, "it is now a part of the crime scene."

"You're right," said Wilson, "it is a part of the crime scene. We'd better make our way over there right away."

"Does anybody mind if we all go out for a late lunch first?" asked Colonel Mack. "I'm starving."

"Not at all," replied Wilson. "Besides, Gretchen must also be starving after all of her travelling. I'd also like to hear her angle on everything she's been listening to."

## GRETCHEN

"Good idea!" said Heidi.

The party of four then made their way out of the office to find a restaurant where they could talk in private.

## CHAPTER SEVENTEEN

## ON THE RUN

By the time the group of four had finished their lunch and made their way to Dr. Konrad's office, they discovered they were able to enter the building but the door to his office was locked. Repeatedly knocking on the door, they discovered no one was going to answer. Konrad had apparently gone home. Rather than to make inquiries and attract suspicion, they decided to leave as quietly as possible and come back the following day.

Returning the next morning at promptly nine o'clock, they were able to enter the building again. This time, however, Konrad's door was wide open. There seemed to be no one inside so they took the opportunity to enter his quarters and soon discovered that everything in the office was gone. This included the furniture in the waiting room, what had most likely been Konrad's office, and an additional room which could have served as a library or file room. Maybe they could find out about the contents of what had been here from the prisoners back at the base but that would have to wait until later. All that remained were a few discarded papers which appeared at first glance to be utterly meaningless.

"Heidi," said Wilson as he picked up the papers, "could you please take those papers and place them in a file? They might come in handy later."

"Yes, sir," she replied as she took the papers from him.

"It seems that we failed to act soon enough," said Wilson.

"You mean my stomach got the better of us?" asked Colonel Mack. "It was I who suggested we go to lunch."

"Well, we don't really know if he was in the office then," responded Wilson, "but, once again, time and speed are of the essence in this whole investigation."

"That's very true," said Heidi. "The immediate attack of the first shrink was followed up promptly by the gang of three. Now, we seem to have reversed the momentum as we are now trailing them, and they continue to move with considerable speed."

"Yes," said Wilson, "but now it's time to find the landlord and ask him some key questions."

As they began to leave the office, the mysterious man with the red fez suddenly appeared. He was walking towards the office and approached them as they emerged from the door.

"Say," said Heidi, "you're the man I saw the other day. Do you have any idea what happened to Dr. Konrad?"

"Hello," said the man in the fez. "My name is Ali Bey."

The man's presence was out of context to the group's acute interest in pursuing this investigation, but his politeness and mood had a calming effect on everyone. Nevertheless, he still had not answered Heidi's question.

"Excuse me," said the general, "I'm General Wilson of the U.S. Army and this is Colonel Mack of the Military Police. We are currently conducting a criminal investigation that concerns military matters. Our leads have led us to Dr. Konrad's office, but we are not even sure at this point exactly who he is. Perhaps you can help us by telling us a bit about him or what your business with him was all about."

Ali Bey looked at them intently but gently, as if he were scanning them. After a short while, he spoke.

"I do not really know Dr. Konrad. I was waiting to see him the other day because he is supposed to be a dealer or collector in ancient manuscripts."

"Do you mind if I ask what you were seeking?" asked Wilson.

"I am a dealer in antiques myself, but I was of the persuasion that he either had or might have knowledge of an ancient mandate concerning the rights of my people to this continent we live upon which is now known as America but was once known as Al Maurikanos, in honor of Morocco. I am a Moor."

"Oh," said Wilson. "Do you have any idea why he disappeared?"

"And," Heidi interjected, "do you think he had anything to do with what you are looking for?"

"Well," responded Ali Bey, "I cannot say for sure, but anything is possible. The document I seek is politically impacting as it could change the social structure upon which so many things are based."

"Could you be so kind," asked Wilson, "as to tell us what has transpired here the last few days? And, do you have any idea why everything is now gone?"

"Perhaps I can help you a little," said Ali Bey. "After this young lady," he said as he pointed to Heidi, "came into the room and peered around for a short time, a professorial looking man soon departed Dr. Konrad's office. Konrad had been having a conversation with him and then escorted him to the door and said good-bye.

"Probably ten or fifteen minutes prior to Heidi opening the door yesterday, Dr. Konrad interrupted his session with the man he was with and came into the waiting room. He was quite distressed and spoke to the only other person in the room, a lady who sat at the opposite end of the room from me. Dr. Konrad said that he had lost a very important book and wanted to know if she could tell him anything about it.

"When the lady asked which book, he said that is was small and black and that it looked like a prayer book, but it was important to antiquity. It seemed to me that he had just suddenly discovered the loss and was hoping that she might have some sort of desperate answer for him."

"She is a psychic," interjected Heidi. "Perhaps that is why she was there. He might have called her to his office — he wanted her to see if she could locate it through ESP."

"Perhaps," said Ali Bey, "but it seemed to me that he had just discovered the loss of the book, and that she was already there for another reason. He appeared to have some degree of familiarity with her.

"Then," continued Ali Bey, "Dr. Konrad took notice of me and seemed to be a little surprised to see me in his office. After all, I came there unannounced. He asked me my business, and I informed him that I was looking for an ancient manuscript that he might either possess or have knowledge of. When he asked me what kind of manuscript I was interested in, I told him and there was a bit of a frown on his face. I'm not sure he knew what I was talking about. He told me that he was very busy with some matters that had just come up and that I could wait or come back tomorrow. I decided to wait. Konrad returned to his office and spoke to the man for about fifteen minutes. You (looking at Heidi) came while I was waiting to see him. A short while after you left, the other man came out and left, too. At that point, Dr. Konrad came out and told me that it would be best if I came back the next day. He then escorted the woman into his office.

# ON THE RUN . . . . . . . . . . . . . . . . . . . . .

"I then got up to leave, but something overtook me. I began to feel a hot flash and soon experienced a problem with my stomach as if I had suddenly become ill. Although I am old, I have not experienced anything quite like this. I was very dizzy and had lost my bearings. My immediate solution was to sit back down in the chair and to gather myself together.

"Although I was mostly preoccupied with my own personal condition, I could not help but hear Dr. Konrad's voice in the next room. He was very upset over the loss of his book and seemed to be making demands upon the woman. I heard her say absolutely nothing, but she was probably speaking to him in a soft tone which could not be overheard. It was easy to tell that he was repressing his rage and was trying not to disturb too many ears with his voice. Had he yelled, it would have been readily heard in the hallways and perhaps in the rooms next door.

"As for myself, I soon realized that I would be best off if I could use a rest room. Seeing a common key on a hook next to the door, I grabbed it and proceeded to the bathroom facility at the end of the hall. While in the rest room, I kind of blacked-out. Although I did not lose total consciousness, I was pretty far removed from any sort of normal state of relative mental relaxation. I recovered fully after what I think was about ten or fifteen minutes. Things were back to normal.

"As I washed my hands, my attention was somehow directed overhead. At the top of the medicine cabinet in the rest room, I saw a small book protruding over the edge. After drying my hands, I reached up and saw that it fit the exact description of what Dr. Konrad was looking for. It looked like a prayer book and even the sides of the pages were pink. The paper was very thin. Taking it, I went back to Dr. Konrad's office to return it to him, but the door was now locked. I knocked several times but no one answered. He had apparently left.

"The next day, I came to return the book to him along with the bathroom key but no one answered the door. I decided to come back early this morning as I also wanted to see him, but I have run into all of you instead."

By this time, much commotion was being stirred up around Dr. Konrad's empty office. A man in work clothes appeared and approached General Wilson and his group.

"Mind if ask what is going on?" he said in a tone that was mocking but somewhat friendly. "I'm the building superintendent."

"Excuse me, I'm General Wilson and this is Colonel Mack of the Military Police and we're conducting an investigation of a crime committed on our base. Although Dr. Konrad is not necessarily in the military, we need to question him. He seems to have suddenly moved. Can you tell us anything about that?"

"I certainly can!" said the super. "I got a couple of calls around midnight. The residential tenants on the top floor were all in a row about all the noise being generated from the movers. It was disturbing their sleep. I live on the third floor, too, but I am stashed away in the corner. It was not so loud to me. When I came down to the second floor, I saw a moving company taking all of his items from the office and placing them in a van on the street."

"Do you remember the name of the company?" asked Wilson.

"Most certainly," said the super. "It is rather hard for me to forget. The name of the mover is Lion's Paw. The logo depicted a big lion's paw with the face of the lion superimposed upon the paw. Not a bad logo and quite memorable."

"Do you have any idea where Konrad was going or why he was in such a hurry?" asked Wilson.

"I have no idea," said the super. "People who leave like that are usually running from something, but I know he was up-to-date on his rent payments. No problems there. He was not a problem tenant."

"OK," said Wilson. "Do you have any idea what he had in that back office?"

"Oh yeah," said the super. "He had a lot of books in there but mostly files in large metal filing cabinets. There were a lot of them."

"And now they're all gone!" said Colonel Mack.

"Not gone but in transit," said Wilson.

"Sir," said Wilson to the superintendent, "do you have a business card or phone number that we can contact you in case we have further questions in the future?"

"No problem," said the super as he gave them a card from his pocket.

## ON THE RUN

"And you?" said Wilson as he nodded towards Ali Bey.

"Yes," said Ali Bey as he handed him a card. "Call me if you like. I've enjoyed speaking with all of you, and I hope you find everything that you're looking for. It sounds like you have quite a mystery on your hands."

"That's for sure," said Wilson. "Now," he continued, addressing his three colleagues, "we've got to get our way down to Lion's Paw. As we have already learned so many times in the last few days, speed is of the essence."

·······CHAPTER EIGHTEEN········

## THE CHRISTENING

Accompanied by the Wilson Brothers, Aleister Crowley arrived at the Fleming estate for a reception in honor of Victor Fleming's new son, Ian, who had just been christened. It was a joyous day amongst the Fleming household and their friends, most of whom were aristocrats or in the international banking trade. Victor Fleming's father, Robert, was still one of the world's most prosperous men and was a great sponsor of technology. Having made several trips to America, he was responsible for many innovations in that new country.

Reaching the outside of the house, Crowley recognized John Ambrose Fleming, the man renown for developing the vaccuum tube.

"Look," said Crowley to the Wilsons, "There's John. I thought you fellows might like to see him today as well as some of the people who are financing and putting your genius to work."

Seeing his benefactors approach the estate at the same time as himself, John Fleming came over to say hello.

"Greetings, my friends," said John Fleming. "The help you gentlemen have given me is beyond words. You should take a lot more credit than you do."

"I think you do pretty well yourself," said Crowley. "These Wilson boys may feed you ideas, but you are the one doing the actual development."

"Without their guidance, I'd probably be fumbling along. Again, I can't thank you all enough," said Fleming to the Wilsons. "Are you absolutely sure you don't want any credit? Maybe I could name a device or two after you."

"True genius does not desire attention," said Crowley.

"If that's true," laughed Preston Wilson, "you have certainly not ranked yourself in that category!"

All of them laughed.

"If you take the time and effort to study my work closely, real closely," said Crowley, "you will see that I never claim any proficiency or notoriety in the areas where I am most proficient. Most of the world is not psychologically prepared to deal with me. My reputation makes it impossible for them to consider me seriously. Those who know me are the ones I want to know me. It is a closed circle," said Crowley.

"Are you saying you are a ruse?" asked Marcus Wilson. Crowley smiled.

"The outer planets," said Crowley, "are the best tools of the magician. Uranus, which you all should know, is the ruler of electromagnetic energy. It is chaotic and haphazard but is nevertheless full of unbridled energy that can be tapped. There is nothing Uranus cannot accomplish, but it is completely unpredictable. Neptune is the ruler of illusion and deception. With Neptune, you can keep your opponent preoccupied with dancing bears, or perhaps something even more enticing, as you cut his jugular."

"What about the planet Pluto?" asked Marcus Wilson.

"*That* planet has not been discovered yet!" said Crowley. "It's not really a planet anyway."

Reaching the door of the Fleming estate, the party was greeted by Victor Fleming and escorted into a parlor full of interesting and powerful people.

"Come and say hello to the new grandfather," Victor Fleming said to Crowley as he directed him to walk towards an older man. Crowley in turn signaled for the Wilsons to follow him.

"Congratulations!" said Crowley to the banking genius known as Robert Fleming. "I thought you might like to meet the vehicles by which so much of this new technology is coming into the world. These are the mechanics behind your investment."

"Technology is the key ingredient in maintaining superiority. Rule Britannia!" said Robert Fleming.

"Robert Fleming," said Crowley, "this is Preston Wilson and this is Marcus Wilson."

"It is a pleasure to meet you and acknowledge the service you have provided for the Empire. How do you do it?"

"A lot of time at the drawing board!" interjected Crowley before either one of them could give an answer. "A lot of time at the drawing board!"

"Mr. Crowley," said Robert Fleming, "we are so lucky to have you on our team. Is there anything I could do for you? You have done so much for us."

"Well, you could let me see your grandson," said Crowley. "After all, he's the reason that brought us all together on this day. Again, congratulations to you, sir."

Robert Fleming then escorted Crowley and the Wilsons to Ian Fleming's baby carriage. They all soon surrounded the tiny infant.

"He's got beautiful eyes and a cute little face," said Marcus Wilson.

"A handsome devil indeed!" said Crowley.

"Do you think he will become a banker like me or that he will tend more toward the political life such as his father?" asked Robert Fleming.

"As requested, I did a horary analysis of him," said Crowley. "The little fellow has a predisposition towards athletics and will be suited for both of these fields in his future. Unfortunately, he will suffer the loss of someone close to him. His stern character and his passion for activity will enable him to overcome this. My intuition tells me that I will be seeing a lot of this little fellow, and I will do my best to guide him."

"Splendid!" said Robert Fleming. "It's always good to have a guardian angel looking over one."

"Hardly!" exclaimed a smirking Crowley.

Robert Fleming then took Crowley by the arm and escorted him to a private room.

"You know," said Robert Fleming, "I was entirely serious about helping you. Is there any small favor I could bequeath to you?"

"My German brethren have been corresponding with me about a certain matter for some time," said Crowley. "They are particularly concerned about persecution by the Russian Czar and have solicited my help and advice in this matter. They seem to view me as someone who has influence with the Crown, but they do exaggerate my influence."

"I understand," said Fleming, "that intelligence has put you in touch with a monk who has access to important circles in Russia."

"Hardly!" laughed Crowley. "They did succeed in putting me in touch with such a person, but they did not know that he was already one of my own friends! It is true, however, that he could prove himself to be quite useful in alleviating the persecution."

## THE CHRISTENING . . . . . . . . . . . . . . . . .

"Persecution is not the way of good government," said Fleming. "It is not necessary. I not only sympathize with your German brethren but will support you in this endeavor. Please tell me what I can do."

"One of the Germans, Rudolph Steiner, has suggested we set up a holding company for the purpose of setting up an effective fifth column inside of Russia. He is supporting a man named Lenin. Steiner has an impeccable reputation and is quite gifted in his own right but I feel that Lenin is vulnerable to other influences."

"Consider it done!" said Robert Fleming. "I will fund it."

"Oh!" said Crowley. "There's one more thing that I almost forgot. George (H.G. Wells) said that I should meet Winston. He said that he would be here and soon be taking an active role in intelligence."

"Winston?" asked Fleming.

"Yes," said Crowley, "now I remember. It's Churchill, Winston Churchill."

"Certainly," said Fleming, "I'll introduce you right now."

As Marcus Wilson amused the baby by playing with his toys and gadgets, Crowley was escorted to meet Winston Churchill.

"Hello, Mr. Churchill, I am Aleister Crowley. George insisted I meet you and extends his best compliments to yourself."

"How is George?" asked Churchill.

"Scheming and dreaming as usual," responded Crowley in a wry but not quite sarcastic tone. "He sees great things for you in the future of the Empire. He is most preoccupied with maintaining the trade routes and dispersing civilization to the outer edges of barbaria."

"Hah!" laughed Churchill.

"He says that the future of Mankind depends upon what we do here and now. It is his utmost concern that an international network of communications be established to not only enhance the British Empire but the human race itself."

"The enhancement of the population, most unfortunately, comes at the hands of turning a dirty deed here and there," said Churchill. "It is most unfortunate that real work requires so much sacrifice on the part of people. The pyramids of Egypt are only one such example."

"I couldn't agree more with you," said Crowley. "Sacrifice is an essential part of the natural order."

"And quite Christian, too!" said Churchill in an almost jocular manner.

"Enjoy the festivities," said Crowley.

"Very well," said Churchill. "I think I will have a very good time."

As Marcus Wilson played with the baby, Preston Wilson looked around the room and gazed at everyone. Something gave him an uncomfortable feeling, and he walked over and cornered Crowley privately.

"I am not so sure what you have gotten us into," said Preston. "If it is true what you say so often — that technology is the key ingredient to maintaining superiority in empire, I would certainly hope that the people surrounding us here are worthy of possessing such technology. Something is making me feel funny about all this."

"Would you have me cancel all our plans and have us take a trip to Japan or China?" asked Crowley as he snickered. "Maybe they would do a better and more ethical job with technology."

"I certainly wouldn't feel good about that," said Preston, but I would consider the United States."

"America!" exclaimed Crowley. "They have more war lords and industrial abuse than anyone in the whole world. Of course, that might apply to anybody who has the biggest industrial base. Yes, I might consider them. But Germany will overtake them in the future. Germany will have the best technological base, but we hold the strings to Germany. We've already laid the groundwork for that."

"I still don't feel good about the people surrounding us," said Preston.

"To be perfectly honest, Preston," said Crowley, "there are no guarantees in life, particularly when you are dealing at this level of society. I can guarantee one thing though. Any of these people, in their normal course of doing business, wouldn't hesitate to go for the jugular. That is the way of the world and it is particularly true in the business world. If they were not strong like that, they wouldn't be here."

"Don't get me wrong," said Preston. "I certainly follow your logic, but there's still something missing here."

## THE CHRISTENING................

"Indeed," said Crowley. "There's a lot missing. There's a lot missing indeed! That's why the world has to change."

## CHAPTER NINETEEN

### THE BOOK

After the party of four made their way rapidly down to the headquarters of the Lion's Paw moving corporation, they immediately informed the secretary that they were pursuing a criminal investigation for the military police. She immediately volunteered to get the manager.

"Hello," said the general manager as he entered the lobby and saw the four strangers, "how may I help you?"

"Good day," said General Wilson as he extended his hand to shake. "I'm General Wilson of the U.S. Army and these are my colleagues: Heidi, Gretchen and Colonel Mack of the Military Police."

"What can I do for you?" asked the manager.

"Well, sir, we need to question Dr. Karl Konrad and we have discovered that your company moved him some time around midnight last night. Your company is not under any sort of investigation or suspicion, but we would very much appreciate it, and it would help our investigation, if you could be so cooperative as to tell us the destination of Dr. Konrad's materials."

"If you just want to do some questioning," said the manager, "I don't see any problem at all. I'll just get the work order and find out the address they are all headed to. If you have any questioning, you can pursue it there. You just might want to do me a favor though. Please don't mention how you got the address."

"No problem," said General Wilson.

The manager of Lion's Paw retreated to his office for a minute and then emerged with a work order.

"I've got it right here," he said. "The address Konrad is moving to is 321 Old Montauk Highway, Montauk, New York. That's about eight to nine hours away. Could be a little longer or shorter depending upon traffic conditions. Anything else you need?"

"No," said Wilson, "you've helped us quite a bit."

"Oh," said the general manager, "one more thing. It might make finding the place a little easier. It says on the work order

# THE BOOK . . . . . . . . . . . . . . . . . . . . . .

that 321 is the section of Old Montauk Highway that is five or six miles beyond the town itself and maybe a mile or so before the lighthouse. That might save you a bit of grief in trying to find it."

"Appreciate it," responded Wilson.

As the general manager returned to his office and the party of four made their way back to their car, Wilson spoke to the group.

"I'm not going to hesitate to reiterate once again that time is of the essence. If there's anything we've learned in this investigation, it is that we have to move fast. Every time we do not, it seems that we are put at a disadvantage. I suggest that we all head to Montauk. That's at the extreme eastern end of Long Island. We can easily make it there by the end of the day if we leave right now. We'll even have time to visit Dr. Konrad at his brand new address and even before he's unpacked. Any counter offers?"

"Yes, I have a counter offer," interjected Gretchen. "Time may be of the essence but there is also such a thing as moving too fast. From what I have seen thus far, this is a highly complicated investigation, and I think you just might be overlooking something that could be very important."

"What's that?" asked Wilson.

"The book," replied Gretchen.

"Oh my God — the book!" exclaimed Wilson. "How could I have overlooked that?"

"Yes," said Heidi, "the man with the fez said he had come to return the book to Dr. Konrad. He must've had it on his person when we saw him, but we were too eager to get to Lion's Paw and forgot to ask him about it."

"Indeed," said Colonel Mack, "an oversight by all of us."

"I think it will be best if we split our forces," said Wilson. "Colonel Mack, I suggest you accompany me to Montauk. We'll put the feminine touch on Ali Bey. Heidi and Gretchen can pursue that end."

"Don't you think," asked Gretchen, "that it might be a good idea to get the book first and return it to Konrad? That way you'll have something that he wants and you could possibly use it as leverage."

"No," said Wilson. "There is no guarantee that Ali Bey will still have the book or that we can readily obtain it from him. We have to get going as speed is of the essence. You ladies can follow up the trail on the book though. It is too important to overlook. I think that Colonel Mack and I can handle the field trip by ourselves. There are weapons in the trunk if we should need them. Any objections?"

Everyone shook their head.

"It's agreed then. Gretchen and Heidi, take a cab over to Ali Bey's place. Try to get the book, but do not offend him or insist upon it. At the very least, please try to get a photostat copy of the entire contents."

Wilson and Mack drove the ladies to the nearest busy corner where they could easily catch a taxi.

When Gretchen and Heidi made their way to Ali Bey's import/export shop, they were not only impressed to see that it was in a nice part of town but that it was filled with many beautiful and exotic items. Although there were different types of wares and furniture, most of them were either of Middle Eastern or African design. The predominant theme of the store seemed to be lamps.

"It looks like you could find Aladin's lamp in here!" said Gretchen as they entered the store.

There was no one in the store when they entered save for Ali Bey who was seated in back. Hearing the bell ring as the door opened, he came forward and smiled when he saw the two familiar faces.

"Hello, my friends. I did not expect to see you so soon, but it is most certainly my pleasure."

"It's nice to see you again, too," said Heidi. "Should we call you Ali or address you by your full name?"

"You can call me Ali. That will be quite fine. Now tell me, what brings you to see me again so soon? Could it be this?" said Ali Bey as he presented the mysterious book that they had come for. He held it in his hand in front of them as if he was putting it on a pedestal.

"Why yes!" said Heidi. "In our haste to go to the moving company and discover where the doctor moved to, we soon remembered that we had abandoned a very important lead in our investigation: the book!"

"Indeed! On my way home, I realized it could be of some importance to you. It is a most interesting and unusual book."

"Have you read it already?" asked Gretchen.

# THE BOOK . . . . . . . . . . . . . . . . . . . . .

"Very much so. In fact, since it came into my possession less than two days ago, I've spent most of my waking hours reading it and wondering about it."

"What can you tell us about it?" asked Gretchen.

"It primarily consists of copies of an odd series of manuscripts and letters, each of which features a designation whereby the manuscript or letter in question can be referenced in a library or official document file. What is most puzzling about the letters and manuscripts, however, is that they all seem to predate major inventions or breakthroughs in technology."

"How do you mean?" asked Gretchen.

"Well, one example is the vacuum tube. History tells us that it was primarily developed and invented by one John Ambrose Fleming, but if you read this book, you will see manuscripts and letters that were written either by a Marcus or Preston Wilson. Their names appear on every one of the documents. It seems as if they either invented the vacuum tube themselves or guided Fleming to its invention. It doesn't stop there however.

"These letters and manuscripts also apply to the development of the zeppelin, wireless transmission, various aspects of the early development of radio, and even a letter to Albert Einstein prior to his discovery of relativity. All of these manuscripts are either by them or put together under their supervision as they are constantly referred to.

"In summary, my friends, it appears that these two men instigated the major technical developments in our civilization's history but that others got credit for them. The trick here, however, would be to look up the references and documents that are cited and check them out. This would verify that the book is not a hoax or ruse of some sort. I must say, however, that if it is a ruse, it is a ruse that was performed on a scale that not even an advanced man could think of let alone take time out to perform. There is something in this book that is of the highest order but a very bizarre order indeed."

"This is most peculiar," said Heidi. "Ali, we realize there is a confusion with regard to the ownership of this book. It is by all rights the property of Dr. Konrad, but it is of great interest to our investigation. We would at least like to copy the pages if you do not mind."

"I have already taken the liberty to copy it for myself, but I will give the actual book to you as I have no expectation of seeing Dr. Konrad. It is more likely that you might do so.

"I must say, however, that it was not an accident that it passed through my hands. That is evidently why I suffered the affliction and was driven to the bathroom astride Dr. Konrad's office. It was only by reason of my temporary suffering that I discovered it.

"I so want to check out the validity of these references when I get the opportunity. If you can, please get back to me when you have the time and let me know what you find. After all, this book was placed in my hands for a reason and perhaps I will have further answers for you in the future."

Ali Bey extended the book to them and placed it in Heidi's hands.

"By the way," said Gretchen. "You have a beautiful store here. It looks like it has come out of time itself."

"Indeed!" laughed Ali Bey. "And thank you my friends. I will look forward to seeing you both again. Please extend my regards to General Wilson."

As the two ladies exited the store, Ali Bey smiled.

# THE BOOK...................

· · · · · · · · **CHAPTER TWENTY** · · · · · · · ·

## MONTAUK

Wilson and Mack had made the trip to Montauk at breakneck speed. It was almost nine at night when they pulled up to 321 Old Montauk Highway. As per the instructions from the moving company, they proceeded to the "second dwelling" at the back of the property. The primary house on the ground was evidently unoccupied at that time. There were neither lights nor cars.

When Wilson and Mack came to the front door of the second unit, they discovered that the door was ajar. The room was filled with boxes and furniture that had yet to be put in its final resting place. When they walked past the main conglomeration of boxes however, and much to their surprise, they discovered a corpse. By all appearances, it seemed to be the body of Dr. Karl Konrad who had evidently been murdered via gun shot from the front. He was lying on the floor face-up.

"Damn it!" said Wilson. "This doesn't seem to quit. We're about to question him, and someone beats us to the punch."

"Before we do anything," said Colonel Mack, "I want to follow some standard procedures. First, let me go back to the car and get my camera. Also, I will immediately call the local police department. We should not touch the crime scene, the body or anything else. I can, however, take some photographs and we can positively identify Konrad either with Ali Bey or with Heidi's tarot reader."

Mack then returned to the car and used the cell phone therein to report the crime to the police. While the police made their way to Old Montauk Highway, Mack took photographs of the crime scene and of Dr. Konrad. He then returned to the car and tucked away the camera.

A policeman arrived in about fifteen minutes. He was alone and approached the second dwelling in his car as Wilson and Mack stood outside. Leaving his car, the officer was greeted by Colonel Mack.

"Hello, officer," said Mack. "I'm Colonel Mack of the Military Police, and this is General Wilson of the U.S. Army.

# MONTAUK..........................

We came up here from Virginia in pursuit of a criminal investigation that we are conducting on behalf of the Military Police. Some of our suspects indicated that we should interview Dr. Konrad, the man we presume to be dead inside. Although he was not a direct suspect himself, we thought that an interview might prove invaluable in our investigation and we were in a hurry to talk to him. We are not sure why, but for some reason, he moved suddenly and unexpectedly to Montauk and had all of his materials moved up here today. We trailed him and arrived here about twenty minutes ago. Now, we discover that he's dead."

"I'm Officer Tom Hailey. Nice to meet you."

The police officer then walked into the dwelling and scrutinized the entire crime scene.

"Somebody killed him all right," said the officer. "I'm going to have to call this one into the office and get the coroner and detective out here to do some forensics and what not. I'll take it over from here guys."

"Certainly," said the Colonel. "I would only request, and let me talk to your superior if needed, that we be informed every step of the way and on the initial summary of the findings."

The policeman suddenly changed his personality and became inordinately more pleasant.

"That won't be a problem at all," said the officer. "I guarantee it. We're used to cooperating with the military around here. After all, we're used to having the Air Force right next door. You guys have had a long day. I suggest you get yourselves something to eat after your long trip and find yourself a motel and get some sleep. You can check in with us tomorrow. I'll personally be available in the morning and I'll introduce you to the coroner and the detective. Right now, procedure would dictate that I get the guys out here and let them do their thing. If you're around, they might second guess themselves. You fellows don't mind do you?"

"No," said Wilson. "We appreciate your cooperation."

As the policeman went back to his car, he went to the radio and began talking. Wilson and Mack entered their own car and began driving away.

"Do you think we can trust them to do a halfway decent job?" asked Wilson.

"I don't think we have much of a choice," replied Mack. "If I were to take over the investigation at this point or in anyway interject myself where I do not belong, this case is going to be blasted all over the higher echelon of the Pentagon, and we just might find ourselves restricted from the case entirely," said Mack. "Personally, I'd like to watch every move these guys make, but I don't want to be an irritant, or worse, get busted off the case. Let's go check into a place."

"Fair enough," said Wilson.

General Wilson and Colonel Mack soon found out that trying to find a motel in August can be nearly impossible at Montauk. It is the height of the tourist season. The best they could do was to find a motel room in Riverhead, a little more than an hour away. It was out of the way, but they really had no choice.

The next morning, Wilson and Mack arrived at the East Hampton Town office building and sought out the police department. It was only nine-thirty and they wanted to get an early start and speak to the coroner and Tom Hailey, the officer who had assisted them the previous evening. They were, however, more than a little surprised at the response they got when they arrived at the police station and asked the secretary for Officer Hailey.

"I'm afraid I do not understand," said the secretary in response to their inquiry. "There is no Officer Hailey on the East Hampton police force. Is it another jurisdiction?"

"No. The crime we reported and where Officer Hailey arrived were both at 321 Old Montauk Highway."

"That is our jurisdiction all right. Let me check the police blotter," said the secretary.

The secretary got up and went to another desk. After a few minutes, she came back.

"It's quite odd, gentlemen," she said. "There is absolutely no mention of anything on the police blotter that concerns Old Montauk Highway. Are you sure you said Officer Hailey?"

"Absolutely," said Mack.

"There used to be an Officer Hailey who had the beat out at Montauk Point, but he committed suicide over a year ago. Are you sure you are not mistaken with the name somehow?"

"Absolutely not!" said Mack. "There is no doubt in my

mind. He said his name was Officer Tom Hailey, and I certainly had no reason to doubt him or scrutinize his credentials. After all, I was the one who called 911. If they didn't send Officer Hailey then who the hell did they send out there?"

"I'm afraid I don't understand," said the lady. "Perhaps you'd like to talk to the Chief of Police."

"Yes!" said Colonel Mack. "I think that would be a good idea at this point."

"He's not here this morning, but you could speak to his deputy, Lieutenant Cowens. He's in the next room."

The secretary then went and retrieved Lieutenant Cowens who came out and greeted the two army officers in a professional manner.

"What can I do for you?" asked Lieutenant Cowens.

"I'm a little distressed," said Colonel Mack. "We came up here on Military Police business, all the way from Virginia. We drove up here yesterday in pursuit of a Dr. Karl Konrad who had suddenly and unexpectedly moved to Montauk, 321 Old Montauk Highway to be exact. He was not a direct suspect in our investigation, but we determined that he was absolutely crucial in helping us to uncover some data. We were not able to reach him before he moved and arrived at approximately nine last night and entered the second dwelling at 321. There, we discovered a man we presume to be Dr. Karl Konrad, shot dead. My training and protocol dictated that I call the local authorities. I dialed 911 from my car cell phone and was told that an officer would be there right away. In ten to fifteen minutes, a man who identified himself as Officer Tom Hailey arrived and took over the crime scene. He knew we were returning this morning and that is why we are here, to coordinate and liaise your findings with our department and investigation."

"You're telling me that a man was killed on Old Montauk Highway, you called the police, a policeman came and that we know nothing about it?"

"Yes," said Mack, "and the officer in question, Officer Hailey, seems to be an imposter. Your secretary told us that a real officer named Hailey died of a suicide over a year ago."

"True," said the lieutenant. "This is one hell of a mystery. First thing we better do is get our tails out to the crime scene."

The lieutenant then turned to the secretary and said, "I'm going out there myself. This sounds like a big one."

"Indeed!" said the secretary.

The lieutenant then escorted the two officers out of the building and into the parking lot.

"Follow me in your car," said the lieutenant. "It's about a twenty to twenty-five minute ride to the crime scene from here and traffic is usually a little busy this time of year. If it is, I'll turn on the siren and you just follow me."

When they arrived at the crime scene, Lieutenant Cowens pulled in first as Wilson and Mack followed him to the second dwelling. They immediately noticed that things were just a bit different. The door was no longer ajar. It was closed. Getting out of their cars, the three men went to the porch. The lieutenant tried to open the door, but it was locked.

"When we came here yesterday," said Wilson, "the door was ajar."

They then looked through the windows and could plainly see that there were no longer any boxes and certainly no dead body. Everything had been cleaned out! The crime scene, including any ostensible evidence of the crime, had been successfully obliterated. Further, the alleged policeman called in to investigate it had no tangible evidence of even existing.

"This is crazy," said Wilson. "I don't know what to say. If my fellow officer here hadn't seen it with his own eyes, I might wonder if I'd gone around the bend. This is definitely the house and there was definitely a crime."

"This is most peculiar," said the lieutenant. "I've had cause to liaise with the military throughout the years, and I've never been dealt with dishonestly. Personally, I have no reason to distrust you or even question your judgement, but I am at a loss to explain what happened here."

"The most obvious explanation," said Colonel Mack, "is that your 911 line is not secure and was compromised. It was intercepted virtually in anticipation of such a call, and an impersonator was sent out to avoid any proper discovery and investigation of this crime."

"I can't disagree with you," said the lieutenant. "Of course, I'm going to have to report this to the chief and we'll conduct an investigation ourselves, beginning with the possible interception of the 911 line. Is there any further evidence you know of that might be of interest? You didn't take any pictures did you?"

"No, I didn't take any pictures," said General Wilson. "Something definitely happened here though, and I hope you can get to the bottom of it."

"Have you ever had security problems like this before?" said Colonel Mack.

"No," said the lieutenant, "I can't say that we have, but this is going to be at the top of my priority list. You know, Montauk is mostly a quiet little fishing village. Other than the occasional drunk or outrageous partier, there is not much police work to do out here. Look it fellows, I appreciate your bringing all of this to the department's attention. I can only offer to do my best in order to find out what happened here. Give me your cards, and I'll be sure to liaise with you on what we find."

"Thanks a lot," said Colonel Mack. "We'll report this on our own lines. There's a lot more to this investigation than we can even talk about right now. Make sure you do a thorough job."

"Will do. We'll talk in a few days," said the lieutenant.

"Fair enough," said General Wilson.

The politeness of the conversation was belying the fact that neither party trusted the other. Wilson was quite sure of this. He had no respect whatsoever for the Lieutenant, but he was not going to spill his hand and upset the apple cart. In his judgement, and Colonel Mack wholeheartedly agreed with him, it was better to let these jokers choke themselves by their own hand.

"I'm sure glad that you did not volunteer that you took any pictures," said Wilson when they entered their car.

"That doesn't make me a liar," retorted Mack.

"That's why I said that I didn't take any pictures," said Wilson. "Got you off the hook, but those pictures are our trump card if we need it. At this point, tipping them off that we have photos is only going to invite us being targeted for a counter-maneuver by whoever the hell is behind this. I propose that we go back to Riverhead as soon as possible. There, no one will be looking over our shoulder, and we can make multiple copies of the photos and send them out so that we cannot possibly be contradicted on this. We can then come back here to Montauk and do some investigating on our own. I'd like to find out what makes this town tick."

Returning to Riverhead, they developed the photographs and sent multiple copies off. One set each went to the office addresses of Wilson, Mack and Heidi by certified mail. Another copy went to their respective homes. They also sent a copy to Ali Bey. They chose the latter as he was innocuous in regards to these matters and no one would be likely to hunt him down. To Ali Bey, they included a cryptic but brief letter of explanation which included a statement that they wanted to positively identify Dr. Konrad.

It was three-thirty in the afternoon by the time Wilson and Mack made it back to Montauk. They proceeded to drive around the circle in the main part of town.

"Yes," said Colonel Mack, "a nice little sleepy fishing village. Looks like a great place to have a good time at the beach. Where do you want to head to first?"

"What are we thinking?" asked Wilson. "We should question the neighbors at 321. They just might give us some sort of clue as to what is going on."

The officers then proceeded back to Old Montauk Highway. When they explained themselves to the neighbor to the north of where Konrad had been killed, the proprietor was none too friendly. He said that he knew nothing of his neighbor and certainly had no idea that a murder had been committed next door. Most surprisingly, he showed no fear or concern that there might be somebody on the loose who could harm him. He seemed desensitized at the very least. Pursuing him was a dead end.

The neighbor to the south was considerably more friendly. She had been a minor movie star herself and knew something about her neighbor. Explaining that she was not close to her neighbor, she said that the original proprietor had starred in early swashbuckling movies and that his German descendants now owned the property. She had occasionally spoken to them and exchanged a few pleasantries but that was about it. The only thing significant she revealed was a German connection with the property. This made sense because Karl Konrad was obviously German. The shrinks who had accosted Wilson were also of German descent. Being that Wilson was investigating Rudolph Hess, this came as no big surprise.

## MONTAUK . . . . . . . . . . . . . . . . . . . . .

When they told this lady the odd circumstances of the police not recognizing the murder, she told them that they should not be surprised by anything that occurs around here. She explained that next door is an old military base that has provided a constant stream of rumors and weird happenings for years. Asking her why she did not move, she said that this was her home and that she had never been seriously disturbed. She loved the beach as well.

The two officers decided to inspect the base next door. When they drove up to the base, they saw that it was fenced off with "no trespassing" signs. There was, however, a guard house with a gate that was wide open. Driving in, they readily saw that the base was abandoned and utterly derelict. They saw a huge radar reflector atop a very large building. They were both already informed that this base had once served as the home of the 773rd Radar Squadron of the U.S. Air Force and acted as the first line of defense with regard to spotting potential enemy aircraft entering U.S. air space. The Air Force had abandoned it many years earlier.

As they drove around the inner base, the officers came upon an ugly and disturbing sight. It was a large white-tailed buck deer that had been severely mutilated, but it had not been destroyed by any normal means. It looked as if the carcass had been crushed to the ground as the legs were spread out at ninety degree angles from the torso of the carcass. Further, the skull looked like it had been pushed into the ground. Virtually all of the meat was still on the deer.

"This deer makes no sense whatsoever. What do you think happened?" asked Wilson.

"Got me," said Colonel Mack. "I've never seen anything like it."

"If you ask me," said Wilson, "my guess is that someone was trying out some sort of super secret weapon. Sometimes the military uses secluded areas of abandon bases to experiment. I can't tell you for sure though."

As they continued to patrol the area, a New York State park ranger drove by. Seeing them in uniform, he paid them no attention.

The officers then made their way off the base and eventually ended up at the famous Montauk Point Lighthouse. After taking in the view of the ocean from the lighthouse area, they made their way down the hill and examined the sea shore by the base of the lighthouse.

"Look at that!" said Wilson. He was pointing to what looked like a mine shaft that was big enough to drive a tank through. The lower part of the shaft was filled with rocks and one could not penetrate it as the top half was filled with dirt.

"An underground facility of some sort," said Mack. "I'll bet it hasn't been used in a long time."

"The base was used during World War II as a first line of defense," said Wilson. "The base inside was made to look like a fishing village. It got a new life in the fifties when the radar system you saw was developed but that became outdated quite a few years ago. I couldn't tell you when this particular tunnel was last used."

As they began to make their way back to the trail that would lead them back to the parking lot, they saw an old wino staggering along the trail. When the wino saw their uniforms, he made a mocking but partial salute and spoke.

"Hello, sir! May I report for duty?"

"Are you a vet?" asked Wilson incredulously. "If you are, I could certainly recommend a place where you might get some assistance."

"Am I a vet?" asked the wino. "Do you mean 'could I fix your cat'? I don't know. They've got some pretty strange animals around here, and I'm not sure I could fix them whether I was a vet or not."

"What do you mean by strange animals?" asked Wilson, knowing that the best way to get information out of a drunk was to treat what he said literally and lead him along.

"They've done some strange experiments on animals around here."

"Like deer?" asked Wilson.

"Deer? Damn right! You'd be surprised. I've seen so many deer running around here like crazy, like they were bumper cars or something. There's a place called Salivar's down at the docks. They have a mural on the window of a deer crashing into the window. It really happened! They turn that big radar transmitter on up on that big building over there and it makes everybody go crazy — people and animals alike."

"Yes indeed," said Wilson, "I've heard this is a very strange place."

"Are you conducting any of these experiments yourself?" asked the drunk who noticed that Wilson wore a military uniform that represented a significant degree of authority.

"No, I'm here investigating a murder. Perhaps you could tell me a thing or two more about this place."

"A murder!" said the drunk. "My God! They used to murder people out here all the time."

"No kidding?" said Wilson in an attempt to indulge the drunk's line of conversation.

"No kidding indeed! They used to send people out into time from here — to their death."

Deciding to entertain the logic of the drunk, the general decided to ask him another question.

"How is it that these people went into time and met their death?" asked Wilson.

"Well, if you send somebody into time, you have no idea where they're going. They could be going to a cafeteria or into the middle of a tornado. They might be going into the middle of outer space or into an ocean. Who the hell can tell? Believe me — I know. I've been to some pretty hairy places myself."

"If that's the case," said Wilson, "and you were sent into time like you say, how come you were so lucky as not to die?"

"I always carry this rabbit's foot," said the wino as he showed him a two-toned green rabbit's foot that he carried in his pocket.

"Remarkable," said Wilson. "Utterly remarkable. Thanks for your time, sir."

"No problem," said the drunk as he began to stumble away.

"Oh!" said Wilson as he pulled out his wallet and presented a ten dollar bill. "I forgot something. Here is something to help you along."

"Thank you! Thank you! Thank you! Since you have been so nice to me, I'll tell you a dirty little secret, but please don't tell anybody. You promise?"

"We promise, right Colonel?" said Wilson to the Colonel who nodded in agreement.

"And," said the wino, "you're sure you're not involved in those experiments with regard to the animals or time?"

"Most certainly," said Wilson. "I've never heard of anything like that."

"Well, if somebody was murdered and you can't find the answer, let me tell you something. This whole town is run by the military and the military runs the police department. They run around and intimidate everybody and that is why people like me run around and get so drunk. It's hard to deal with."

"The military?" asked Wilson. "I'm in the military, and there is certainly no military presence out here that I've ever heard of, and I have full access to such records."

"They operate underground and they operate in secret and its the Navy. You're in the Army, right?"

"Yes, that's right," said Wilson.

"It's the Navy, and they're the most secretive of all the military. Just don't tell anybody that I told you," said the drunk.

"Well, that won't too hard," said Wilson. "We don't even know your name."

"Good point!" said the wino as he stumbled off.

Wilson looked at Colonel Mack and spoke.

"I'll bet you never thought you'd hear anything like that, especially from a drunk."

"I've never heard of anything like that. This investigation has gone from the bizarre to the very very weird," said Colonel Mack. "Do you have any idea of what the hell is going on?"

"If Heidi were here," said Wilson, "she'd happily remind me not to be too surprised at anything and consider all possibilities. I can't overestimate that angle at this particular time."

"Do you think there's any thread of truth in what the wino said?" asked Mack.

"There might be. There well might be, but we've got to get back on the trail of our investigation. But first, I want to check out this place called Salivar's that he spoke about."

After asking directions, the two officers made their way to Salivar's and saw the pictorial evidence of a deer having crashed into the restaurant window. Going inside, they met several of the customers who were all too ready to talk about the day a deer ran uncontrollably through the front window. Some of them had seen other deer lose control at different times. One had even reported seeing a deer run head first into a phone booth and commit virtual suicide.

As they headed off from Salivar's and back towards the main part of town, General Wilson spoke up.

"I think we've seen enough to determine that this is one crazy place. I propose we head back to our motel, give Heidi a call and prepare for the trip home tomorrow. I want to do some prowling around at the Pentagon about what might be going on here."

"Do you have any clear ideas at this point?" asked Colonel Mack.

"Clear? You've got to be kidding! There's absolutely nothing clear about what's going on here."

"General, let me be completely frank. I know you spent a lot of time dealing with highly classified stuff when you were in Germany and all those super secret Nazi programs. Does that give you any insight into any of this and can you tell me anything?"

"Quite oddly," said the general, "much of the stuff I saw in Germany isn't even in the realm of being classified. That's because too few people know about it, and I cleverly kept my mouth shut. I'm not too restricted in what I can talk about, but I'm loathe to say much of anything for what it might incur in terms of consequences."

"But there's nothing that might shed light on what we saw today or on the Hess matter?" asked Mack.

"On the Hess matter, yes; but not on what we heard today."

"What about Hess?"

"Well, we've got a long drive back to Virginia tomorrow. It's about time I fill you in on a few things you don't know."

## CHAPTER TWENTY-ONE

## SPYING

In America, George Sylvester Viereck was the primary agent of Germany when it came to foreign affairs that were not suitable for proper diplomatic channels. As the grandson of Kaiser Wilhelm, this should not have surprised anyone. It certainly did not surprise Aleister Crowley when he was called upon to visit Mr. Viereck.

"What is all this about Sylvester?" asked Crowley to the well known magazine editor and publisher. "You said you wanted to see me."

"Yes, I do. With America entering the war, pressure is increasing for me to relinquish my position as editor and to keep a lower profile. It becomes a more sensitive issue everyday."

"And?" asked Crowley.

"I would like you to take over as editor for *The Fatherland*."

"You would? Why not pick someone who is German with German sympathies?"

"My people in Germany have advised me to pick you."

"You are kidding?" laughed Crowley betraying surprise over his selection. "Why on Earth me?"

"You have a literary background and a wide education, but that only makes you qualified. My advisers in Germany....."

"...are apparently inundated in the matters of secret societies!" interrupted Crowley. "Sometimes I think it is nothing other than a routine compulsion with such people to use my name every time there is an opportunity. What you need — don't you think — is a German agent, someone who has the sympathies of the heart of Germany?"

"You seem to know more about Germany and her patrons than the average German and even those in the aristocracy."

"How do you know that George didn't send me over here to drum up President Wilson's support to get America into the war? It is said that I have a great power of persuasion."

"Whether that is true or not," said Viereck, "you have been recommended to me by people I trust and support. Your sarcasm notwithstanding, I would like to ask you if you will take the job. After all, we both know that the inner hierarchy of Germany and England are closely related."

"Do we?" asked Crowley in a mocking but playful tone.

"It would be nice if you would give me an answer rather than to answer my questions with further questions. I am not ignorant to the ways of manipulation and neither are you. I have a job to do here, and I am simply asking your help, but perhaps you can answer another question for me. How is it that you have captured the imaginations and credibility of so many societies in Germany?"

"That is an intriguing question," said Crowley, "and it certainly deserves a considerably higher degree of response than working for a German propaganda paper, but let me tell you one thing, my friend, and that is that these secret societies don't give a damn about these war games and who wins. I have come to America to execute my will and to fortify an island."

"What on Earth do you mean?" asked Viereck.

"Let me say this," said Crowley. "Diversion is one of the best tools of war. If the theater of war is in Europe, I would look elsewhere in order to see what is going on. Do not think that I do not know about the German factions that settled on Long Island years ago."

"Is that the island you were sent to fortify?" asked Viereck. "Anyway, will you take this god damn job?"

"The English and the Germans are both pawns," said Crowley. The Americans are perhaps the most expendable of all. You should not need reminding, but remember your oath to the Rosy Cross when I tell you what I tell you. The codes that Telefunken used were broken and this is what got Tesla in so much trouble and made him a suspect of the American government. Codes and ciphers are first and foremost a province of secret societies. No matter how brilliant or knuckle-headed, intelligence services are only working with a sliver. Beware of becoming a patriot of Germany or anyone else. It will be your undoing. It is a lesson worth learning."

Crowley turned around to walk away. Just before he reached the door, he stopped and turned around.

"Oh, by the way," said Crowley, "when do you want me to start?"

"Come in as soon as you can," said Viereck.

## CHAPTER TWENTY-TWO

### THE DRIVE

After breakfast, General Wilson and Colonel Mack made their way to the Long Island Expressway to begin the long ride home to Virginia.

Colonel Mack said, "Anytime you are ready to talk, I am ready to listen."

"There's so much I could tell you, but I'm going to have to stick to the most relevant facts," said Wilson. "First, I'm going to discuss a general outline of the circumstances and will eventually get back to Hess. Exactly how this fits in with the attacks of the shrinks, I still cannot figure out at this point; but if I give you the background, it will certainly help you in getting to the bottom of it."

"Yesterday," said Mack, "you said you were going to start with your nonclassified experiences at the end of the war."

"Right," said Wilson. "If there is nothing else that I learned in the war, the most flagrant lesson is that common history is full of lies. The truth is not a highly regarded commodity when it comes down to writing down an actual legacy.

"At the war's end, I was with Patton's Third Army when everyone thought we were going to be assigned to Berlin and beat the Russians to Hitler's bunker. Instead, we were ostensibly assigned to go after the German National Redoubt, sometimes colloquially known as the Werewolves. The press and public were fed a line that Otto Skorzeny was gathering the remains of the German army for a final last stand. It was further said that Hitler was living in a bunker there as well. Historians have always questioned why Eisenhower sent his best general on such a lark when intelligence reports clearly indicated there was no national redoubt that was of any threat to anybody. Actually, there was a redoubt of sorts, but it had nothing to do with the military. It was all about technology, but we'll get to that later.

"Historians are also puzzled as to why, when Hitler's general who was defending Berlin asked for more troops, Hitler insisted upon leaving sizable forces in Norway, Prague,

# THE DRIVE . . . . . . . . . . . . . . . . . . . . .

and in the south. There should have been nothing to defend in any of those areas. As a matter of fact, Hitler stated in his refusal that these troops were the key to Germany's future. Most of these comments have been attributed to Hitler being insane, but there is a far deeper story.

"Our real mission with Patton's army was to go after the sizable fortresses where the Nazi's had developed avant garde weaponry and flying technology. This also included their development of the atomic bomb. Allied history has been concocted and distorted to tell us that brilliant Germans like Heisenberg, the German who gave us one of the first theories on quantum physics, were not quite smart. This also included the man who discovered nuclear fission. It really makes you wonder how much crap people are capable of swallowing. If you look closely, you will note that America was only able to figure out the atomic bomb after Germany surrendered and the Americans were able to obtain full access to their technical archives and scientists. It is so simple."

"I also heard that the Japanese had developed an atomic bomb prior to the war's end," said Mack.

"Yes, they did," said Wilson. "Where do you think they got the uranium from?"

"I don't know — where?" responded Mack.

"I'll give you a hint. As the war ended, a German submarine was found clearly transporting uranium to Japan."

"Well," said Mack, "they wouldn't be sending it there unless they had a good reason."

"You bet," said Wilson. "They helped the Japanese develop a bomb. This was why Tojo and his generals were not ready to surrender. Ultimately, they bowed to the Emperor but mostly because they no longer had an adequate air force that could deliver the bombs.

"Several soldiers," continued Wilson, "including at least one German pilot, witnessed a test bombing in Germany that featured an atomic mushroom cloud.

"While the bomb was certainly the most forceful and useful of the technologies discovered in the German arsenal, there was also a host of exotic craft and engineering designs. Many of these were not perfected yet, but some had reached a significant degree of evolution. These included flyer saucer craft, flying wings and mysterious radar jamming weapons."

"Radar jamming?" asked Mack. "You must be talking about those Foo Fighters. Did you see much of that stuff?"

"I didn't see too much of it. I saw a craft or two flying in the distance, but most of them were in hiding by the time we arrived on the scene. I did see some that were partially constructed in underground hangars, and I saw plenty of blueprints, but I never studied them. After all, I am not an engineer.

"The point here is that Patton's army collected a vast array of technological information. This included the German war department's files which had been moved out of Berlin. It was all waiting for us in the south, and that's why Eisenhower sent Patton. It was the most important assignment of the war, and he needed his most effective general."

"What about the rocket scientists?" asked Mack. "Were you going after them?"

"No, other people were put on that. We were primarily conquering territory and securing locations. Of course, Patton had reason to interview many top people and had access to all sorts of information. You must remember, however, that all of this stuff was written in German and might well have been Chinese to most of us. When it came to technical matters, it created a gap with the translators unless they themselves were already sophisticated engineers."

"Does this tie in with the murder of Hess?" asked Mack.

"Apparently, "said Wilson. "I'd say very much so, but I do not know the exact details because I never got a chance to speak with him. We'll get back to that later though.

"As most of the rail lines and major roads had been bombed out by the end of the war, the Nazis had become incredibly clever at moving their facilities and reconstructing new ones. They would use natural caverns under mountains but were also excellent at boring tunnels and making underground bases.

"One of their generals was unsurpassed with his efficiency in constructing underground facilities. His name was Hanz Kammler, and he was ultimately in charge of all technologies and factories. It didn't start out that way though, but his remarkable ability as a builder and adaptability in establishing new locations earned him almost unparalleled rank in the Third Reich. Even Walter Dornberger, the paperclip scientist

**THE DRIVE . . . . . . . . . . . . . . . . . . . .**

who Werner von Braun was subordinate to, both at NASA and in Nazi Germany, was put under General Hans Kammler. This was by order of Hitler and thus Kammler became the technology czar. All technical information and capability was under him."

"Boy," said Mack, "that must've made him one of the most powerful men in the Third Reich. What happened to him? Did he end up at Nuremburg?"

"That is an excellent question," replied Wilson, "and while Rudolph Hess was not in a position to observe the events at the end of the war, I always thought he might be able to give me a clue. Hanz Kammler was never found."

"Do you think," asked Mack, "that he might have been repatriated under another name?"

"One has to consider the possibility, but I wouldn't necessarily vote for that theory. The best guess would be that he went to the so-called legendary Nazi base at New Schwabenland."

"You mean in Antarctica?" asked Mack.

"Yes," said Wilson, "that is one of the best Nazi survival myths. The biggest telltale sign of an actual operation in that area, at least as far as common history is concerned, is Operation Highjump. That is when Admiral Byrd was heralded in leading an expedition to Antarctica in 1946. It had a stated military objective, but inside knowledge in the military will tell you that the ships on that operation got their asses kicked and some of them never made it home. The operation was heralded in the press and in newsreels as a successful polar expedition, but it was really nothing of the kind. It was a humiliation and military disaster, and Byrd later warned the public that our greatest threat was from high speed objects flying from pole to pole."

"Didn't the Nazis have something on the North Pole, too?" asked Mack.

"There are several stories of a base in subarctic Canada or Greenland. This might explain why Hitler maintained so many soldiers and U-boats in Norway at war's end. It could serve as an escape route or as a strategic launching base for a facility near the North Pole. What is known is that Kammler would've been the perfect candidate to construct and develop an underground city in a remote part of the planet."

"What is the official version of the Nazi's original expedition to Antarctica?" asked Mack.

"Essentially, they went to claim a piece of the continent for Germany. Enormous money was expended to build a ship for that express purpose. They dropped swastika flags from planes and claimed that area as New Schwabenland. This was in the late 1930's and prior to the war. As a matter of fact, Admiral Byrd was invited by the Nazis to accompany them on the expedition. He even flew to Germany to advise them and gave a lecture. Byrd was going to join them on the expedition itself but backed out of it at the last minute."

"Do you know why?" asked Mack.

"I do not know, but he was a Mason and the Nazis hated Masons. Perhaps he found this out and had a change of heart. I am sure they were more than polite to each other in their official capacities. It is also likely that Byrd had a secret agenda of his own in going to Germany. He was very high up in Freemasonry and always insisted that his immediate subordinates be similarly inclined and had each one take an oath of allegiance to him. I also understand he was full of a lot of crap and would grandstand for the cameras. His crews resented him for this type of behavior and did not care too much for him.

"Also keep in mind that Byrd was not really a military admiral. Actually, he was a ballet dancer. He was only nominally in charge of Operation Highjump. His purpose was at least twofold. As a geophysical explorer, he provided an ostensible credibility for polar explanation, but he also knew the Nazis firsthand and would have had direct experience with the original mission."

"The early expedition to the Antarctic though, perhaps surprisingly to you, is an area where Hess fits in. I was very interested in asking him about this directly, and I was damn close to being able to get an interview with him.

"Hess was in charge of the Auslands Organization or Germans Abroad organization. He was literally assigned the responsibility of being in charge of all Germans who served the Reich from abroad. His title and role were never abolished so, technically speaking, it could be construed that he was the officer of senior rank over the Nazis in Antarctica and anywhere else abroad. It might seem ludicrous that a broken

# THE DRIVE...................

down old man in his nineties had any such influence or power, but the hundreds of millions of dollars it cost annually to keep him incarcerated was a testament to the fact that he was more than a token power.

"You see, there are still many legal technicalities that are still unresolved with regard to present day Germany and it being an occupied war zone. When Admiral Doenitz succeeded Hitler as the Fuhrer of the German people, he was forced to surrender unconditionally. Although he was primarily a soldier, Doenitz was found guilty of war crimes, mostly by reason of the political winds of the times. Incarcerated with Hess, Doenitz was only one of seven inmates in Spandau Prison but was released after about ten years.

"The Allies, however, had a bit of a problem when Doenitz surrendered. They had to install a new government in what became known as West Germany, but they had no real or credible people to serve as heads of state that were not dyed-in-the-wool Nazis. What they did do, however, was take a giant leap of faith by declaring the old Second Reich as the legitimate heir with regard to being the true government of the German people. They refused to acknowledge the Third Reich and declared it an illegal government. For all practical purposes, they instituted a new democracy in West Germany and things have run at that level ever since. When it comes to technical legalities, however, and the honoring of true and unbiased international law, some problems could arise."

"How's that?" asked Mack.

"If you study Hess, you will find that he is more influential in the rise of the Nazi Party than Hitler himself. You see, Hess was into the Friekorps before he ever met Hitler. He was also studying under Karl Haushofer and was part of the Thule Society. It was he who first recognized the talent of Hitler and Haushofer readily came on board, but that was not Hess's only contribution. Hess was not only a competent street fighter in the Friekorps, but he was a superb organizer and excellent at raising money. He not only used his connections in the Thule Society to raise huge amounts of money, he was in charge of it.

"When I say he was a good organizer, he had a reputation for being meticulous. This not only applied to organization in finances but to technology."

"Technology — you're kidding?" said Mack.

"No, I'm not. He had a meticulous and technical mind, and I even saw some of his lectures on technology. They had to be translated by an interpreter though. He knew a lot about the flying technology that was developed, but that was in the years prior to his flight to Scotland. It is clear, however, that he inspired, financed, and encouraged so much of this alternative research. NASA scientists, up to his very death, always wrote to him and kept him regularly informed of developments with the space program. He was always quick to respond and share his views on how people might survive better in space."

"In other words," said Mack, "he was respected for his technical prowess and not just because he had served as the Deputy Fuhrer."

"Exactly," replied Wilson. "You do not get to a position like he held by being much of a dummy. I think he is one of the most complex and interesting personalities of the Twentieth Century.

"Now, let me get back to the legal issues with Germany. Hess was meticulous in legalizing the Nazi Party within the framework of the legal German government. If you study up on it, you'll notice that Hess himself took incredible care to dot all the i's and cross all the t's when it came to their assumption of power within the German state. They certainly strong-armed people at different junctures, but Hitler made his way through channels of law. Laws were legally and formally passed that literally made the Nazi Party the only political party in Germany as well as the head of state. Hitler, as Fuhrer of the Nazi Party, was by that reason legally in charge of the entire German state. Hess, as the Deputy Fuhrer, was second in command. In terms of technicalities, declaring them an illegal state is more of an opinion and a judgement as opposed to a good hard loophole in the law. In fact, the Allies had no loophole save for the fact that they declared the Nazis to be bad and evil. Without regard to the truth, the legal argument as I have stated presents certain inconsistencies with regards to the structure of the current West German government and any future government the Allies would be likely to approve. Hess was a very key figure here."

## THE DRIVE . . . . . . . . . . . . . . . . . . . . . . .

"Do you mean to say that the current West German government might go down the tubes?" asked Mack.

"I do not mean that at all, but there are many powerful and influential Germans who resent the fact that their government is one that was set up by an occupying power. When you go back to the original faction of Germans who ruled the German state, you are dealing with the last legal head of state and that is the Third Reich. Before he died, Hess could have been construed as the legal Fuhrer."

"Well, I could never see that having happened," said Mack. "Do you think that is the reason they killed him?"

"I think it contributed to the reason. There are many problems surrounding Hess. Although his membership in the Nazi Party may or may not have been accurately rescinded, a good lawyer could have construed a good argument on his behalf. When you look at all the obvious facts or even consult the more complex facts underneath, there is no question that his flight to Scotland was as an emissary of peace. It is a war crime to incarcerate him on that basis. This may all have come to nil, but they are certainly questions that would have been raised by his allies if not himself. He certainly represented quite a predicament for the English who had literally lured him into a baited trap."

"How does East Germany fit into the picture?" asked Mack.

"From all of my intelligence sources, they are about to fall flat on their face. Hess's death just might be the final piece of the puzzle that will allow Germany to reunify. You see, the Russians can no longer maintain East Germany. It is a lost cause as is the Soviet Union. The scenario in East Germany presents new problems. If the Russians should relinquish East Germany, it would revert to its prior government and that, according to the technical argument I have presented, would be the Third Reich. Again, these are legal technicalities and are not likely to be enforced."

"Yes," said Mack, "but they wouldn't seem to mean anything now that Hess is dead."

"These matters are not without significance because there are plenty of highly influential Germans who insist that the Third Reich itself never surrendered. More importantly, it still survives albeit in an underground faction that is sometimes referred to as the Fourth Reich. This includes the possible colonies in the poles, South America and perhaps elsewhere. This so-called New Reich has long since become the master of a powerful underground military culture."

"So," asked Mack, "why are these shrinks chasing you? Is it because you have such an inside track on these technicalities and their implications?"

"I'm not sure," said General Wilson. "All I know is that I have struck a nerve and it seems to be connected to a major artery."

"I can't disagree with you," said Mack. "The disappearance of Dr. Konrad is nothing short of remarkable. A problem, however, is that the perpetrator is quite invisible and somewhat intangible, if not utterly so."

"You are alluding to a hidden force, and you are quite correct," said Wilson. "That is the same as an occult force and that was a primary aspect of the Nazi regime: occultism."

"I've heard you say before," said Mack, "that the occult records of the Nazis have remained highly classified to this day. Were they part of the records that Patton's army collected?"

"Yes and no," said Wilson. "I could tell you stories and then more stories, but I have to be honest with you. The enormity and complexity of the Nazi paradigm is such that it is one of the greatest philosophical and historical puzzles presented to modern man. Most people, of course, do not know anything about it and would just focus on what history has told us — that the Nazis were sadistic racists who hated Jews. Indeed, there might be considerable truth in that statement, but that is like examining an elephant by only examining one of his feet and not the whole body. You miss too much. So, most people are not even aware of the puzzle. Solving it is an entirely different manner, and I myself would not even be keenly aware of it had I not survived the war the way I did."

"OK," said Mack, "you've struck a nerve and you should not be surprised by anything. An open-ended investigation is going to have to embrace the occult factor."

"True," agreed Wilson, "and you see it breathing right into the situation with the tarot cards. This even extended to Heidi's reading when the gypsy witch pulled the Hanged Man

# THE DRIVE...................

card without even knowing that she would soon be involved in an investigation concerning such."

"And then the gypsy witch shows up on the trail of the crime," said Mack. "A little too coincidental or just plain weird?"

"This is what Carl Jung referred to as synchronicity. It is a divine happenstance. In other words, a synchronization of events reveals meaning that might not otherwise be perceived under ordinary circumstances. In this case, the gypsy reads for my colleague, but she is also involved with the man who apparently sent these wanna-be thugs to apprehend me," said Wilson.

"That clearly represents an occult force that is trying to stop you. She is tied to the force and it comes through her. That's why she picked the card," said Mack.

"We do know, however," said Wilson, "that she most likely had nothing to do with the murder of Konrad and neither did the shrinks that came to get me. We would therefore have to associate the murderer of Konrad with the murderer of Hess. This is a tier that we have to reach up to and investigate. They might not be the same person, but we know we have a level of association that cannot be denied. We also have to consider the extreme likelihood of a link between Montauk or Berlin. Otherwise, it couldn't have been pulled off in the way that it was."

"Your clearest link there is the military at Spandau Prison and the alleged military force at Montauk," said Mack.

"Good point," replied Wilson. "I'm glad you mentioned that, but we're jumping ahead a bit. Let me backtrack a bit with regard to what happened with General Patton.

"Patton was killed. A contract was put out on him and that was because he had the best insight into the technology of war. Had he been a scientist or an administrative soldier, it might not have mattered too much. He might need to have been eliminated anyway, but he was a warrior general and a damned powerful one, too. Remember, technology is the key martial ingredient in war. Superior technology wins. Genghis Khan developed fire power and beat the Chinese and everyone else. Napoleon's crummy little cannons far surpassed the cavalry of the Mamalukes in Egypt. Every which way you look, technology wins the war."

"If you want to pay attention to that funny little drunk back at Montauk," said Mack, "someone is playing with the technology of time. Now that is some advanced technology!"

"Yeah, that was one weird encounter. Carl Jung would have considered it a meaningful event in terms of the investigation. We'll have to leave it in the bullpen for now though," said Wilson.

"Patton was a very gregarious and engaging individual," he continued. "He was the military governor of Bavaria and was specifically charged with maintaining order and distributing life giving services to the defeated population. Of course, he knew that the most reliable and sure fire way to do this was to utilize the Germans and Nazis who had held the fort previously. That was not really so bad. The real problem the authorities had with him is that he was such a virulent anticommunist that he wanted to network and coordinate the new technology we had discovered into literally destroying the Soviet Union and all remnants of communism. In this respect, he was fully in agreement with Nazi political doctrine. Remember, their hatred of the communists was at the top of the list. They considered the communists and Jews one and the same. Homosexuals were not far behind either.

"What made him politically questionable was his carousing and fraternization with the Nazis. We had a lot of fun during those days. One of the things he did was to gather all of these films from the Nazi film depository and we would watch them at night. There would be drinking, carousing and even some gambling amongst the Germans and Americans. What I found to be most interesting was when these films were shown and Patton would have one of the English-speaking Germans translate them for us. It was not as good as watching a subtitled movie, but we saw some fascinating stuff. The instant translation made it hard to follow, but it was always damned interesting. The Germans would always point to the films afterwards and say something like, 'Look, we had a pretty interesting civilization, didn't we? Isn't it ashamed to see it all go down?'

"This is where I saw some of the lectures of Hess. I wish I would have written down the information that I gleaned from them or at least followed them better, but they were beyond my technical grasp."

## THE DRIVE . . . . . . . . . . . . . . . . . . . . . . . .

"Do you mean to tell me," asked Mack, "that this stuff is not highly classified and you are free to tell me?"

"No doubt about it," said Wilson. "These films literally disappeared from the face of the Earth. If I begin talking about it, people would accuse me of making it up. In any case, there is no evidence to back up my assertions about the films. The soldiers I was with knew better than to talk about it or were otherwise gotten to or eliminated. Let me put it this way. Talking about it is not a good way to win friends and influence people, particularly with your superiors in the military. There is more to this aspect of the story, but we will get to it later."

"To the best of your memory, what did Hess say in those films?" asked Mack.

"He talked about the designs and inspiration for a vast new array of flying craft. These lectures were either to or sponsored by the Vril Society which was a secretive society. Its purpose was to revive the ancient Atlantean culture. This included not only the Vimana flying craft that Atlantis was reputed to feature but also the psychic characteristics of the Atlanteans, most prominent of which was the vril itself."

"What exactly is the vril?"

"Vril refers most basically to the life force but also the ability to activate that life force and mobilize matter. That is essentially what life, when you consider it in its most pure spiritual form, does. It activates and mobilizes material objects. You can see it in DNA — that would be its most basic construct; whereby a computer code is activating matter and conjuring it into a specific mode. The age old question for philosophers and theologians is, of course, 'Who is writing the program?'"

"Well," interjected Mack, "all of us human beings are, at least to some degree, a spin-off of that primary program, at least to the extent that we have or think we have free will."

"I follow you," said Wilson, "and it is significant to point out that the concept and etymology of *vril* and *will* are intimately related. The will determines a program. It is the highest form of computer programming. All codes, directions and protocols are for the express purpose of serving the will, goal, or stated function of what is to be done.

"According to one theory, there is a vestigial organ in the human body which is programmed into our DNA and resides between the heart and the throat. Its function was once to activate, with some degree of automaticity, the emotional feelings of the being into a pronounced activation. In terms of human speech, this would evolve through the throat and up into the brain. The heart would be considered the clearing center of the lower survival functions. It is this vestigial organ or dormant program which was originally designed to activate the full potential of the human being or the spiritual entity which resides in and through the physical vehicle."

"A super race?" asked Mack.

"There you go," replied Wilson. "According to theory, man de-evolved into his current state. The idea of a new super race is actually a regenerative program of an original template. Certain Tibetan masters were said to push this agenda."

"Why would the designer of this program allow for a race that devolves?" asked Mack.

"That's a good question," said Wilson. "The designers of evolution work on a much broader scale. It is complicated to explain let alone understand. There is also an adjunct to this vestigial organ that features an inherent ability to communicate with the entire species. It is also linked to the brain. This linkage, through a telepathic frequency, connects the heart or feelings of all consciousness to the respective brains of all beings. In the case of the massive Nazi rallies at Nuremburg, this vestigial function was activated to a certain extent. It would be a perfect system if only it worked perfectly. In the case of the Germans, they were and are less than perfect.

"The human race has fallen away from such perfection. The theory of devolution suggests that we have been compromised as a species but also that there is an inherent corrective capacity within the human structure. All evolutionary programs, mistaken or successful, are contained within the memory structure of the DNA and are accessible. Life responds accordingly. That is pure mechanics of computational evolution and can theoretically be applied to the mechanical structure of atoms and molecules of matter as well. Once again, when we consider the concept of the vril, it implies a conscious will and a senior life function of exercising an intention. Of course, there is a whole hierarchy with some conscious entities at the top of the food chain. The individual act of a conscious will is prone to conflicting with other wills.

# THE DRIVE

Referring back to the grand design or universal will, it is also possible to tap into the grand design and align oneself with that scheme. Here we are talking about something on the order of the Tao which espouses the most basic components of nature."

"Essentially," interjected Mack, "there is a primary will that would serve as the senior functionary of the universe."

"Yes," said Wilson, "and aligning oneself with that will, in some ways, is not much different than people trying to become president. It is a position of power that many seek and few attain. The only ones who have any hope of ultimate success are those who align themselves the most naturally and in accordance with the Tao or some similar principle. This is where the will of an individual or group goes awry. It becomes shortsighted or embraces a scheme that is not inclusive or valuable to the larger design. Life is a haphazard proposition."

"So," said Mack, "you could say that exercise of the vril, being life itself, could be evil or good?"

"Exactly," answered Wilson, "but the key principle is functionary purpose being exercised. There are certain aspects where the Nazis demonstrated themselves to be very advanced with their lack of prejudice in examining metaphysical and scientific concepts. They were functional because they did not share the same myopia or prejudicial thought that has been so prevalent elsewhere in the Western world. They were also eager to pursue the sky's limit when it came to these various ends. All of this research has been taken underground and has virtually disappeared from sight."

"As far as Hess and the Nazis are concerned, where does the evil or undermining influence enter the picture and was it there from the beginning?" asked Mack.

"That gets even more involved," said Wilson. "I think we'd better pull over for lunch right now. I can finish the story during the rest of the way home."

## CHAPTER TWENTY-THREE

## AMALANTRAH

In 1918, Aleister Crowley indulged in one of his greatest magical workings with the help of a psychic medium by the name of Roddie Minor. Virtually all of what is known of this working is from the notes of Roddie Minor herself. It was called the Amalantrah Working and was named after Amalantrah, a small wizard who appeared in Minor's visions and claimed the name. The purported intention of the participants, and there were a few others besides Crowley and Minor, was to obtain communication with a higher intelligence and thereby bridge such into the world via the lives of the participants.

The ingredients of ceremonial magick are designed to awaken the various sensibilities of the individual and thus form a pathway into those dormant or infrequently unused areas of the brain which are sometimes designated as terra incognita and are a blank to modern science. One is awakening old and slumbering patterns or units of consciousness that are generally not recognized or even assumed to exist in modern culture. Often, due to the lack of familiar references or the frequent perversion of such, magicians who practice such an endeavor are not guaranteed a certain result. It is for this reason that such acts can deliver a result that is either tragic, hapless or not worth mentioning.

In the case of the Amalantrah Working, common threads were laced into the individuals who participated and these stayed with them throughout the rest of their lives and beyond. Without regard to goodness or badness, the network woven by these various threads was to spawn new contacts for different individuals. The pattern of this working thus increased through expansion of the loom and the further weaving of the threads.

The unfamiliarity of these patterns or "cobwebs" of the mind are such that they often incline individuals to perceive them as incredibly fearsome or exceedingly strange. After studying these for decades, Aleister Crowley knew well that the universe was primarily nothing more than a series of continuing repetitions. Creation and all it could manifest was eventually reducible to numerical designations that could represent both quantity and/or quality. The number "one" has certain characteristics and properties and so does the numeral two and so on. All complex constructions could be reduced to patterns of

# AMALANTRAH

*numbers or patterns of geometry, each with their own particular characteristic.* Knowing and understanding these patterns eventually resulted in philosophical machines such as the Qabala and Tarot. As sober and accurate as this realization was, it hardly solved the basic problems of society and one's own physical existence. The infinite permutations that could ensue from the creative principles associated with the numbers of life are generally more than the above average person can get a handle on, let alone control. But, the aforesaid insight does give insight into how to compare unforeseen or unpredictable permutations that raise havoc or create chaos. One seeks to find the pattern and compare it or trace it back to that which has already existed before.

Part of this study of comparisons is known in magick as sympathies. A two and a four are more sympathetic than a seventeen and a nine. In seeking out the function of a higher intelligence such as in the Amalantrah Working, one is seeking to discover qualities and characteristics in such intelligences or otherwise hidden aspects of the mind and explain and solve problems in the physical plane. In a sense, this could be interpreted to be the highest aspiration of a human being in that one is trying to seek solace and union with the creative forces or determinations that gave way or yielded to provide the original consciousness eventually recognized as oneself.

It was with the above in mind that Aleister Crowley placed an ad in a newspaper seeking bizarre people of all types that included circus freaks, sexual deviants, dwarves, perverts, homosexuals and anything else that might seem reprehensible to those who might consider themselves solid citizens. He did not share in the ad, however, that he was really only seeking dwarves. The rest of the ad was to hide his true purpose.

Due to his strange predisposition towards the components of drugs and magick, Aleister Crowley did not view or experience the world in the way ordinary people do. Thus, it should not come as too much of a surprise when he answered a knock on his door one day only to discover a dwarf by the name of Amalantrah. This dwarf did not fit the description as laid out by Roddie Minor in her notes or verbal descriptions, but he was close enough. In magical terms, he was a "sympathy." The ad that Crowley had placed was an overt gesticulation designed to further a magical ritual he had performed previously.

"Yes?" said Crowley as he opened the door to find a dwarf dressed in the robes of a bedouin.

"My name is Amalantrah, and you have summoned me. What can I do for you?"

As Crowley assessed and mentally took in the dwarf, something he always did when meeting someone for the first time, he could not help but think of what he had just come to realize a few days earlier: that the name Amalantrah is an anagram for *alah mantra* which was no different than "mantra of Allah." He always paid attention to names, and to him, this was most significant. He was also struck by the appearance of this live physical dwarf. Although he had summoned a dwarf, seeing it alive and breathing was an altogether different experience.

He could not help but contemplate that a dwarf represented his own "dwarf-self" or lower nature. Dwarves traditionally live closer to the ground and even in the underground. They love and hoard precious metals and jewels. Traditionally, the dwarf-self comes into one's life to destroy the personality or "false self" and thereby escalate one's soul by leaving oneself with their own higher or true self. With complete disregard to any personal danger it might represent to him, Crowley greeted the dwarf named Amalantrah.

"Do come in, Mr. Dwarf. I am distressed that the Kaiser has constructed an underground complex at the eastern end of Long Island. There is a secret German contingency that still resides there even though this country is now officially at war with that country. When it comes to matters that go below, my previous experience has told me that it is best to consult you people as you have an inside track."

"That is true," said the dwarf.

A certain percentage of the population has always believed in the wee folk who are sometimes described by different names such as fairies, leprechauns, brownies and a host of other names. While dwarves and physical "little people" are not necessarily of the same variety, they are only one step away from each other. Such creatures, like Aleister Crowley himself, exist in a confluence of dimensions and reach into this world on occasion. The fact that they are not believed to exist by most people acts as a protection mechanism and enables them to operate with impunity. Those close

# AMALANTRAH

to nature are often able to see their traces in the case of toadstool rings or other energetic manipulations of flora.

The dwarf then grabbed a loose piece of paper and scribbled out a name and address.

"Contact him," he said to Crowley, "and tell him you will pay him to escort you out to Montauk and show you what underground secrets he can."

By the next day, Crowley had prepared a sleeping bag and an assortment of camping equipment and made his way via subway to the Coney Island address that had been given him. The location was not far from the Coney Island amusement park which featured a famous and popular freak show. Arriving at a rather small house, Crowley knocked and a new dwarf came to the door.

"Hello," said the dwarf. "May name is Gibby. I was visited yesterday by Amalantrah and he told me to expect you. I am ready to travel today."

Crowley, having assured him of payment, walked with the dwarf to the subway so they could make the connection to the train which would take them to Montauk.

After a long train ride, Crowley and Gibby arrived at Montauk and walked to a small house that was not too far from the station. There, Gibby knocked on the door. A small man of about four-and-a-half feet emerged. His skin was very dark with the features of both a Mayan and Egyptian.

"Mr. Crowley, this is my friend, Chewey," said Gibby, "and Chewey, this is Mr. Crowley who has some business underneath."

Chewey nodded with a look of understanding.

"I'll be with you and ready in a minute," said Chewey.

After a few minutes, Chewey came out of the house with a backpack and the three caught a ride to Montauk Point where they planned to spend the evening. It was about seven miles to the east.

Crowley immediately noticed that Chewey was a character who liked to be delightfully funny. At least, he would appear funny to some people. He would often make faces to Gibby, but Crowley seemed to be out of synch with this type of humor. To him, it seemed something to be shared between two little people even though Gibby's demeanor was much more matter of fact and less playful.

When they arrived at Montauk Point and made camp, Chewey ran around and talked at and to the animals as if he was actually saying something to them. He was laughing continuously. This seemed to go over the heads of his companions, even Gibby. In some respects, people might have regarded his behavior as insane, but he was really just out of tune with the habitual characteristics of ordinary humans.

As soon as Crowley mentioned that they should prepare to eat soon, Chewey surprised them by going into the bushes and emerging soon after with a decent-sized game bird. Equally impressive was that he skinned it in almost no time and presented it to Crowley. This was a pleasant surprise as all they had to do was put it on a spit and roast it. While the bird was roasted, Chewey took the group to a vantage point where they could view three pyramids.

"We will explore these a little bit after dinner and sleep there tonight," said Chewey. "This will prepare you for further exploration tomorrow. These pyramids are temples, one being built after another. They are all falling apart. The one to the east is the oldest but also the most damaged."

The structures were, however, all erect and clearly visible as pyramids.

After dinner and just before dusk, Chewey escorted them to the pyramids and indicated he would sleep in the eastern most one while Crowley would sleep in the pyramid furthest west. The latter was in the best condition of all the pyramids.

Each of the structures seemed to be variations on an Indian longhouse except that they were pyramid-shaped. The two western most pyramids had earthenware that appeared to be a combination of both Mayan and Egyptian design and inscription. There were also figurines representing animal totems. In the eastern most pyramid, a wooden ladder led to a chamber below.

As nightfall came, each of them went to sleep in their respective pyramids. Glad to relax after a long day of travelling, Crowley fell asleep immediately but soon found himself tormented in the dream state. He dreamt that fairies and other little people had tied him up while he was sleeping and then pounded him relentlessly. It was only their small fists and arms that made their blows tolerable. Still, it was not easy to endure. When they finished pounding him, they took off his clothes and then played with his penis until it was erect. Once it was erect, they began to flick it with their fingers and hit at it but not as hard as they had pounded him previously. It was painful and irritating but was just at the threshold where he could barely tolerate it.

When morning came, Chewey emerged from his pyramid to see Crowley lying naked on the sand as if he had indeed been dragged out of the pyramid by the little people. Crowley was just waking up as Chewey approached him.

"What happened to you?" asked Chewey.

"I am not sure. I thought I was dreaming that fairies had pummeled me and stripped me," said Crowley.

"You have bruises on your body. Are you OK?" asked Chewey.

"No, I'm not all right!" said Crowley. "What in the hell has happened? It seems as if my dream was true and that I was humiliated and carried out here."

"I think you forgot to pay the rest of the party," said Gibby who had just emerged from his pyramid and was taking in the conversation.

"I thought I paid you — damn it! And you were to pay the subcontractors," said Crowley.

"Well," said Gibby, "I certainly made arrangements with Chewey, but I didn't know we had partners. Chewey?"

"We'll be fine. They've already extracted their payment," said Chewey.

"They could've asked first!" complained Crowley.

"They play by their own rules," said Chewey. "You have to know them. When you are ready, we will do some exploring."

After a quick breakfast, Crowley took a quick swim to ease his bruised body. Chewey then led them into the eastern most pyramid, the same one he had slept in. Caved-in somewhat and partly exposed to the air, it needed repair. There was no earthenware in this pyramid and there was no maintenance of any sort. Chewey led them down a ladder to a chamber below. The chamber was musty and uncomfortable. Chewey then motioned to a corner of the chamber where there was a remnant of a cave that was filled in with boulders and rocks.

"We have to clear this away. It's an old passageway and is almost inaccessible. We have to put all the rocks to the other end of the chamber so they do not get in our way."

After an hour of heavy work, they had removed the stones, boulders, and dirt blocking the passage. Some of the boulders were heavy but the quarters were cramped and dark. It made the work difficult.

"Now," said Chewey, "we will go on our knees for hundreds of yards. Wrap cloth around your knees as they could get sore."

"I'm sure this is not how the Germans get to their underground!" said Crowley.

"No," said Chewey, "but I will show you far more than most of them get to see."

The tunnel was no more than three feet high and headed downwards. It was sturdy and in good shape despite its clogged condition at the entrance. After what seemed like almost a half hour of crawling, they emerged into a natural rock chamber that was about ten feet by ten feet. Beyond that was a much bigger chamber, but it was hard to see with the limited light they had.

"A natural yoni," said Crowley. He was referring to the Hindu word for a receptacle or a female characterization.

As there was not much light in the cave, they took notice of a spherical area that seemed almost phosphorescent except that it vaguely suggested the colors of the rainbow.

"This is one of the locations I wanted to show you," said Chewey who then, with seeming abandonment, jumped into the center of the sphere and promptly disappeared.

"Where did he go?" asked Crowley.

Chewey then jumped back from the sphere and reappeared. Beckoning with his hand for Gibby to join him, the two of them disappeared into the sphere . Crowley had no idea where they were. After a short while, the two jumped back. They then began jumping back and forth, disappearing and reappearing, as if trying to demonstrate to Crowley that they could come and go as they pleased. Finally stopping, they looked at Crowley and beckoned him to join them.

"This is the Inner Earth," said Chewey. "Is that not what you wanted to see and learn about?"

Crowley looked around in a paranoid manner. His eyes then went blank to the point where they looked completely devoid of life. He then jumped into the orb.

# AMALANTRAH . . . . . . . . . . . . . . . . . . .

When Crowley came to, he was dizzy and a little perplexed. He took in his surroundings, but there was no sign of Chewey or Gibby. There was a rock chamber that had been contoured with a metal bulkhead so as to keep anyone from entering except via a push door that featured a sign in the German language. The phosphorescent sphere, however, was still there. He could jump back in if he wanted to. The push door was of a somewhat modern variety. Crowley, who could read German, read the sign which featured a headline which said "WARNING." The rest of the sign told him that if one were to exit via this door that one's return could not be guaranteed. It specifically said, "Return from whence you came or proceed at your own risk. We repeat, we cannot guarantee your return."

Crowley gave the matter little thought and went through the doorway. It was of little concern to him whether he would return or not, and he considered his own bold action in this regard to be a great accomplishment and feat of discipline with regard to the mind.

When Crowley went through the door, he found a manmade corridor that eventually emerged onto a rocky beach. Turning around and looking up, he saw the same Montauk Lighthouse that he had witnessed before except that it had been renovated. It was a bright and sunny day. The surf was almost sizable and pounded on the shore. He climbed the pathway back towards the campsite he had been at, but the terrain was quite different. The pyramids were no longer there, and there was no sign of the campground, at least as he knew it. When he got to the top of the hill, he could see that things were altogether different. The automobiles were of a totally different variety than he had known and they seemed more reliable and efficient by their appearance and the way their motors sounded. The dress people wore was also different than he had known and the roads were incredible compared to anything he had ever seen.

Looking out to sea, Crowley noticed a fleet of German U-boats that had surfaced and were basking in the sun. There were even some German seamen sunbathing on the decks. The vessels were about two hundred yards from the shore.

Seeing a handful of ladies picnicking nearby, Crowley was keenly aware that they would have no knowledge of his predicament. Nevertheless, he approached them and hoped he could still exude the same animal magnetism that had worked so well on ladies from his past.

"Excuse me, ladies, could you be so kind as to let me interrupt you for a minute?" he asked.

"Why yes!" said one of the ladies who seemed quite friendly. She had dark brown hair and looked as if she was in her early forties. "I think we could suffer a bit of attention from a strange man we do not know," she laughed.

"How can we help you?" said one of the other ladies.

"I was doing some camping down on the beach last night," said Crowley in his most friendly tone, "and I must confess that I have a bit of an affliction. I suffer from amnesia from time to time; consequently, I sometimes cannot remember who I am or where I am. It usually resolves quite readily if I can gather someone around me to tell me a few facts and circumstances such as the time and the date. This usually unsnags things for me. Could you be so kind as to help?"

The eyes of the women all gleamed. They all seemed intrigued by this stranger and the bizarre mental construction he had just portrayed.

"Looks like he might be one of them!" said one of the ladies under her breath as she snickered.

"Certainly!" said the brunette to Crowley. "What would you like to know? The time and the date? It is August 12th, 1943 and you are at Montauk Point in the state of New York. It is twelve-thirty in the afternoon. Does that help? And, would you like to know more?"

"Well," said Crowley, "that's certainly a good start. I certainly do remember coming to Montauk Point, but I had some companions and I don't see them anywhere around. And, what are those submarines doing out there? I don't recognize them?"

"Those are German submarines," said the brunette, "our allies."

"Allies?" asked Crowley. "Please remind me, who is at war?"

"War?" said the brunette. "The war is over. It ended when all the false information and perpetrators were uncovered."

Crowley was perplexed by his circumstances, but he was too well trained in too many disciplines to be too perplexed.

# AMALANTRAH...................

Gauging their responses and the surroundings, he was well aware that he was in a different time and place than the Montauk Point of 1918 that he had been in this morning. He decided to play upon their sympathies and also seek further information.

"You ladies are certainly kind and helpful, but I am perplexed that this is not helping me to jog my memory loose. I think I need to read a newspaper or something."

At that point, Crowley stumbled purposely and in such a way as to feign illness and gain sympathy.

"I think I need to rest," said Crowley as he eased himself into a sitting position near a tree.

The brunette came to his immediate aide and sought to comfort him. As she tended to him, Crowley could hear one of the other women speak softly to one of the others.

"I think he is indeed one of them!" she said.

"Could be," said one of the other ladies in a barely audible volume. "I haven't seen or heard of one in quite a while, but they do come through now and then."

"All you have to do is look at his clothes," said another. "Rather old fashioned, wouldn't you say?"

The brunette was no less certain than the others. In fact, she had noticed his clothes immediately and had recognized that he did not fit-in in this time or place. It was obvious to her that he was a traveller and she would do her best to comfort him.

"Just lay down and get your bearings," she said in a comforting tone. "You will be all right. I can take you to a doctor if you wish. He can help you."

Crowley's survival instincts told him that he should avail himself of all the hospitality he could. He also thought it would be a good idea to cover his tracks and see if it were possible to return from whence he came.

"I would appreciate that very much," said Crowley to the brunette, "however, I have left some things on the shore. Could a couple of you accompany me just to make sure I don't get lost?"

Saying that they needed a little walk after lunch, all of the women decided to accompany him. The party then followed Crowley to the area from which he had emerged. Coming to the exact area, he could not find the door he came through.

"I seem to remember a door here," he said. "This is exactly where I left my equipment and now I can't find it."

"See," said one of the ladies under her breath, "it's just like we thought."

"Don't worry, sir," said the brunette to Crowley, "it will be all right. If you're suffering from amnesia, you might not be coming to the right place. Let's get into town and get you some help."

The brunette took Crowley to her car and said she would drive him home. Once they were alone together on the highway, she spoke.

"Look it, I know you come from a different place. We understand that there are anomalies in time associated with this area. We do not see travellers very often, but they are known to come here from time to time. More importantly, we have scientists who are aware of such phenomena and they are able to deal with people such as yourself and the phenomena surrounding them."

"What do you mean by 'the phenomena surrounding them?'" asked Crowley.

"There can be dangers for you people. I do not mean to frighten you but sometimes travellers have come through and exploded into fire. It is not necessarily common, but there have also been psychological or physical disturbances with individuals. This might explain your amnesia. Are you physically OK?"

"Physically, I feel OK. I was a little dizzy when I arrived, but the amnesia is completely feigned on my part. I was concerned that you ladies might not understand my predicament so I made up a story. I am pleased that you at least speak my language."

By the end of the day, Crowley had a chance to read some newspapers and glance through various magazines and books. From these and further conversations with the brunette, he was able to surmise a synopsis of the new culture he had suddenly and unexpectedly stepped into. He was careful, however, not to give the woman his full name and said that he was simply "Edward Alexander." These were the first and middle names given to him at birth. He was well aware that the name "Aleister Crowley" might possibly disturb things in his current situation or any given situation for that matter.

# AMALANTRAH..................

To Crowley, it seemed that he had entered a future that was an extenuation of the planet and circumstances he had come from. He had been propelled twenty-five years into the future. Even though Germany had suffered a bitter defeat in World War I, their army never surrendered. The German soldiers considered it a cowardly and traitorous surrender by their political leaders which was exacerbated and orchestrated by the German Minister of War, a Jew who was in kahutz with various profiteers. Germany was then forced to accept an impossible treaty which strangled it economically and punished the entire country which resulted in wheelbarrow inflation and other nightmares for the German people. The United States, however, had not been a party to the treaty and this act of gratitude pleased the Germans to no end. As a result, Germany and the United States formed a strong alliance, particularly in the realm of technology. They worked on various projects in secret.

In the 1930's, the World Jewish Congress had declared war on Germany which resulted in economic boycotts and caused great suffering for Germanic people. Some of the worst sufferings of the Germans were in Poland and tensions ran very high. Poland, backed by the war declaration of the World Jewish Congress and the reassurances of England and France, baited the German government by inflicting further punishment against the millions of Germans living in Poland. This had been exacerbated by Franklin Roosevelt who, in collaboration with Winston Churchill, engaged in a treacherous series of events designed to further encourage Poland to tease Germany by humiliating their countrymen living in Poland. A stunning series of incidents then occurred.

A young man in the U.S. foreign service by the name of Tyler Kent, a communications clerk for Joseph Kennedy, the American Ambassador to the United Kingdom, exposed communications between the President of the United States and the Prime Minister of England which clearly demonstrated that they had engaged in treasonous behavior by conspiring and intriguing to enter the United States into a war with Germany and Japan. Kent had saved all of the correspondence between these world leaders and fed them to Charles Lindbergh who used his celebrity and contacts to start a revolution in the United States. Churchill and Roosevelt were both forced to step down and were prosecuted for treason and war mongering. As a result, a special act of Congress resulted in new elections whereby Charles Lindbergh was elected President of the United States.

A violent war had broken out when Germany, in retaliation, invaded Poland, France and the Netherlands. England soon capitulated to Germany and King Edward VIII took back the reigns as King of England. As for the present, the relationship between Germany and America had never been stronger.

Off the record, Crowley learned that scientific collaboration between the Germans and Americans had resulted in experiments and research at Montauk. He was told that there was an underground complex beneath Montauk Point and that the two countries had played with the science and technology of time. This was why he had suddenly appeared in this particular locale. The woman, however, could not tell him where he had come from or how he had been delivered here. She only told him that there was a certain doctor who might be able to help him go back to where he came from but the result could not be guaranteed.

To Crowley, who had experienced so many bizarre and abnormal events in his life, this was certainly the most interesting of all of them. His home and ordinary references that he depended upon, however, had been completely taken out from under his feet. He now found himself at the mercy of the universe and the people in it that he would meet, at least for the time being.

After a few days, the brunette arranged for a meeting between Crowley and the doctor she said could help him. When they arrived at the doctor's office, Crowley was surprised to see a very short and somewhat Oriental man. For Crowley, who had lived in China, it was not easy to distinguish this man's nationality. Indeed, he looked a bit odd. His shortness, however, was far more noticeable than whatever Oriental heritage he might have possessed.

"Hello," said the doctor in a very positive and friendly tone. "My name is Dr. Soto. I understand that you have had a remarkable experience, no?"

"Nice to meet you, sir," said Crowley. "My name is Edward Alexander and you are quite right about my having a

# AMALANTRAH...................

remarkable experience. I've never experienced anything quite like it. I am mystified, however, how any doctor might help me in such a circumstance. Can you enlighten me?"

"I think I might," said Dr. Soto. "From time to time, we have mysterious people suddenly appear in the neighborhood of the Montauk Lighthouse. Unlike you, they do not always speak English, but over the years we have collected a considerable amount of anecdotal evidence suggesting that all of our different visitors seem to come from a different time. Do you have memories of coming from a different time, Edward?"

"You might say that!" said Crowley. "What mystifies me most is that I came here with a couple of others and I can't seem to find my companions or any trace of them. There is no camping equipment for myself, and I am positive that I arrived at Montauk Point with such."

"So," said the doctor, "it was from Montauk Point that you came to this new situation?"

"Most certainly," said Crowley. "There were pyramids that we slept in, three of them..."

"Pyramids?" interrupted Dr. Soto. "You saw pyramids at Montauk Point?"

"Most certainly. I slept in one and my companions slept in the other two. In the morning, we climbed through a passage from underneath the eastern most pyramid and climbed for hundreds of yards until we reached an underground chamber. We encountered a remarkable sphere that was suggestive of phosphorescence but was even a little more vague in nature than phosphorescence. Additionally, it had the colors of the rainbow strewn about it.

"After seeing my companions step back and forth through this, they treated it as if it were a joke before imploring me to come through. When I did so, I ended up in a natural rock chamber contoured with metal. Besides the phosphorescence, which I could still see, there was a push door with a sign in German that warned me that I might not be able to return if I passed through the door. I took the dare and came through into your world. It was only after that experience that I met the ladies, one of which brought me to you. I did not come from 1943 but from the time period of 1918."

"From what you've been able to learn of our history thus far," asked Dr. Soto, "is it the same history as your world?"

"As far as I can tell — for the most part," answered Crowley. "I couldn't guarantee that though. There might be some differences, but I would have to check a bigger library to see if there are discrepancies."

"Sir," said Dr. Soto, "it sounds to me as if you have come through a dragon path. Did they have Einstein in your world?"

"Yes," said Crowley. "He had the Theory of Relativity and the Special Theory of Relativity."

"So, you will understand then, to put it in simple English terms, that the universe is a reference frame that we look through and that there are other reference frames that we look through besides that. The world that you and I are in right now is just one reference frame. Do you understand?"

"Yes," said Crowley, "I understand that very well, but I do not understand how I could jump ahead in one reference frame and go to a time in the future."

"This is why you are referred to as a traveller. The dragon paths lead from one place in time and are in a higher dimension than what we see. It is not unlike a cube. You are being taken from a three-dimensional cube and being put in another place on the cube."

"Yes, I understand," said Crowley, "but we are talking about a cube that is moving in time. If you consider that the cube has a consecutive appearance every fraction of a second, I have left Point A on the cube and suddenly disappeared. Then, while all the other continuous fractions of a second pass by, with a 'separate' cube appearing in a repeated linear fashion, I suddenly appear at Point A Prime on the cube where Point A Prime is the "same place" but at a different time period. In actuality, it seems to me that I have only disappeared from Point A and reappeared at Point A Prime which is almost the same as Point A. It would therefore appear that A Prime is the future but this has yet to be determined, i.e. I might not be in the future at all but somewhere else. The essential ingredient, however, might have more to do with disappearing. It appears that I have disappeared for some twenty-five years and am now back at a point that looks like Point A. I have referred to it as Point A Prime because it is on the same 'cube' but in the future. It may even be possible that I might be somewhere other than my own future."

## AMALANTRAH

"The physics and math can be complicated to communicate," said the doctor, "but the dragon path is not as simple as I have explained. A true dragon path is like a dragon with many necks and heads. You could have returned to a later point on your own time-line or have come to a parallel time line that is similar. Some people come to us with no recognition at all of the world we live in."

"Perhaps," said Crowley, "we could reach some common ground if you could tell me how these dragon paths at Montauk were discovered. There was certainly no mention of them in my time although I came out here because I was suspicious that the Germans were up to something."

"The Germans did discover these dragon paths at Montauk," said Dr. Soto. "Kaiser Wilhelm had people out here. They were exploring everywhere they could and they found these dragon paths underneath. The Germans have always been interested in theories of a hollow Earth. The Kaiser had tunnels and bunkers constructed so as to augment the natural tunnels and chambers already present.

"They also discovered traces of a civilization of small people who had once occupied the original tunnels. These portals were apparently already known to the little people and were something of religious significance, but they do not appear to have been well understood and seemed to have delivered disaster to them. The Germans experimented with the dragon paths and came to understand them to some degree. I came along as a scientist and have been able to get something of a handle on them but even I cannot claim to know everything there is to know about them. May I suggest something?"

"Why, of course," said Crowley.

"It is interesting and entertaining for us to talk to each other, but I think it would be most important if I do a diagnostic procedure on you to make sure that your body is wholesome and that you did not suffer any molecular damage when you passed through the dragon path. Do you have any objection?"

"A diagnostic?" asked Crowley.

"Yes, I just need you to take a few pills so that I can do what is called an x-ray and ensure that your bones have not been affected. If we want to send you back and you want to go, and I cannot guarantee the results, we want to at least make sure that you are in good shape at this end."

"Go ahead. It sounds reasonable to me," said Crowley. The doctor then retrieved small black pills that looked like charcoal. After receiving a glass of water, Crowley consumed the pills. Within a few minutes, Crowley was out like a light. These pills were going to be used for a diagnosis but not the one Dr. Soto spoke of. In fact, they were a drug that would allow the doctor to question Crowley about his actual history and motivations. It was a virtual truth serum.

After Crowley went into a hypnogogic trance state, Dr. Soto, who was expert at such methods, began to apply certain aromas to the olfactory senses which stimulated the audio and speech center of the brain. In this state of mind, Dr. Soto was able to extract and tape record the biographical history of Crowley and the major events in his life. Had this been any ordinary person, the circumstances of a life would be rather routine. In the case of Aleister Crowley, his life was anything but routine and seemed to pinball all over the world.

Understandably, Crowley's well-travelled life made Dr. Soto's work a little more interesting than usual. Things became hazardous however, and filled with pitfalls and booby-traps, when Dr. Soto approached Crowley's magical studies, particularly those associated with the Enochian calls of Dr. John Dee and Edward Talbot Kelly. Although these could only be described as memories within Crowley's mind, they came with all sorts of strings attached, memories or not, and strings that were indeed superstrings that reached beyond a mere memory as well as the limitations of space-time itself. The memories in Crowley's mind were deposits of cells of thought which remained dormant unless activated. The uninitiated activator was at peril to even approach such, but Dr. Soto knew nothing of this. He merely probed and asked questions. When he did not understand, he asked for more information. This is what got him into trouble.

When asking Crowley's mind to describe the particular nature of the 33rd Aethyr, Crowley's head jerked back and looked devoid of life as an auric blackishness suddenly and unexpectedly emerged from his mouth and enveloped the head of Dr. Soto who also jerked back. Soto was taken over as he slumped to the floor. He had just become possessed, not

**AMALANTRAH**.....................

by Crowley but by specific forces working inside and through him. Soto slumped and together, with Crowley, they both remained unattended and in an unconscious condition. Whatever plans Soto had for Crowley were now clearly compromised. Crowley, who had no plans whatsoever, at least as far as his own personality was concerned, was now on a path that would be dictated by forces he was already carrying inside of him. Soto had been mastered, not by Crowley, but by the forces the time travelling magician carried with him.

..... CHAPTER TWENTY-FOUR .....

## UNBOUND

After having stopped for lunch at a roadside stop off of the New Jersey Turnpike, Colonel Mack and General Wilson set in for the second half of their long journey. It was now time for Wilson to divulge the rest of what he had to say.

"OK," said Wilson. "Before lunch you asked about Hess and where the evil all began. That's like asking when the egg first became a chicken, but we'll begin by tracing the aftermath of World War II and tracing back some of those events.

"As I said earlier," continued Wilson, "it is well known that Patton hated communists with Jews and homosexuals not being too far behind. His passion for fighting the communists in the name of preserving the United States, however, was directly frowned upon by the people in power. He was removed from his post war command in Bavaria due to being accused of fraternization with the Nazis and utilizing them in key positions.

"Although his removal seemed like a rebuke, Command actually needed him for a much more important task: compilation of the history of the war, particularly with regard to the German viewpoint. No one was more in the middle of things with regard to the European theater than Patton, but not even he knew everything. The Allied Command needed a history compiled, but they needed the German vantage point because that was a key factor they did not have a handle on.

"Through their interrogations of Hess and based upon their evaluation of routine and non-routine intelligence reports, there were a lot of secrets that needed to be ferreted out. Although they did not expect to unearth all of the secrets, they knew that an outline of the history of the war would be invaluable towards this end. Patton had not only been in the middle of the action, it was well known that he enjoyed superb camaraderie with the Germans. Now, Command was going to utilize Patton's fraternization — they had turned the tables on him for cavorting with the Nazis."

"So," asked Colonel Mack, "Hess became an instrument upon which evil was used for intelligence purposes."

"Most definitely," replied Wilson. "But, he was being worked prior to the interrogations. The Brits, in no small part through the personages of Ian Fleming and Aleister Crowley, were working on getting Hess over to England. Besides usual diplomatic gestures, black magic was also applied."

"How so?" asked Mack.

"Ian Fleming and Crowley were both voracious students of Dr. John Dee, the occultist who formulated the British Empire, but this is getting a bit off topic. What was important with regard to Hess was the information they found out through interrogating him. This consisted of wild stuff that caused some to think Hess was a madman, but it was never brought out to the public."

"How did you find out about it?"

"Through Patton, but it was all rather sketchy, even for him. All I know is that he was briefed on the Hess interrogations and was to dig up every last bit of flying craft the Nazis had. He was specifically told to look for 'Martian' vehicles. 'Martian' did not refer to Mars per se but suggested craft that might have been suited to the fiction of H.G. Wells. All he was told was that the German flying crafts were very advanced and looked like vessels from outer space. There was no intimation that beings from outer space were involved. Patton, however, told me quite emphatically that he would not discount the possibility. First, however, let me get back to Patton and the history project.

"Patton gathered a large crew of German soldiers and officers for compiling this history. This included General Fritz Kraemer of the S.S. who appeared on German war crime dockets at the Dachau Trials but was almost immediately repatriated through the actions of John McCloy. Kraemer is still in the Pentagon today, and he pulled the strings for Henry Kissinger to get to where he is to this day.

"Kraemer?" asked Mack incredulously. "I've certainly heard of him. Do you mean to say that the Fritz Kraemer in the Pentagon is the same one you're talking about?"

"Well," said Wilson, "there is a bit of a debatable point on that. When they repatriated him, they created a false biography which Kissinger always referred to in his writings about the man. Just look at the photos of the American Fritz Kraemer versus the Fritz Kraemer of the S.S."

"So," asked Mack, "he really is the same Fritz Kraemer?"

"Well," answered Wilson, "I suggest you make up your own mind because I possess a rather unfair vantage point."

"What is that?" asked Mack.

"I knew him!" said Wilson. "In fact, I think I'll have a talk with him. He owes me a few favors, and I think he might be able to give me a clue about this Rudolph Hess business."

"There is your double agent then," said Mack.

"Not quite," said Wilson. "Keep in mind that there was a changing of the guard after World War II. Kraemer was only a soldier in an army of double agents that worked for, and some still do, a powerful management corps that is invisible to John Q. Public. And further, I'm one of those soldiers just by reason of knowing what I know."

"Boy, this is getting interesting," said Mack, "but to tell you the truth, it is becoming a little more disturbing than interesting."

"It might become more so," said Wilson, "but if you're going to help me solve this case, you're going to have to know the truth about certain things. Sure, I could just retire and be done with it, but I am nearing the final phase of my life and there are so many things I just don't care about anymore. This, however, is not one of them. It has been my passion and still is. I would sacrifice anything to get to the bottom of where we are headed."

"Well then," said Mack. "Don't let me stop you. Please continue."

"Very well," said Wilson. "When you consider that the British effectively used diplomacy to kidnap Hess as a public relations coup, the equation does not make any sense. In fact, they did not utilize the propaganda value at all other than the initial coverage in the press and a few brief follow-ups. There had to be another reason they wanted him, and I have already alluded to some of these points. But when you ask where the evils begins, this is just one stepping stone. Hess was a puppet on a string, but a very key puppet who was not allowed to talk."

"As far as evil is concerned," said Mack, "was Hess involved in the Holocaust?"

"I'm glad you brought that up," said Wilson. "Hess, as Deputy Fuhrer, was both a pragmatist and idealist. Keep in mind, it was he who discovered Hitler's talent as a leader.

Hess is as responsible as anybody for the inception of the power movement behind the Nazi Party. As an idealist, he embraced the highest aspirations for Germany. As a pragmatist, he knew that the communists in Germany could only be overtaken by violence in the streets. Hess, an excellent street fighter, did his fair share here.

When the Nazis took power, however, he also saw the pragmatic value of softening the violent atmosphere that surrounded Hitler's power struggles. As Deputy Fuhrer and as Minister Without Portfolio, he could change laws and countermand harsh punishment. Many people who were the victims of Nazi atrocities, some of them without cause, sought Hess out to receive justice. More than often, he was quite accommodating to these requests and became the primary source to petition in the Third Reich. He even "Aryan-ized" known Jews to protect them. There is even, believe it or not, evidence to suggest Hess was himself part Jewish."

"You're kidding!" exclaimed Mack. "Could that be what all the fuss was about?"

"Hardly," said Wilson, "but we'll get back to that tangent. In tracing the evil surrounding Hess, I want you to learn some things about the history of Germany that almost no one has paid attention to let alone heard. Keep in mind, however, that what I am about to tell you was compiled by Patton's staff — and this included me — from the German generals, soldiers, gestapo, bureaucrats, and civilians that we talked to. It is not an official history, but keep in mind, Patton wrote two histories. One was rather pedestrian and was intended for general consumption. The other one was filled with candid information about what was really going on in and around the Third Reich, at least from the German point of view. What I am going to tell you is not necessarily what the report is all about. I am going to tell you what I learned from the Germans in the years following the war. It is their story mixed with a little insight and tiny portions of data that I have discovered.

"Virtually every German I spoke to was mystified about the Allied persecution of Germany after the invasion of Poland. There is no question in the mind of the Germans that they were tricked into invading Poland. It was not something they wanted to do. Just as in the case with Hess, the pendulum points to manipulation by the British.

"The situation goes back to at least World War I. In 1916, Austria and Germany had actually restored the Kingdom of Poland. They thought they had done them a great favor. Poland, however, decided to side with the Allies and began setting up concentration camps in 1918. These were for containment of — guess who? The Germans! Keep in mind, the Poles were with the Allies and the Germans were now enemies of the state. Based upon very old themes of animosity and war, the Poles took advantage of the post World War I scenario to annex huge portions of territory so as to maintain sovereignty over some two and a half million Germans. These were the first concentration camps and most of them were stuffed with Germans.

"Prior to the German invasion of Poland, there was more than a decade of German persecution by the Poles. This eventually resulted in ten thousand Germans being massacred between May and September of 1939. Besides this, tens of thousands of German refugees were held in Polish concentration camps. Keep in mind, most of the concentration camps utilized by the Germans and virtually all of the extermination camps were in Poland. These camps all existed long before the Germans came to town, and the Germans will tell you that they were for dispensing with the German population.

"The animosity between the Poles and Germans goes back hundreds of years. Although I would never discount the possibility, we cannot blame the Brits for that. They did, however, exploit the situation when they promised to back the Poles up in any conflict with Germany. They had no such intention. This only encouraged the Poles to keep up and increase their abuse of Germans within their borders. There is no question in the minds of the Germans that Hitler, after several entreaties and suits for peace were refused, had to invade Poland. Any other tact would have been viewed as an act of cowardice and, more importantly, a betrayal to the German people. This is one of the reasons the people supported him so blindly. They were confident he would redeem Germany."

"So," said Mack, "there were basically two international empires before World War II: England and Germany, right?"

"Not exactly," replied Wilson. "Britain was still the major sea power, but the U.S. had invaded Spanish territories and became an imperialist style power at the turn of the century. Japan had also become active to save their own skins. Germany was a major power, too, but World War I was designed to destroy them."

"What about the Russians?" asked Mack.

"They were always the foils of the Brits or the Jesuits, at least to some degree," said Wilson.

"I thought they were Orthodox and not Catholic — and what about the Jews?"

"Stalin studied with the Jesuits but their infiltration of the Russian secret police goes way back. World War I is where the Jesuits and Brits meet on common ground which results in abolishing the Ottoman Empire. That is the real prize of World War I. The lies that Lawrence of Arabia told to the Arabs resulted in the fall of the Ottomans, but the Arabs were betrayed. They did not get the land promised to them. The Brits divided up what had once been Arabia into all these countries that make trouble into today's world. Keep in mind, it was the fall of the Ottoman Empire that gave rise to fundamentalist Islam and the terrorism that accompanies it. It plays right into the hands of war mongering financiers."

"Jews?" asked Mack.

"That's what the Jesuits and Brits would like you to think. It creates conflict that they prey off of."

"Jews are bankers though. You can't let them off the hook," said Mack.

"Some, sure. No question. Jewish hysteria has been around as long as history and some with good reason, but hysteria is a tool. Wiping out Jews is easy to stir up as a cause. So much of Christianity is based upon hating Jews."

"Perhaps because Jesus was Jewish and too many of them hate their own founder," laughed Mack.

"You've got a point there," said Wilson, "but when common people think they know the world's problems are caused by Jews, it tells you that it is probably not the case."

"Why?" asked Mack, "because people are so stupid?"

"It's like buying stocks because the shoe shine boy is doing it. Look for sources that are not so obvious, like the Brits and Jesuits," said Wilson. "They both got rid of the Ottomans with World War I. Germany went by the boards, too. The Brits wanted empire and the Jesuits got even for Martin Luther."

"If you listen to the Germans, every act of militarism was based upon prevention and defense of Germany. This comes to a head once again with Operation Barbarossa when Hitler attacked the Soviet Union. This was the result of a Christmas party by the Russians which was spied upon by the Nazis. The Russians were quite drunk and became unguarded and quite vocal about Stalin's plans to invade Germany. At that point, there were less than 4,000 German tanks and Russia had more that 20,000. Does that sound like a fair fight to you? Hitler had no choice but to attack. He beat Stalin to the punch by fourteen days and this stopped the Reds from totally overrunning half of Europe. In essence, Germany was targeted for slaughter, but there was a reason for this.

"There has long been an intent by the Brits to wipe the Germans off the face of the Earth. The German people are incredibly industrious. Just look at where our technology comes from. After the onset of the Dark Ages, it took hundreds of years to wipe out the German culture and to browbeat Christianity into their way of life. Even the name of Germany is misleading, and this was perpetrated by the British. The real ancestors of the German people are the Goths and not the *Ger*. The *Ger* are a small tribe from Belgium. This is British superiority at work: complex, clear and simple. They changed the name.

"Actually, this purge against the Germans began in 1871 when Masonic Lodges convened in Lausanne and laid out a plan for three world wars. Ultimately, this was about reducing Germany's ability to reign supreme. That role was to be reserved only for the British or their ruling partners.

"After having been completely humiliated by the Treaty of Versailles at the end of World War I, the Germans had nowhere to turn. For those who wanted to embrace radical change, they did not have much of a choice: become a communist or a National Socialist. This was, after all, the era of wheelbarrow inflation.

"One of the biggest secrets of Germany's success, and why it became the most prosperous country in the world, was that Hitler introduced radical economic changes that benefited the majority of the German population. He detached German currency from the gold standard; thus removing the economy from the undermining influence of international markets. In this way, he based the economy on barter and trade. This was so successful and so out of bounds with what the international bankers wanted that it has remained hidden history. While all of this was going on, the United States was in a depression.

"When Britain was still going through the motions of negotiating for peace, they absolutely insisted upon Germany abolishing this economic system. They were well aware that other countries might copy it and thus reduce their own international influence.

"As far as the concentration camps went, most of the deaths in concentration camps were the result of spotted fever and typhoid. This had been purposely conveyed by the Russians through their own soldiers who were used as unwitting victims. The infamous gas known as Zyklon B was actually found in the delousing chambers because it was used as a sterilizing agent against the lice which carried the diseases. Zyklon B is normally thought to have been used for mass exterminations in the gas chambers. Believe it or not, it was actually used to save lives.

"The mounds of bodies that you so often see in newsreel footage were stacked due to hygiene reasons. They could not be buried in the ground for fear of epidemics. It might surprise you and everyone else to know that the International Red Cross made regular visits to the camps and estimated that a total number of 400,000 to 500,000 died and that sixty percent of the casualties were Jewish."

"Just a second," said Mack.

"What's the matter?" asked Wilson.

Although Mack had no reason to disbelieve Wilson, he was struck by the utter amazement of the information he was hearing. It was as if the world had been turned upside town within the brief span of part of a conversation. As a loyal colleague of Wilson's highly secretive patriot group, Mack was an extreme advocate of defending the Constitution of the United States, but he had never heard the full story of the behind-the-scenes politics of World War II and certainly not this aspect.

"General," said Mack. "I knew things were awry with many aspects of our government, but I never thought about how sordid and sinister it might be. My head is reeling from what you have been telling me. If anybody cared about what you're saying and was not able to just dismiss it as idle and misguided chatter, you could be tried for treason."

"Ah!" exclaimed Wilson. "It's not me who needs to be afraid of treason charges. That's the boys in power."

"You are talking about an intelligence war," said Mack, "and this is exactly what this has become."

"Ya think?" asked Wilson. "Why do you think we're being dogged right now? You're damned right it has to do with intelligence. Intelligence is created as an adjunct to war in the first place. When Patton was wiped out before our very midst, it got us all to thinking. Over the years, we have been mostly silent and very careful. That is the only reason we've survived. There are others, however, who have not been so bright and have gone off the deep end. One of these was Larry Patton McDonald, General Patton's cousin.

"With people like you, we've only taken in people we can trust. Now, it would appear that somebody thinks our number is up. Perhaps somebody has been watching us all along and has just decided that now is the time to strike."

As Wilson looked ahead on the road, he could not believe his eyes.

"Look," said Wilson, "there's a Lion's Paw Moving Company truck right in front of us. I can't believe it! Do you think it's the very same truck that moved Konrad?"

"Good point," said Mack. "I think we'd better trail him and then ask a few questions."

Before another question could be asked or another statement could be made, the truck from Lion's Paw suddenly slammed on his breaks. It was too late for Wilson to react. He slammed hard into the rear of the truck at upwards of fifty miles-per-hour. Wilson lost consciousness.

# UNBOUND............

## CHAPTER TWENTY-FIVE

## THE CORPORAL

Awakening from his passed out condition, Crowley looked up and saw the doctor who had manipulated him lying helplessly on the ground. With no hesitation whatsoever, Crowley promptly proceeded to tie the little doctor up firmly to a chair so that he could not escape. When the doctor began to awaken, Crowley found the same small black pills that had been given to him and placed these under the doctor's tongue so that his system would absorb it. When the doctor went into a hypnogogic state, Crowley then proceeded to question him.

"Why did you put me to sleep?" asked Crowley.

"It is hard to explain," said the doctor. "You are a visitor from another team and this area has special properties, much of what we do not fully understand."

Crowley then grabbed the private parts of the doctor and spoke forcefully.

"If you do not answer me truthfully, I am going to ensure that you will regret it forever."

"I will tell you anything you want, just ask," said the frightened doctor.

"To the best of your knowledge, how did I end up in this world?" asked Crowley.

"As I told you, there are dragon paths that connect one universe to another. They go from one location at a particular time in a particular domain to another point in space-time. If you want to know the way out of this universe, it is right underneath the lighthouse. To find it, go beneath the lighthouse. There is a stairwell that goes down into a well. You will find a manhole cover or something similar. From that you can penetrate a cave and find your way back home. I must warn you, however, that there are dangers involved. You might go into the orb and then end up in another world.

"I was not going to hurt you," continued the doctor. "I just wanted to find out where you are from."

"I would like you to come with me" said Crowley. "Tell me and be honest — would it help me if you came along and, if you did, would you be cooperative or adversarial?"

# THE CORPORAL..................

"It might help you," replied the doctor, "and I would not be adversarial. Personally, I would find it interesting."

"Have you explored these areas on your own?" asked Crowley.

"Not too much," replied the doctor. "You see, I have brethren or relatives who are much more suited towards this type of exploration. I live in this world as a doctor. In a sense, you could say that I live on the cusp of two worlds, but I am mostly in this so-called regular world. They need people like me here."

Deciding that he wanted the doctor to accompany him, Crowley knew that he would first have to wait for the effects of the drugs to wear off of the doctor. As he waited, however, he proceeded to ask questions of his captive. He found out that the man's Asiatic appearance had something to do with his being related to a small people known as Dropa, a hybrid race of people and aliens who had crash-landed in Tibet thousands of years ago. They had memories of a different star system from which they had come and which was their real home. Dr. Soto, however, was only part Dropa as his genetics were a mixture of other people.

Crowley also learned from the doctor that, to the best of his knowledge, Crowley had found himself in an alternative future. This was the course of action that things would become if he did not change them. Germany and America would have been great allies to the detriment of the British. Crowley also learned from the doctor that travelling in time presented no danger of killing your grandfather and thereby nullifying your own existence. He explained that every time you "travelled in time" you were creating a new time-line and existing in a new dimension.

With all of this in mind, the doctor warned Crowley that wherever they ended up would be a crap shoot. Crowley, however, knew that he could direct things by the use of will alone. He also realized that there was more than one will working inside of his own gray matter. Crowley was very curious about the world he was in but felt a compulsion or duty to get back to his own time. In fact, he was experiencing a homesickness of sorts.

When the doctor awoke, he found the doctor to be very cooperative. Insisting that they bring along a considerable amount of food as well as a compliment of medicine and drugs, Crowley left for the Montauk lighthouse with the doctor.

Accessing the secret door, the area was just as the doctor had described. It was almost identical to the space he had been in earlier with Chewey and Gibby. There was the same phosphorescent orb as well. This time, Crowley would enter the sphere accompanied by the doctor. Before he did, however, the doctor warned him that they should only enter the sphere after it had faded out. If not, there could be problems for them. The sphere pulsated so that it would come on strong and then weaken. They entered the area of the sphere only after there was an ebb in the power.

After entering the portal, Crowley and the doctor found themselves in a tunnel. They could see light at the end. Once again, it was unclear if he had returned in time to the same place from which he had originally come. This time, however, he was in an environment where he had no idea where he was. Emerging from the tunnel, it was clear that he was no longer near Montauk Point. Walking along a cobblestone road, Crowley observed that the signs were written in Polish. There were also German signs.

Soon, they noticed a large building on the road. As they approached, Crowley could see a guard in front of the building. As the guard was wearing a German military uniform, Crowley realized he would have to think fast on his feet. It was clear from the signs that this building was a hospital. Crowley, who spoke fluent German, was able to convince the guard that he had business with the commandant of the hospital. He simply explained that he had arranged to bring this excellent doctor to help the patients inside.

When Crowley was ushered in to meet the commandant, he quickly explained that he was a personal friend of General Karl Haushofer, a renown German general. This caught the commandant's fancy and resulted in a warm greeting for Crowley as well as a German medico being assigned to assist them in their efforts. It was thus that Crowley was directed to one of their more difficult and hopeless patients, a corporal who was suffering from blindness and psychohysteria as a result of being exposed to gas on the battlefield.

The problem with the patient, according to his doctors, was that he was speaking hysterically in a language that no one

# THE CORPORAL..................

could understand. One of the doctors suggested that it was something like the Pentecostal phenomena of speaking in tongues. When Crowley heard the patient himself, however, he recognized that it was a language and certainly not the rantings of a Pentecostal. It was quite obviously the Enochian language that he knew so well from his own studies of magick.

Crowley could readily see, however, that it was really not the patient who was doing the talking. It was an entity within the patient. The best Crowley could translate these rambling outcries was as "please release me from this madness!" The phrase was often repeated in Enochian variations on this concept. There were also lesser rantings complaining of his condition. The entity also said that it needed morphine to be more comfortable and that more drugs put into the body would enhance its perception. The entity repeatedly pleaded for succor and more morphine.

Crowley directed the Asian doctor to administer medicine. The doctor, who was knowledgable about Oriental medicine, worked on the patient in different spots and then gave him a pill of an unknown substance. After the body received the medicine, the entity that had been residing in the patient emerged and attached itself to Crowley. The corporal's body then relaxed and went into a deeper and deeper state of relaxation. Crowley was shaken by the reception of the entity and he staggered to a chair.

"What happened?" asked the doctor.

"Whatever was inside of this man has now attached itself to me," replied Crowley.

"That does not sound good," said the doctor, "but I feel a deja vu about this moment. It is as if we have done it before or perhaps many times before."

"Do you mean," asked Crowley, "that it is like this particular point in history was pivotal and has been accessed or manipulated many times so as to achieve a different result?"

"It wouldn't be like that exactly, but I think you are right for the most part. Whenever time is 'altered' so to speak, it creates a new time-line. There is, however, a phenomena which is even more ephemeral than that. I am talking about the consciousness of each time-line. The consciousness of each time-line always seems to leak from one time-line to another because they do not consist of the same property as the constituents of time itself."

"Sort of like ideas having a separate constituency than matter or energy?" asked Crowley.

"Exactly!" said the doctor.

"Perhaps that is all fine and well," said Crowley. "In fact, it's damn interesting, but it does not relieve me of my current condition!"

"Oh, don't worry about that!" said the doctor. "You saw me fix the corporal. You're a breeze compared to him."

"What are you going to do?" asked Crowley.

"Just lie down on that bed and I will do some healing on you."

"You mean you'll rid me of this entity?" asked Crowley.

"It wouldn't be the first time!" said the doctor. "I can't guarantee what will happen except that you will relax, feel better, and get back to a more normal feel about yourself."

Crowley reclined on a hospital bed whereupon the doctor began to work on him. After about fifteen minutes, Crowley went into a deep sleep and relaxed.

# THE CORPORAL..................

## CHAPTER TWENTY-SIX

## A SUSPICIOUS COINCIDENCE

Colonel Mack picked up the telephone as rapidly as he could and spoke excitedly into the mouthpiece.
"Heidi! We've just had a horrible accident. General Wilson has suffered a bad concussion and is in a coma. He was rushed to the hospital, and I'll give you a report as soon as I get one. I am whiplashed but do not need immediate hospital care. In the meantime, we've got to continue on this investigation with the general. In so many words, I'm not so sure this was a pure accident. We've got to move and move fast."
"Why is that?" asked Heidi.
"You're not going to believe it. Just before the accident, we were coming upon a truck from the Lion's Paw Moving Company. Just as we were wondering if it was the very same truck who moved Konrad, the truck came to a sudden and completely unexpected halt. It was as if they slammed on the brakes to make sure we collided with them. We crashed into the rear. If you ask me, I think it was done on purpose. The ambulance has taken the general to a local hospital. I've already investigated the driver in cooperation with the local police. His name is David Crowley..."
"What did you say the name was?" asked Heidi. "Did you say Crowley?"
"Yes, that's right," said Mack.
"I can't believe that!" exclaimed Heidi. "That's too much of a coincidence."
"What are you getting at?" asked Mack.
"Crowley — the name is just like Aleister Crowley. Find out if this driver is at all involved in any form of ceremonial magic or occult activities."
"I haven't even thought of asking that," said Mack, "but there's plenty of strange activity going on here without that additional factor. Wait until you hear the work order that David Crowley was working under.
"It turns out," continued Mack, "that this was indeed the same truck that moved Dr. Konrad. The previous work order was from D.C. to Montauk and the papers were still in the cab.

## A SUSPICIOUS COINCIDENCE.........

It was making its return trip but featured a very strange cargo. The truck left Montauk with a cargo that consisted of electronic equipment that featured strange coils, some of which were pyramid-shaped. That cargo was taken to the Brooklyn Navy Yard where it added on additional cargo which consisted of lamps. Most of the truck is filled with antique lamps, some of which appear to be very exotic. The kicker is that the work order has them being shipped to Ali-Bey, the same character we ran into at Konrad's.

"I have to tell you Heidi, the town of Montauk is weird, damn weird; and now we can't afford to let Ali-Bey off the hook. He's as much in the middle of all of this as the Lion's Paw Moving Company. Why are they bringing him this weird truckload of coils and apparatus from Montauk that is supplemented by exotic lamps and other old-fashioned electrical appliances? You'd better get on him right away and start finding out some answers. I will personally stay with the general until I can arrange a security watch for him. I will need some medical attention myself, but my current condition is not so bad that I cannot continue the investigation."

"There's a lot we have to talk about," said Heidi, "and I'm referring to things we've found out on our end, but I believe it's best to keep it off the phone. This line is not secure. Just take care of the general as you are doing. I suggest sending Gretchen as a backup for you. Go ahead and do your regular routine but order and insist that Gretchen be with the general at all times."

"Excellent point!" said Mack.

"I'll make arrangements to have her sent up to you right away."

"Very good," said Mack. "I'll be ready. Then I'll get a chance to see a doctor for myself."

· · · · · CHAPTER TWENTY-SEVEN · · · · ·

## FRITZ

General Wilson was not used to being stopped. Besides having a particularly strong constitution, he was a Scorpio. This not only indicated he was secretive and powerful but that he possessed a natural characteristic of being unkillable. Not even the battlefield of war had delivered such an effective blow upon him as Wilson had received from the moving van from Lion's Paw. He was not, however, about to be stopped.

Rising to the occasion, Wilson committed himself to the exact destination he had set for himself upon his return to Virginia. He was going to visit his old friend and colleague from World War II, Fritz Kraemer. When Wilson entered Kraemer's office in the Pentagon, he extended his hand.

"Hello, Hugh," said Kraemer in his patented and unmistakable German accent as Wilson nodded.

"What can I do for you, my friend?" said the monocled Director of War Planning.

Kraemer's warmth for Wilson was quite genuine. The general had in fact protected Kraemer all of these years by simply remaining silent about the former's role as an SS officer during the war.

"Perhaps I should have come to you a long time ago, Fritz, but I didn't want to burden you. The issues I've been dealing with are highly sensitive, but that is not the point. They are quite out of the ordinary," said Wilson.

"What is it then, my friend?" asked Kraemer.

"It is essentially about three items. First, it includes the Hess affair, and then an attempt to either abduct me or kill me. Thirdly, it involves a strange place called Montauk."

"Oh?" asked Kraemer who raised his eyebrows after the word Montauk was mentioned. "Perhaps you can enlighten me on these matters?"

After giving Kraemer a general synopsis of what had happened since Hess's death, the old German looked quizzically at Wilson.

"Why did you not come to me before all of this?" asked Kraemer. "I think I could have saved you considerable grief."

# FRITZ

"I don't like to call in my favors, Fritz, but it is true that I have overlooked our old connection. I never really thought that you might be up-to-date on the Hess affair, but this Montauk business has made it very clear to me that there is a fifth column within our military."

"You mean like your own?" asked Kraemer.

"I think you know my primary interest has always been in defending the Constitution and dealing with all the bullshit that happened in the wake of Patton's death. He was your ally just as much as mine."

"Very true," agreed Kraemer. "He was a true man, a gentleman, and a great soldier. Kissinger, as you know, turned into an opportunist and an ass-hole. It is very hard for me to trust anyone these days, but tell me, how can I help you?"

"You can start by answering some questions if you can," said Wilson.

"I will do my best," said Kraemer in a sincere tone.

"Number one, who in the hell are these guys trying to kill me? Number two, what in the hell does Konrad have to do with this? Number three, where do Hess and Montauk fit in?"

"Montauk has been a German outpost for a long time. There was considerable technical collaboration between the Americans and Germans in the 1930's. This was prevalent on Long Island and Montauk made a convenient geographic rendezvous point for our Irish allies. The lines of intelligence between Berlin, Ireland and Montauk have always been close. Montauk was a nesting ground for the Germans and the Irish. In the old days, we all fit together quite nicely.

"The Hess affair is very messy and what was done to my old comrade is a shame and a travesty. At first, it was the Allies that wanted him imprisoned. As time evolved, however, it was the old German guard who, after enjoying the spoils of World War II, then wanted him to remain behind bars. They didn't want to risk upsetting their own apple cart."

"Do you mean to suggest," asked Wilson, "that Hess would have exposed all the secret power ploys if he were released?"

"There was always that danger. It was too big of a mess for everybody. Personally, it would not have bothered me if he were released. I thought everyone made too big a deal out of it. Then again, I now have a legitimate role and do not think

I would have been subjected to much scrutiny. Others had a lot more to lose in the equation."

"Why would my interest in Hess be of such vital concern to these people, particularly if he is already dead?" asked Wilson. "Their actions were drastic in the extreme."

"I can't answer that directly," said Kraemer, "but perhaps I can still help you to some degree. You know, when Dulles was fired by Kennedy as the CIA Director, he made a comment to the President. 'You can't fire me — you don't even know who I work for!' was what he said. I must tell you that I have a similar feeling with regard to the people I work for. I have worked for every president in the post World War II era. Nobody can fire me because they do not even know who I work for. But you are an old friend and a trusted companion. I don't need you now, but I needed you when I did, and you have been good to me.

"With regard to Montauk, I can tell you — quite unofficially by the way — that you have penetrated the deepest of mysteries with regards to our government and world politics. You have become embroiled in forces that want to consume you. This is clearly beyond my control. If I were to place orders or suggestions on your behalf, it might not do much at all, if anything. I am not that powerful. Essentially, you are stirring up a hornets nets for which you do not have the army or capacity to deal with."

"So, Fritz, you are essentially telling me that it is in my best interest to beg off?"

"Yes, I would, but that does not get the monkey off your back. You are in a tough position. People have come after you, and you have not relieved your adversaries of their plight. You are a threat and a rival to them."

"Is there something that they want from me? Perhaps I could satisfy them in some way," asked Wilson.

"I can make some inquiries," said Kraemer, "but this is obviously a very sensitive matter. I will try to help, but for your own sake, please do not count on me. I am on your side in this matter. I do not want to see a friend hurt."

"There is one other thing," said Kraemer. "In an official capacity, I suggest you contact Senator Goldwater on these matters. He can tell you what is going on officially as he has looked into the events and circumstances at Montauk."

"Barry?" asked Wilson. "I had no idea. When you put it all together, I guess you and he would be logical allies against communists, but I'm not so sure this Montauk connection is communist. Is it?"

"Quite the opposite," said Kraemer, "but it is still highly secretive. Whatever you do, just be careful. Also, it is probably best that you keep your distance from me on these matters. If I can assist, I will let you know."

"It's not a whole hell of a lot to go on, but it's better than nothing. I still have some cards to play."

"The prisoners?" asked Fritz.

"That's one of them," replied Wilson. "But it may hearten you to know that there are forces at work here, occult forces. They have influenced this investigation and even perpetrated it. Whether I like it or not, I feel that they will determine the outcome in the end."

"Indeed!" said Fritz. "Occult forces were abundant in the Third Reich. Everyone knew about them, but it was always deemed wise not to say too much. In America, it is virtually impossible. The Americans have been robbed of their soul!"

"I'm afraid what you say is only too true," said Wilson.

"By the way," said Kraemer as he scribbled a name and address on a piece of paper and handed it to Wilson, "there is one other thing that might help you."

"What's that?" asked the general.

"When you finish with Barry, you might want to look this person up," said Kraemer.

Wilson looked at the name on the paper and then extended his hand to Kraemer. After the two men shook hands, Wilson left the office.

## CHAPTER TWENTY-EIGHT

### THE SENATOR

"Barry," said Wilson after having entered the senator's Congressional office, "I've stumbled into one hell of a mess. I sure as hell hope you can help me with it."

"Hugh, I'll do anything I can to assist you," said Barry Goldwater, "but why did you come to me?"

"It's Fritz, over in the Pentagon."

"Kraemer?" asked the senator.

"Yes — he told me that you had investigated Montauk."

"You're kidding? This is about Montauk?"

"It sure the hell is," said Wilson who proceeded to explain his entire story.

After listening intently to Wilson, Goldwater spoke.

"I'll be frank with you, Hugh. This Montauk business comes from the strangest and most mysterious factions of our government that I've ever encountered. I still haven't gotten to the bottom of it. Not even my associates in the Freemasons have been able to give me a good clue."

"What can you tell me about it?" asked Wilson.

"When I was placed on the Senate Intelligence Committee, I began to hear rumors through the grapevine of a highly specialized intelligence activity going on at Camp Hero on Long Island."

"At least somebody was owning up to something!" exclaimed Wilson.

"Not as much as you might think. I couldn't get a damn straight answer out of anybody. It kind of goes back to my early days when I asked Curtis LeMay about UFOs. That was back in the sixties."

"What was that about?" asked Wilson.

"As you know, I've been interested in unidentified flying objects and have wanted to get to the bottom of that ever since I first encountered one. Knowing LeMay personally, I asked him about getting into the blue room at Wright-Patterson. That was the room that contained all the secret files on the UFOs. He not only clammed up on me like the son-of-a-bitch that he was but yelled at me and told me never to talk about it again. With friends like that in authority, it curtailed my ability to look further into these matters.

"As for Montauk, I sent my nephew out to Long Island and told him to find out what he could. There is no question that there was activity going on out there that is above and beyond the so-called FAA station they had running out there. It's on the order of the MK-Ultra stuff. This is so hush-hush that anybody who is involved gets apoplexy when you mention it. It is like there are two major divisions in the Government: those who know and those who do not know. I'm on the cusp, but I've always been politely encouraged not to venture too far across the line."

"Are you saying that they're mind-fucking people out there?" asked Wilson.

"That line of inquiry is a good place to start," replied the senator. "I've talked to some pretty strange characters from there myself. It's disinformation of the finest sort. The people are so fractured in their communication that you can't make much sense out of it."

"How does this fit in with the flying saucer factor?" asked Wilson.

"It's even kookier. It's not that I think flying saucers are kooky. In fact, I've seen them. The problem is, however, we're dealing with a security issue but it is a security issue that cannot be touched by an elected official or even through generals like ourselves. In these matters, we are more like pawns than generals."

"What's the bottom line?" asked Wilson.

"The bottom line," said Goldwater, "is completely and utterly nonsensical. All I can tell you is that people have been messed with and messed with on a large scale. Funding was arranged through clandestine means. It's all black budget that I could not begin to deliver the goods on. In fact, I've been warned rather severely. I have to insist that you not let anyone know what I've told you. It could only create trouble for the both of us. For you, I'm doing it as an old friend."

"The most intriguing thing I heard concerning this investigation," said Wilson, "had to do with this old wino we ran across near the Montauk Lighthouse. He talked about literal experiments in time. It sounded like stuff from H.G. Wells. Of course, it's hard to believe a drunk."

"You heard that?" asked Goldwater. "If that's the case, I suggest you talk to Preston Nichols. He'll indulge you on that line of investigation. It's pretty far-out stuff."

"Fritz already gave me his address. I'll be seeing him next," said Wilson. "By the way, as an Air Force officer, can you give me any insight regarding the history of that place?"

"Camp Hero? Sure," answered Goldwater. "It housed the SAGE radar system which was the premier device in what was known as the Eastern Shield Defense system. It was our first line of defense against projectiles or planes coming from overseas. Its primary function was during the late fifties and early sixties. The radar is antiquated, but they still run it. It is one damn off-the-wall operation if you ask me. Over-the-horizon radar makes that system obsolete, but they still use it for god-knows-what.

"They have a gymnasium and bowling alley, too, but those are no longer in use. In its heyday, Camp Hero was used as an R&R depot that went well beyond the designs of what they purported was a crummy little Air Force Station. There are also some strange rooms on the base, psychedelic paint and what not. It looks like the work of Tim Leary and his boys. We know he was out there with the MK-Ultra crowd and one of his spook programs."

"Did you ever ask any of your Mormon friends about this?" asked Wilson. "They can't lie you know."

"That applies only when they are talking to each other," answered Goldwater. "I'm not a Mormon, only a Mason."

"Well," said Wilson, "I suppose the Mormons who have backed you in your election campaigns are also Masons, right? Maybe the Mormons could share with you on that basis."

"As a matter of fact," said Goldwater, "you've got a point. There's something I can share with you about the Masons. Ever heard of Ezra Taft Benson?"

"The name is maybe vaguely familiar. Who is he?" asked Wilson.

"He's currently the president of the Mormon church. They call him the Prophet and he is the highest official of the Latter Day Saints. His father before him was also one of the twelve apostles of the church."

"I haven't heard of him," said Wilson, "but I don't follow the Mormons or their history."

## THE SENATOR . . . . . . . . . . . . . . . . . . .

"Perhaps you should," said the senator. "In any case, when I asked him about all this, he confided to me that those experiments at Montauk were being done on land his family had swindled from the Indians in that area. I think he told me this because my family had similar issues with Indian land. He thought he had a sympathetic ear."

"What was that last name again?" asked Wilson.

"Benson," said Goldwater.

"Interesting," said Wilson. "Is there any more Mormon involvement at Montauk?"

"He didn't seem to know about the experiments, but he was keenly aware of the property," said Goldwater.

"How and why would he be so keenly aware of that property at Montauk?" asked Wilson.

"The Mormons, not unlike us Freemasons, keep a lot of records from antiquity. There is a reason he knew about it, but I could not tell you. I was basically trying to find out what the military was doing from my position on the intelligence committee. I was not doing an investigation on my own, as a Freemason, or on behalf of any other secret society. I can give you Benson's card if you like," said Goldwater.

"That's not a bad idea," said Wilson as Goldwater fetched him a card. "I guess I'll check with Nichols first though. Trying to track down the Latter Day Saints is like chasing butterflies. After all, this is basically a criminal case."

"I agree with you, but do not sell the Mormons or their information short," said Goldwater. "I agree with you that Preston Nichols would be an excellent place for you to go next. He's full of information, and you can tell him I referred you. That's the only person...better yet, don't mention me at all. Say it was Fritz."

"Thank you, Barry," said Wilson as he stood up to leave.

"One thing," said the senator.

"What's that?" asked Wilson.

"Let me know what you find out."

## CHAPTER TWENTY-NINE

## 7 DORIS PLACE

As General Wilson approached the home of Preston Nichols at 7 Doris Place in East Islip, New York, Nichols emerged form his laboratory, an oversized and extended garage that seemed to go on and on. As soon as Wilson saw Nichols, he began to go into a daze and lost his balance. It was as if, for a moment, he lost his reference to time itself. In other words, Wilson's mind was no longer in synch with the normal stream of space and time. It had something to do with Preston's eyes meeting his.

Seeing the general stumbling, Nichols came to his aid and helped him to his acoustic room in the front of the garage. The general had come unannounced and Preston was not familiar with him but saw that the man obviously needed help. The general laid down on the cushions of a makeshift couch, apparently unconscious. After about forty-five minutes, the general woke up and looked around.

"Where am I?" he asked Preston.

"You are at Space-Time Labs in East Islip, New York. I am Preston Nichols. Who are you?"

"Oh! I know who you are. Now I remember. As soon as I saw you, I began falling apart. I'm not sure why I had such a strange reaction. I came here to ask you about time experiments at Montauk."

"There is some sort of odd connection here," said Preston. "Perhaps you remember me from Montauk. I hear that a lot from people these days."

"I have no recollection of you whatsoever," said Wilson. "I came to talk to you at the suggestion of Fritz Kraemer from the Pentagon. I am hoping you can tell me all you know about that strange place out there."

After giving Preston a brief synopsis of the events with the psychiatrists and his subsequent trip out to Montauk, he asked Nichols what he had to say about it all.

"I came across Montauk many years ago," he said, "but I had no idea of its full implications until just a few years ago. Originally, I was interviewing and testing psychics. I had determined that telepathy was a genuine phenomena that behaved in the same manner as actual radio waves. As I worked with different psychics, I discovered that they were all blocked at a different time each day. Eventually, I got my radio-direction-finder and started searching for the signal that was blocking them. I took my van across Long Island until I ended up at that strange radar installation at Montauk Point. You know the one I'm talking about?"

"Yes," answered Wilson. "I saw it. It's a monster-sized device."

"I visited the area more than once," said Preston. "Initially, I found that the base had been utterly abandoned with all sorts of equipment strewn about. Making inquiries, I eventually discovered that no one formally claimed to own any of the equipment. The Air Force claimed to have no record. Eventually, I contacted the GSA, and they put me in touch with a security force officer, a Mr. George Anderson, who let me take so much of the equipment that is in my garage back there. It was from a highly classified spook project.

"Lately, I have had quite a few people recognize me from Montauk. Although I have no memory of the place and had never even been there, various people have continued to swear that they worked for me out there. It almost resulted in a fight with my cousin's husband. He insisted that I was his boss, and I thought he was crazy. By all appearances, I have some sort of mysterious connection to the place. As I said, I have also acquired much of the equipment that was used there."

"I have no idea what sort of secret op they have going out there," said Wilson, "but the oddest thing I have heard in my investigation was from an old wino who talked about experiments in time. I thought he was nuts. Have you ever heard stories like that?"

"Sure," replied Preston. "You've talked to Goldwater, haven't you?"

"Yes," answered Wilson. "What made you ask?"

"He called me. To further answer your question, I have heard stories about people disappearing, but I also heard stories about animals running wild and kids going on crime sprees. Apparently, it had to do with the transmitter being directed at the population. When it was turned on, the mood of people and animals would change and change drastically.

## SPANDAU MYSTERY

There is a whole science of mood control that they worked on and it's very secret. This is why Goldwater was stopped. Congress disapproved this work in the fifties, but they started it up again anyway. It was, however, done behind the back of Congress. This is what pissed off Goldwater."

"Understand," continued Preston, "that everything I'm telling you is speculative. I've interviewed quite a few government contractors and associated personnel. By fitting together bits and pieces of what I've learned, I've put together a story of what I feel is best circulated as a legend. Do you want to hear it?"

Wilson nodded.

"It all goes back to the Philadelphia Experiment of 1943. The Navy was trying to make a ship appear invisible to any sort of electromagnetic surveillance such as radar. There are many different theories as to what actually happened with this ship, the *USS Eldridge*. Whatever they did, however, the ship disappeared and left this continuum. It resulted in a tragic catastrophe. Nobody could account for the sailors aboard.

"Unfortunately, when the ship finally did return to Philadelphia — it has also been witnessed off the coast of Norfolk and Montauk during this period — the entire crew had been dramatically affected. Some were on fire, some suffered spontaneous combustion and one was even amalgamated into one of the bulkheads of the ship itself. Those who did not suffer ostensible physical consequences were traumatized mentally. When the ship disappeared, into what we now know was an electromagnetic bubble, they completely lost their references to their environment. It was extremely disruptive to their mental state."

"The Germans have got to be tied into this somewhere — I know it, but I'm not sure how," interrupted Wilson.

"You're right," said Nichols. "The Germans were part of this project from the thirties, before the war. There was still a very secretive liaison during the war, but the situation was too troublesome to continue serious research. If the Germans had been fully involved in the research, it might not have had such devastating effects. Tesla was involved but bowed out before he died. The Americans, under the tutelage of John von Neumann, pressed for a weapon that could help them win the war. With the resulting disaster, it was evident that it was no good as a weapon so it was shelved. After the war, the Germans were reenlisted to help in the project, including all the research from the empirical experimentation they conducted upon their various subjects.

"The effort to figure things out began with the Germans and it occurred right where the Nazis had their biggest headquarters outside of Germany: Yaphank, Long Island. This area featured two real estates parcels known as German Gardens and Camp Seigfried. Also in that area was Camp Upton, an old army camp from World War I that served as a convalescent center for some of the *Eldridge* crew. This began a full psychological studies program. All of this occurred right along side the development of what was to become the premier atomic laboratory in the world: Brookhaven National Laboratory. The Germans were a crucial element in both."

"I was not unaware of these elements but am fascinated how this might tie into Hess and Montauk," said Wilson.

"Montauk is easy, but Hess I'm not so sure about," said Nichols. "It might interest you to know that the work of Josef Mengele was used extensively at Montauk, particularly his studies of twins. Mengele showed no qualms when it came to experimenting on people and there were obviously entities working through him and his sadistic methods. In some cases, torturing people forced them out of their body or normal consciousness and induced various psychic abilities. This was particularly prevalent in the case of male twins. Pleasure or sexual energy was also used to induce these abilities. Hess, however, I cannot answer for. To my knowledge, Hess was not involved in the death camps."

"That's true," said Wilson. "They had a very hard time convicting him at Nuremburg and eventually had to trump up charges on him. Quite brainwashed, too, but that is another story. I'm sorry that I have interrupted you. Please carry on and tell me how this relates to Montauk."

"All of the initial research was conducted at Brookhaven until it was fully established that the human mind could generate a tangible radio wave. A telepathic wave is essentially a psychic wave. The true test of the matter is when you have a person think a thought and it has a tangible or demonstrative result in the physical plane. This was clearly proven in the established world with the Ingo Swann experiments conducted at the Stanford Research Institute. They took Ingo and some of the other psychics who were adept at moving material objects and surveyed the electromagnetic phenomena surrounding them. To make a very long and involved story very short, they amplified their psychic or electromagnetic thoughts by using amplification techniques that are peculiar to the audio electronics industry. As I was already deeply involved in the recording industry, I became a crucial part of this development. I was working at Brookhaven Labs as a youngster and ended up being recruited for the project at Montauk. It took a good while for me to realize it all."

"Were you brainwashed, too?" asked Wilson.

"Something like that," answered Nichols. "I did not remember what was going on until later. Actually, I believe I was living on two time-lines but that is another story.

"Eventually, the experiments at Brookhaven were moved out to Montauk because of the huge radar dish they have out there. Congress forbid any further research on this project at Brookhaven because they were afraid that their own minds might be controlled. It then went under the table and eventually emerged in full at Montauk in the seventies. The lure of Montauk was the big radar transmitter which operated at 435 megahertz, the same frequency that is found to align with the human consciousness.

"The empirical experiments originally conducted by the Nazis became much more sophisticated at Montauk. Many times they were not so brutal. A discovery was that the thoughts of certain individuals could be promulgated along a carrier wave and could influence certain outcomes. The more esoteric aspects of all of this had to do with the manipulation of matter, energy, space and time itself. One of the breakthroughs occurred when one of our psychics could manifest a can of beer, but it would appear at different times of the day than when he thought he was manifesting it. This was the key to penetrating time. If one concentrated on a different time, one was precipitating quantum leaks. Theoretically, we might have a can of beer moving from one time line to another. It is hard to say exactly how things fit into what time line as that is a rather infinite schematic but suffice it to say that we had a very weird and avant garde project going on.

## 7 DORIS PLACE . . . . . . . . . . . . . . . . . . .

"The time experiments were quite interesting. Essentially, and from all of the data I can gather, vortexes were opened according to and in alignment with ancient biorhythms where known worm holes would appear. Montauk certainly is not the only point on the globe that is conducive to this, but it is an excellent candidate if not the best.

"You would probably be very surprised to see what happens when a very powerful group of psychics come together. We were measuring the quality and energy of space itself along with the electromagnetic variations. When you put together the 435 megahertz function — which is, remember, representative of the window frequency to the human consciousness —you have a very interesting set of circumstances by which quantum tunneling and other phenomena can occur. With one of our more adept psychics, we could literally open a vortex to another domain. In the beginning, we sent in bums and other derelict type people and equipped them with television gear. We found out that with proper modifications, they could transmit back to us in 'real time.' These people, however, were expendable and many of them never returned."

"The whole proof in the pudding here," interrupted Wilson, "centers around whether or not you can get a tangible result."

"Exactly," said Preston. "You could see animals running around in crazy patterns as I alluded to earlier. You will find time anomalies as well. Short of giving you an actual time travel experience though, I can't prove the more spectacular aspects."

"I find what you have said to be utterly fascinating. Although it might explain some of the madness I have encountered at Montauk, it seems to open up more questions as opposed to providing real answers," said Wilson. "Essentially, I am conducting a murder investigation. It is important that I do not lose sight of that. On the other hand, I am also being pursued by some pretty shady characters. I cannot lose sight of that either. In any event, I realize that these funny aspects of Montauk could be involved here. What do you make of the phenomena I ran across at Montauk?"

"Do you want me to speculate?" asked Nichols.

"Exactly," replied Wilson.

"I think that your investigation has led you into a very precarious position because it has triggered something very major. The Nazis have been tied to Montauk; and although I have no logical reason to guess why Hess might be involved, it apparently has to do with leadership issues that affect the brass behind Montauk. You're crossing wits with someone important. Be careful."

"I should tell you one thing, Preston. I'm a battle-tested soldier and am afraid of nothing. I want to pursue this Montauk angle further. I am going to take a drive out to Montauk when I finish with you. Would you like to come along? I could use some company to say nothing of your insight."

"As a matter of fact," said Preston, "I've been meaning to take a trip out there anyway. There are some signals I'd like to check out."

It was late morning, and there was plenty of time in the day for an investigative trip out to Montauk. The two made their way out to Preston's van and departed.

**7 DORIS PLACE..................**

......... CHAPTER THIRTY .........

## PASEWICK

By the strangest of fates, General Karl Haushofer was not too far from the Pasewick military hospital when he received news that Aleister Crowley, a member of his secret brethren, had mysteriously arrived in Poland. Despite the surprise, it was easy for the general to make arrangements and meet the very next day with Crowley and his doctor friend. The latter two had arranged to spend the night at the hospital.

Early the next afternoon, Crowley and Haushofer met at a nearby hotel.

"Greetings, my old friend," said Haushofer who spoke perfect English.

"Do what thou wilt shall be the whole of the law," replied Crowley, delivering his signature greeting line.

"I understand," said Haushofer, "that you have facilitated a most remarkable miracle for one of our soldiers. First, however, I must ask what you are doing here. Your arrival here is most remarkable in itself for I thought you were in America and filling the void left by Viereck."

"What I have to tell you, general, is more remarkable than even I could come up with from my own magical mind. It is true that I was working in America, but at the behest of the British, I became very curious about what the Germans had been doing at the eastern end of Long Island for so many years."

"Oh?" replied Haushofer.

"Yes, at Montauk. I made a trip out there as there are several underground facilities — I'm surprised you do not know about them. Do you?"

"I do know," replied the general. "Our dowsing and research of ley lines led us to discover that there is a so-called ganglion of ley lines that aggregate at Montauk Point. You will see a slight hint of this in Madame Blavatsky's work where she identified an identical word for *vril* as being "mashmak." There is a place-name of such on a map of Long Island. It is now called Shelter Island. This indigenous name caught our attention but further study, based upon legends we had already read or heard, led us to discover that most of the energy of the area was consolidated at Montauk Point. It was an ancient place of worship from Atlantean times as it houses a great source of vril. Our people are only trying to tap it. Had we done a better job, I am sure that the war would not have turned in our disfavor."

"From what I understand," said Crowley, "your war machine has held up just fine. It is just the damn politicians that are fouling things up."

"Agreed," said Haushofer. "Now, tell me how you have come to arrive in Pasewick of all places."

After Crowley shared his remarkable story, Haushofer raised his eyebrows. "Perhaps I should be very surprised," said the general, "but I am not surprised. We have lost the war but things have turned out in our favor. This gives us a great advantage. After all, we are the chiefs."

"The secret chiefs?" asked Crowley, "Is that what you are referring to?"

"Indeed," said Haushofer, "the secret chiefs of Atlantis."

"I haven't even been thinking from that perspective recently. I guess I have been too busy experiencing to have a circumspect view. After all, I am intruding upon your world and not the other way around."

"It is really quite simple," said Haushofer. "At the outset, we were intent on raising Atlantis. Should it surprise us that we have actually arrived? The portal that you have come through is an unexpected gift that suddenly gives us an advantage we did not have before; however, it is also a cavern that descends into Agartha and the people of that realm."

Crowley was silent as he absorbed the information. He looked puzzled as if he was waiting for further revelation.

"You know," continued Haushofer, "there is another secret chief in the United States. On your return journey, assuming you get back with no problem, perhaps you could contact him when you do."

"Who are you referring to?" asked Crowley.

"The prophet of the Latter Day Saints. He is the guardian of another route to Agartha that the Mormons rediscovered through their association with the Indians and by tracing old trade routes left by the Knights Templar. This entry way to Agartha is through deep caverns at the Great Salt Lake."

"Is that why they settled there?" asked Crowley. "Personally, I always wondered if they were trying to keep spirits away from the proximity of so much salt."

"Ah! Exactly!" exclaimed Haushofer. "You never forget that you are an alchemist, do you? Tell me...let me speak to your doctor friend."

The Asian doctor who had accompanied Crowley to this encounter now looked at the general when he realized that he had become an object of interest.

"That's quite fine," said Crowley. "In fact, I can guarantee that he has understood every word which you have said thus far. I do not know how these things you are talking about apply to his world though."

"Indeed!" exclaimed Haushofer. "He reminds me of people I have known from Tibet, particularly the little ones."

"The Dropa?" asked the doctor.

"Yes," replied Haushofer.

Haushofer soon discovered that the two of them shared a common language: Tibetan. The two of them began speaking animatedly for a few minutes. This language left Crowley out in the blue.

"What did you say?" asked Crowley when there was finally a pause.

"I merely suggested that we had some common experiences in culture and should share them," replied Haushofer. "First though, we have to discover what we are now going to do with the both of you. It is not exactly like you have a home here. I would be very curious about sending you back to England, but I do not know how that would work out. Also, I must ask myself, 'Is there another Crowley in this world?'"

"Heaven forbid!" said Crowley. "I think one is enough for this world, if I do say so myself."

After the three men had further discussions, Haushofer insisted upon meeting the corporal upon whom the doctor had facilitated the miracle cure. Crowley, who was content to let the two of them explore that route by themselves, decided he wanted to connect with the elements and go for a walk in the forest. He said it would make him feel like a Druid again.

As Crowley walked into the forest, he was stopped by the energy vectors of the trees. To his surprise, he had never encountered anything quite like this in his days in the forests of England. There was almost no wind yet the trees suggested that something was coming through. Suddenly, he heard a rattling in the bush. It sounded like it might be a wild animal and he put himself on guard.

Before he could contemplate what danger might await him, he saw his two tiny comrades that he had left behind at Montauk. Popping out of the bushes, Gibby and Chewey were muttering and giggling under their breath as they came into full view before him.

"There you are!" said Chewey.

"I'll bet you thought you got away!" said Gibby.

"What do you mean?" asked Crowley. "It was more like you both ditched me! I was perplexed when I lost you and ended up in another world. I suppose I was lucky enough to emerge at Montauk the first time albeit in a different time. Now, I seem to be at the same time period but in a different part of the world. But tell me, what are you two doing here?"

"You are in our realm now and you have gotten lost," said Chewey. "This is not perplexing to us. We were having so much fun jumping between places that we left you behind. When we stopped fooling around, we simply traced you down."

"How did you do that?" asked Crowley.

"Never mind that now. You're not supposed to be here, and it is important that we get you back to where you came from in no time."

"You're forgetting something very important," said Crowley.

"What's that?" asked Chewey.

"You were supposed to show me the underground, but here I am getting a side tour," said Crowley.

"Hmm..." muttered Chewey. "In a sense, you are seeing the underground. We'll talk about all that later. First, it is important that we get you back. Follow me."

Chewey ran ahead and Gibby ran behind Crowley to make sure that he would follow. After running a hundred yards, they came upon a hill and found a cave. Entering the cave, they walked until they came to a portal reminiscent of those that Crowley had recently become experienced with.

Arriving back at the original portal they had left from, circa 1918 at Montauk, they all stood together and relaxed.

"Now that we're here and we have finally got you back to

where you belong," said Chewey, "we can discuss some of those other things you wanted to know."

As Chewy spoke, the spherical portal remained nearby. It began to wax. Instead of listening to Chewey and instead of being relieved that he was back to where he belonged, Crowley deliberately jumped through the portal and disappeared.

**PASEWICK.....................**

·····CHAPTER THIRTY-ONE······

## UNDERGROUND

When General Wilson and Preston Nichols finally made their way to Montauk Point, they turned on Camp Hero Road and found the gate to be wide open. Driving inwards, they continued and drove right by the radar building and the tennis courts. In a field south of a large bunker, they saw a small blue building. Contractors were excavating large chunks of dirt. As the two men walked towards the area, one of the workers saw Preston Nichols and spoke.
"Are you the ones that we are supposed to let down the elevator?" the worker asked.
Nichols simply nodded. General Wilson, who was in uniform, did not hurt their cause by reason of the way he was dressed. As far as Wilson and Nichols knew, however, they were now playing the role of impostors taking advantage of lax security in order to find out what they could. They were then escorted to the blue building where they got aboard a very large freight elevator that would take them several stories beneath the ground.
Emerging from the elevator, Wilson and Nichols made their way down a wide bunker hallway until they reached a room full of technicians who mostly sat in front of screens.
"This looks familiar to me," said Preston. "Just act like you know what you're doing."
Most of the technicians were slumped in their chairs. In front of each one was a crudely constructed video apparatus. The technicians seemed despondent, tired and under fed. To look at them, one would expect they were surveying different time periods via television screens, none of which looked very interesting. They looked to be bored in the extreme.
Wilson, being a general and a commander of people, made himself comfortable and quite at home as he looked around and inspected the place.
"Does anyone have anything to report?" he asked the technicians.
"No, sir!" said one of the technicians. "It's been pretty bleak on my screen."

"Same here," said another technician.

"That's 'same here, *sir!*'" exclaimed Wilson, letting them all know who was boss.

"Yes, sir!" responded the technician. "I'm sorry, sir."

"Now, listen," said Wilson, "we've got a technician here that you might know. His name is Mr. Nichols. He can take care of any problems you're having, not only with your screens but in accessing potential areas of interest. I'm now going to go around to each one of you and ask about the last orders you've been working on. I want to see what you're doing and get you going."

One by one, Wilson went to each of the technicians and began to absorb information from them. After assessing that these technicians had not been doing much of anything and had been left rudderless, Wilson decided to take some fast action.

"Tell me what you are doing," he said to one of the technicians. "What are you looking at here?"

"646 A.D., approximately," said the technician.

"Who in here is in the nineteen-forties?" asked Wilson.

"I am, sir," said a different technician as he raised his hand.

"Very good, we'll start with you," replied Wilson. "Mr. Nichols, come with me."

"What are you focused on?" asked Wilson to the same technician.

"1945," the technician replied.

"Excellent," said Wilson. "Now, I want you to focus in on a particular individual. We might need to go earlier or maybe even later. The individual I want you to focus on is Rudolph Hess, the Deputy Fuhrer of Germany."

Looking at Nichols, the general spoke.

"Between the two of you, Preston, do you think you can find him?"

"That won't be a problem," said Preston. "We'll just have to find a witness that we can locate to that area."

Wilson then watched in amazement as his dream unfolded before his own eyes. He had always wanted to know what exactly had happened during the interrogations of Rudolph Hess. Now, he would discover the truth for himself through the convoluted and remarkable circumstances of time manipulation at Montauk.

Watching the initial interrogations of Hess in 1941, the practitioners and doctors supplied by the British literally got nowhere. Due to either incompetence or just plain ineffectiveness, the information they retrieved was either petty, already well known or completely insignificant. Finally, an intelligence officer with an M.D. background began to get some results by applying narcosynthesis or truth serum.

In response to questions as to his purpose and identity, Hess started off by stating his mission was peace. This did not surprise anyone, but everything else he said on that first day of truth-serum-inspired-interrogation threw everyone for a loop. He identified himself as a member of a secret and important family that was not only related to Holy Roman Emperor Rudolph I of the Hapsburg Empire but to the bloodline of Aaron, the builder of the Ark of the Covenant. He explained that much was misconstrued about the bloodline of the Jews. The Jews, he stated, were not all bad and it is unfair to label all Jews as bad or evil but that it was done for urgent political necessity. The term "Jew" was misleading in itself, but it was useful with the population in eliminating certain so-called "bad seeds" of humanity. In Germany, a country which he described as being betrayed and devalued by Jewish people who were already hated, he said that it was of the most advantageous political expediency to identify them. Drastic measures had to be taken against them, not all of which he was happy about. The Nuremberg Laws, he said, were pressured upon him; but there must be sacrifices.

Besides being related to the Hapsburgs, he said that his mother was Greek and that she not only shared Jewish heritage but Egyptian and that she used to take him out into the Libyan desert when he was young. Much of his heritage was explained in a secret family book, but he did not remember it all because he had never read it in detail. He only knew the general outline.

According to one tradition, his lineage made him an agent of the Temple of Solomon because he was a blood relative of Aaron, the brother of Moses. Aaron was the builder of the Ark of the Covenant and his bloodline had been misconstrued. "Erin," the Irish word for *Aaron*, he said, as well as the word *Aryan*, both derived from the character called Aaron in the Bible. This, he said, was a most secret doctrine and could not be revealed to outsiders or to the public. With regard to Aryans and key members of the Nazi Party, Hess explained that Heydrich, Hitler and himself all had the blood of Jews in their lineage.

In addition to the above, his relatives on the Hess side had also settled in America where they sought the New Jerusalem. Some of these people settled in Pennsylvania and others settled in Stone Arabia in New York. The Americans, he said, had no idea of their own history. In fact, his ancestors had to maintain a hidden history for fear of having it wiped out by the Freemasons in the United States. All of this led to his next revelation.

One of the biggest finds, according to the drugged Hess, was discovered as a result of the raids the Nazis staged against the Freemasons, particularly in Germany. Not only did they find secret writing codes, but they were able to arrest key Masons and trace back the names of loyal Freemasons across the world. In such an abrupt and forceful manner did the Nazis obtain banking secrets and ultimate spheres of influence. Based upon the information thus discovered, the invasion of America was going to become a necessity. The British, he stated to his captors, were in complete agreement and wanted to subdue America. America, he said, was a most misunderstood country, particularly the Indians.

The pro-Aryan theory that he divulged to his captors was that King Solomon represented the father of all peoples and this contained not only all races but good seeds and bad seeds. The problem, he said, was the Judeans who either descended from or carried on the corrupt manner of Rahoboam, Solomon's son who ruled Judeah and alienated ten tribes of Israel. This resulted in the diaspora of the Israelites across the world. The Nazis, to some degree, shared the aims of the Knights Templar and that was to restore the Temple, but there were some philosophical questions that had to be resolved before this could be properly accomplished. Earlier depictions of Hitler as a Knights Templar were to further this end but this tact was eventually nixed by Goebbels who decided it would be better to allay the fears of the German population by not suggesting any possible association between Hitler and the Temple of Jewry. This was only known and recognized by certain elite members of the Nazi Party.

The Pharaoh of Egypt, Hess indicated, was a direct descendant of the Kings of Atlantis and this was broadly recognized by most indigenous tribes of the world. This, however, was forgotten as time marched on. Rahoboam, the King of Judeah who failed the Israelites with his cruel actions, was the keeper of the Temple until it was raided by Shisak of Egypt who took all of the gold and valuables. Rahoboan replaced the gold with cheap metals and imitation artifacts. As this gold had been taken from so many parts of the planet, Pharaoh Shisak took it upon himself to return what he could to the rightful owners. This caused a diaspora of wealth back to various areas of the planet which included Peru, Mexico and the United States.

The best kept secrets of the Temple, Hess said, were the maps of where the gold and riches came from. These were stored with the scrolls and were kept in the caves beneath the Temple. Such was Solomon's power that he could command the jinn and all the gnomes and spirits who were assigned to burying and keeping gold. When Solomon died, the "little people" set things in motion in order to retrieve what was lost when the Kingdom of Israel was erected in all its glory. Shisak was the instrument of these little people. The true Pharaoh, Hess said, would have to be a world leader who distributed all the wealth back to its original sources and did not hoard it at one temple for the glorification of one god.

The entire economy of the world, Hess said, mimicked or followed the gold that went into the temple and was taken from the temple. The Spanish conquistadores, at the behest of the Vatican, sought the gold that had been taken from the Temple. The obsessions of the world, which include both religion and money, are still wrapped around the issues of the Temple. The Freemasons had penetrated many of these secrets through their early contact with the Indians and also utilized the Mormon movement to appropriate and safeguard this gold for a future time.

When asked about much of this information, Hess explained that most of it came from a book that was very secret and was part of one of the society's that he belonged to. He was not allowed to talk about it publicly or even privately.

When asked about his plane ride to England, Hess explained that the Nazis could not easily survive a war on two fronts as well as the fact that they had already arranged to be allies with the British in the first place. The Russians were about to invade and this is why he sought peace with England. It would avoid hundreds of thousands of deaths and would create an alliance of peace, one that Hitler and Churchill had agreed upon earlier. The English already knew this. When Hess made his arrangements to negotiate peace with the British, it was intercepted by intelligence who did not forward the requests but hung Hess and the Germans out to dry. It was deceit through "diplomacy."

It was obvious from the reaction of the British and their subsequent conversations, observed through the chronovisor at Montauk by Wilson, that the statements of Hess were extremely disturbing politically, philosophically and for religious policy as well. It created all sorts of problems whether it was considered seriously or not.

Deciding to move to a future time with the chronovisor, General Wilson consulted Preston Nichols. He was the only technician who knew how to readily shift from one time-space locale to another. Using his own intuition, accompanied by his technical skill, Nichols guided Wilson to a scene where the reports on Hess were reviewed by British superiors. This included an admiral, an intelligence officer and a priest who, after each report, would all prescribe different questions to be asked of their subject.

As Wilson foraged through this information, time stood still for him. Hours became days and days became weeks. His interest was piqued to the degree that he paid no attention to anything else.

Further inquiries of Hess by the British revealed that Nazi submarines in the mid-thirties had sought out an area in the Atlantic that was once known as the City of the Golden Gates, the ancient capital of Atlantis. Although this city had been submerged for millennia, the area had attracted their attention. It was off the coast of South America and not far north of the equator. This city had appeared on ancient maps and was even referenced by the Theosophical Society. Under drugs, Hess revealed that Nazi scientists were able to detect in this area what they determined to be "an electromagnetic bubble" that could not be penetrated. Thorough and meticulous, Hess ordered a study of all applicable data of the area, legendary and otherwise. As a result of his liaison with their Italian allies, he eventually determined that Guiglio Marconi was the most qualified person who might be able to remedy the mysteries of this electric bubble.

Marconi, Hess stated, had gone to work for the British just before the turn of the century. This was right after the Vatican had persuaded the Italians not to foster Marconi's wireless work in Italy. In the 1930's, however, Marconi had convincingly demonstrated to Mussolini that he could neutralize all electromagnetic operations in a given area. This was a completely different technology than the wireless. William Donovan, on behalf of the Vatican and British, brokered a deal with Mussolini which directed Marconi back to the British. Marconi was fiercely loyal to Italy but only went to foreign countries when directed by Italian leaders. All of this was common knowledge to the Axis powers. The British, said Hess, had directed a considerable tide of events through the Vatican by means which were more than a little mysterious. Although this was only an opinion by Hess, it ended up as a closely guarded secret of the Hess incarceration.

Through their association, Marconi gave the British what eventually became their early radar technology. It was, quite ironically, this same technology by which Hess's flight to Scotland was monitored. Marconi, who already was aware of the British and how they operated, became increasingly aware of their imperial designs to exploit the various people of the world. After seeing too much, he decided to rebel and faked his own death. Although he did not have sure evidence, Hess believed that Marconi mastered the mystery of the bubble and entered it.

In the meantime, Hess's Auslands-Organization had his loyal countrymen employed at the highest levels of the American military and industrial world. Through this form of espionage, the Germans learned that the Americans had discovered the German surveillance of the City of the Golden Gates. This was unfortunate but also convenient for the Germans who were already engaged in a joint study of invisibility with the Americans. The British, however, had already engaged the Americans with various aspects of the technology they had learned with Marconi. When everyone more or less found out what everyone was doing, a new joint venture was undertaken. This time, however, the Germans and Americans had to accept the British as a silent but virtually senior partner as they held key patents and literally licensed key technology which had come from Marconi. This endeavor was called Operation Southern Cross and was designed with multifold purposes, only one of which was the so-called "raising of Atlantis."

Despite all of this, Hess explained that the Germans had the upper hand because they not only had superior scientists and cogent psychic mediums from the Vril Society, they also had been working on it the longest. One of the most perplexing phenomena they encountered was that some German submarines would disappear when either attempting to penetrate the electromagnetic bubble or when in its vicinity. The bubble, after it had been recognized, was studied intensely and all avenues of thought were explored.

"All possible analyses of this electromagnetic bottle were pursued," stated Hess. "German scientists in America consulted top physicists at Princeton, the University of Chicago and Columbia University in New York. These great minds contributed many theories as did the scientists of Europe, but it was our own Vril mediums who were responsible for the ultimate breakthrough. When confronted with the problem, they pointed out that the electromagnetic bottle, as witnessed by the disappearance of various craft within its realm, was a matter of reality. In other words, the fabric of space-time reality itself was changing. They informed that there was a consciousness or beings connected to this reality. If one enters the realm of the bottle without connecting with the conscious entity or entities in its realm, there would either be no resolution or a compromised resolution. I am making this sound almost simple but the path of research, particularly the scientific angles, were arrived at by very complicated logic. The Vril mediums, however, pointed out that the ultimate rules in play were no different than arcane spirituality or alchemy. These avenues, they said, would provide simplistic theories or pathways that scientists could emulate into equations.

"They also informed us," continued Hess, "that unless one acquiesced or submitted themselves to this consciousness in the other realm, one was subject to being consumed by it. This added a whole new approach to the subject and the study of the electromagnetic bottle. Recent developments in quantum physics only enabled us to accelerate our pursuit of what could easily be construed as other-worldly ambition. The sky was the limit."

As Hess ended his diatribe for that particular day, Wilson looked up from the chronovisor and had a look of fulfillment.

"Now I know why I was so damn curious all of these years," he said to Nichols. "He's talking about the Philadelphia Experiment — that experiment also featured an electromagnetic bottle."

"Sure sounds like it," replied Preston Nichols. "Those experiments and all that ensued from them were the forerunner of all sorts of technology we use today."

"You mean before the Americans messed it all up," replied Wilson.

"They certainly did mess things up," said Nichols.

**UNDERGROUND..................**

## CHAPTER THIRTY-TWO

## THE LAMPS

In a hurry and breathing heavily, Heidi rushed into Ali Bey's exotic lamp store. Her desperation betrayed her, but she knew she had to act fast. Inside of her, she trusted Ali Bey very deeply. That was woman's intuition. She knew, however, that any typical investigator, including Colonel Mack, would look at Ali Bey with a jaundiced eye as a result of the data that had been found in the Lion's Paw moving van.

"Ali," she called out as she entered the store.

You could have heard a pin drop in the silence. As she went towards the back of the store, she finally saw Ali's old but gentle eye balls peering up at her. He was wearing his fez and rose to greet her.

"My lady," he exclaimed, "how nice to see you so soon. You look troubled though. What is the matter?"

"I am troubled," she replied, "but I would be more comfortable talking elsewhere. I think we might be under surveillance. Just in case, let's go elsewhere."

"That would be fine," said Ali Bey.

The two departed. Once outside, they agreed to have lunch at a sidewalk cafe across the street.

"Ali," said Heidi, "you already know that this investigation has resulted in some very strange phenomena and that includes the incredible book that you copied for us. Do you feel that you need it back?"

"Oh, no," he responded. "I have the notes, remember? I believe the data is far more important than the book."

"I am not so sure about that," said Heidi, "but that is only my female intuition working."

"I would consider that a very important guideline then," responded Ali.

"Essentially, Ali, there is another bizarre incident I must relay to you. First though, I must ask you a question. Are you expecting any deliveries from Lion's Paw?"

"Why do you ask?" asked Ali.

"Because if you are, someone has a lot of explaining to do," said Heidi.

# THE LAMPS . . . . . . . . . . . . . . . . . . . . .

"Indeed," said Ali, "I am expecting a delivery from Lion's Paw. It is an ensemble of antique lamps which, of course, I routinely deal in."

"OK," said Heidi. "Can you tell me where they are coming from? Your answer will help very much in our investigation."

"It should be coming from the Brooklyn Navy Yard. I use an agent there who imports lamps for me."

"Can you please be more specific?" asked Heidi.

"Normally," replied Ali, "I would be very hesitant to furnish this information as it is proprietary. I have a very unique business in exotic lamps. I do, however, trust you. Can I trust you not to reveal my supplier?"

"As far as commerce goes, no problem. As far as the investigation of this murder, it could become very important to the proceedings."

"What would you like to know?" asked Ali.

"I will be quite frank with you, and I feel that I can speak honestly. General Wilson suffered a severe concussion in an accident. He is still in the hospital and is recovering very slowly. The prognosis is 'cautiously optimistic.'"

"I am very sorry to hear that," said Ali.

"Furthermore," continued Heidi, "he was hit by the very same truck from Lion's Paw that not only included your shipment but was also used to move Dr. Konrad to Montauk."

Ali looked like he was in shock. After a while, he spoke.

"Montauk?" asked Ali Bey.

"Certainly. You did not know that?" asked Heidi.

"No, but you should understand that it was through the Lion's Paw company that I found out about Dr. Konrad in the first place. You see, I have used Lion's Paw for a considerable amount of time. I was put in touch with them through my contact at the Brooklyn Navy Yard. His name is Gregory Moore, and he has a strange way of importing things through his connections in the Navy."

"He is in the Navy?" asked Heidi.

"Yes," answered Ali Bey. "It is a rather unusual arrangement and one I cannot completely account for. It was through him and the people at Lion's Paw that I was eventually put in contact with Konrad."

"Why were you put in touch with Konrad?" asked Heidi. "This is becoming a very important piece of the puzzle."

"Earlier I told you that I was a Moor and that I was seeking an antiquity from him but I did not tell you too much about myself and the implications of it all. Before I can tell you exactly why I was interested in Dr. Konrad, I feel it is very important that I must inform you what I was up to. Greg Moore, who had been supplying me for years, knew that I was looking for a specific document. His contacts at Lion's Paw suggested I contact Konrad. They apparently have done several moves for him and know him a bit. They said he deals in antiquities.

"Before you make any judgments about me, please understand what I have to tell you about my Moorish heritage. Most people do not understand and are woefully ignorant of these matters. I cannot expect you to be any different.

"My people come from the ancient Moabites. We are keepers of the Temple. By that, I am referring to the Temple of Solomon the King. Knowing this Temple would eventually fall, Solomon deposited the Ark of the Covenant and its secrets with his son, Menilek. Our ancient customs eventually referred to us as Shriners and we wear the fez that you see on my head right now. It is an adornment that expresses our dedication to the Craft. We represent the original Freemason. The "free" in Freemason is very important. We are free and do not represent any cult, dogma or any institution. We represent the truth and the truth is free.

"As a nation representing the family of man, however, our heritage has been destroyed and mocked by our current civilization. The knowledge that we carry forward to this day is represented as the lamp of illumination. This was often expressed in medieval lore as the lamp of illumination of the Saracen. Keep in mind that the term Saracen is synonymous to the appellation "Moor." The concept of the lamp of illumination is, in no small part, why I deal in exotic lamps. The lamp of illumination is what my people represent.

"You see, our importance and our heritage have been emulated and taken by the original governors of your country as well as by the enemies of Mankind. Today, you will find Shriners imitating our ways and wearing a fez. They are an abomination to our ways. We are free Freemasons and do not subscribe to limited thinking. This all becomes self-evident if you observe the fez that the 32nd degree Masons wear. If you

## THE LAMPS . . . . . . . . . . . . . . . . . . . . . .

notice the tassel on their fez, you will see that it is knotted so that it can only move within the confines of 32° of a circle. The tassel on our fez moves a full 360° because we are indeed free from limitation. To us, the word *Mason* is not just a word. We are builders of the sacred.

"Our people had to remain underground during Roman times and the sack of Jerusalem. Much of our learning and knowledge was held in upper Egypt and at Elephantine Island. Eventually, we were able to come forward with the modern advent of Islam. We were able to use that movement to promulgate our knowledge into upper Africa and the Iberian Peninsula. That civilization was the greatest Europe has ever known and took them out of the Dark Ages. The greatest enemy we have ever known, however, was the Vatican and the same forces therein that committed genocide against the Cathars of France.

"In 1492, there was the Capitulation of Santa Fe. This had to do with the last Moorish stronghold that was in Granada in that year. The Moorish Empire in Iberia motivated the Church to do something which had never been done before: unite the fighting kingdoms of Spain so as pit them against the Moors. This ultimately resulted in the arranged marriage of Ferdinand and Isabella. They brought their armies to the Alhambra and waited for Granada to challenge them, but it was a battle the Moors could not win. Their empire had already been systematically reduced to one stronghold. With the Spanish army at the door, their food supply was cut off. It was a waiting game.

"While the Spaniards waited them out, there were jousting events and games between the Moorish and Spanish knights. All of them were geared towards declaring a winner in the standoff. The events, however, did not result in either side conceding. The Spanish held the upper hand.

"In the midst of the long wait, the royal camp of the Spaniards caught fire. As Ferdinand and Isabella had both come to watch and celebrate the final domination of the Moors, they barely escaped this fire which was caused by a negligent member of their own family. In response to this frightening omen, Ferdinand and Isabella decided to put their still armies to work by erecting houses of stone. In a direct statement of their Christian faith, they built a series of stone buildings so that two streets formed a cross. This was an act of faith which is translated in Spanish to *fe*. The city was therefore named Santa Fe. To this day, that cross stands in the middle of that city and remains as a tribute to the extinction of Moorish wisdom in Europe. The cross, which was originally a holy symbol, has been used to denigrate the memory and advanced civilization or our people. It is a testament to ignorance as well.

"At that time, the Moors were the custodians of Amexem, an empire that stretched from Africa all the way to Al Maurikanos, our name for the continents which are now known as the Americas. Al Maurikanos means El Morocco and means "the home of the Moors."

When Ali Bey paused, Heidi interrupted. "What does all this have to do with the facts of the case?" she asked.

"To an ordinary mind, it might seem to have nothing to do with the case. At the very least, however, it will explain to you how I came into contact with Dr. Konrad.

"You see, at that time, the Moors had custodianship of the Western Hemisphere. It was recognized by all peoples and was actually a matter of international diplomacy. The Vatican, who was behind the advent of Ferdinand and Isabella, wanted to rid the world of the Moorish Empire. It was they who fostered Cristobal Colon, the man you recognize as Christopher Columbus. He was present at the Capitulation of Santa Fe where the Moors did not surrender but agreed upon a capitulation. In this capitulation, they allowed for Spain to become the stewards of what was deliberately referred to as the New Continent in Columbus's charter. They knew it was not a new continent but had to create a fiction. There was no mention of Asia or India in that charter. The missions of Columbus and those who followed resulted in the Triangular Trade Route. They also enslaved the indigenous Moors of Al Maurikanos who had lived there since time immemorial. A most peculiarly cruel people, the slave traders added insult to injury by giving them a red flag to rally around when they were rounded up like cattle. This red flag was also the standard of Morocco and was known as "Old Glory."

"The document of this capitulation at Santa Fe has remained obscure to history, but we do know of its existence. The copies that were originally ceded to the Moors were later confiscated or destroyed.  We do know, however, that the Vatican library will possess the original or perhaps even a deliberately altered version.

"It was in this regard that I sought out Dr. Konrad.  I was told that he had access to antiquities that go back into history.  I was hoping that he might know of this manuscript."

"Who told you this?" asked Heidi.

"It was my friend, Greg Moore, from the Brooklyn Navy Yard.  He told me about Konrad."

"There is still one other thing you must explain to me," said Heidi.

"What is that?" asked Ali.

"The lamps were not the only articles on the bill of lading from Lion's Paw that were directed to you."

"Oh?" responded Ali Bey who appeared to be genuinely surprised.

"There were other items.  Do you have any idea what I'm talking about?"

"Absolutely not, but being that I will have to explain them anyway, or at least try, you might as well tell me what they are."

"Strangely shaped electronic coils and other electronic apparatus."

"Really?" asked Ali who still seemed genuinely puzzled.  "Did they come from Greg?"

"No, they went directly from Montauk to the Brooklyn Navy Yard.  There was a separate order for them, and they must have gone to your friend Greg.  I would have to review the paperwork.  All I know is that everything in the truck, including that equipment, was being directed towards you."

Ali Bey looked dizzy over the revelation he had just heard.

"If what you say it true," he said, "I guess it will be delivered to me soon.  I have no idea what it is."

...... CHAPTER THIRTY-THREE ......

## RESOLUTION

The initial interrogations of Rudolph Hess revealed many things the British Command did not know, but the more he spoke, the more his information turned into a major security leak. It was very clear that Hess's intelligence sources, as well as he himself, knew far too much information about the British and even more than the interrogators themselves should know. It was at this point that the British brought in Dr. Ewen Cameron to deal with their prisoner who was in fact an envoy of the German government. Cameron was brought in because he was a specialist in getting people to forget their identity. Cameron was capable of inducing a person to think he had an identity completely different than what he was known to have had before. Various drugs and procedures were applied by him in an attempt to make Hess forget his past and what he had learned from his top position in the Third Reich. After the Nuremburg Trials, this was further enforced by forbidding him to discuss his Nazi past.

All of the above was very clear to General Wilson as he looked through the time window and saw Hess being tortured to the point of mental compromise. For Wilson, however, the tragedy of Rudolph Hess was not something to be disappointed about. There was not much he could do about a piece of history that had already taken place. At long last, however, Wilson rejoiced for he had discovered the basis behind the mystery of Rudolph Hess and what he represented. As is the case with any good investigation, this only opened more avenues. It certainly did not close the case of Hess's assassination, but it gave an excellent explanation for its motivation: privileged truth.

The knowledge and secrets that Hess had arrived at by reason of his unique heritage and experiences and rise to power was such that it threatened the very power of those who rule. What all this meant was clearly beyond Wilson's capacity to understand. All it really did was answer Wilson's mystery that he had been wondering about all these years. This, in itself, could have been enough, but even if he wanted

# RESOLUTION . . . . . . . . . . . . . . . . . . . .

to rest, he knew he could not. A whole can of worms was now opened in his consciousness, and he would have to see it through. This was a battle, and he was in the middle of it. He knew, however, that the best course of action was for him to take things one step at a time.

In one respect, Hess was an acme of secrets and sacred knowledge that could be very useful to rival aspirants of power. His knowledge ranged from the mundane aspects of political control zones to the secret societies of America and the Far East. It even extended to the most esoteric ranges of sacred knowledge. Hess, if allowed to speak, was like a genie bottle that would spurt out information that was understandably intriguing but chaotic and uncontrollable to the powers that be. It had to be contained. At the very least, it was sure to change the way the world looked at itself.

Even if Wilson did not feel fully qualified to resolve the dilemma of Rudolph Hess's information, he could not sell himself short. Wilson's mind was sharp and brilliant. He fully realized that there was an investigation to be done with regard to the "psychiatrists" who had tried to subdue him. There was also the mysterious death of Konrad. Whoever was behind these actions was obviously interested in keeping the Hess business closed. Wilson did remember, however, that there was another possibility at work here. Someone just might be baiting him and not trying to cover up anything at all. If that was the case, they were indulging him in what amounted to be a very dangerous game that held a prize at the end of an imaginary rainbow. The prize was not a pot of gold but a treasure trove of endless mysteries that were waiting to be unveiled. This alone, he mused, was worth the price he had paid for the adventure. Somehow, he had been miraculously and serendipitously afforded the opportunity to arrive at the Montauk underground and peer into these holes in time. Perhaps, he thought, there was a higher power at work. Whatever it was, he was quite aware that it was a double-edged sword.

Besides the high adventure, there was also the bottom line reality to deal with and that had everything to do with the criminal investigation of the psychiatrists who had tried to abduct him. It was clear to Wilson that whoever was behind the death of Konrad was tied to this Montauk Project scenario. They seemed to operate with impunity, secrecy, and at the highest levels of government authority. The Hess issue, he now realized, was not only a trigger point of major proportions, it might well have been *the* trigger point of the century. After all, Wilson's experiences in the wake of his original Hess investigation were opening quantum tunnels and phenomena that seemed to have no limit. He had plugged into, albeit haphazardly, the adventure of a lifetime.

"It's too bad I'm so old," Wilson thought to himself.

Letting the matters of his original pursuit rest, he began to look around the installation he was working in. Hess was done, at least for the time being. Now, he would concentrate on his role as an impostor of a Commanding Officer of the Montauk underground complex.

"Where are the field reports of all these various activities that you have all monitored?" barked Wilson to the assortment of technicians around him.

"That would be in the archives," said Nichols.

"Of course," said Wilson, pretending he should have known or thought of this. "Let's go."

Wilson was then led down different corridors to a huge chamber filled with video cassette tapes and film cans. Upon entering the large chamber, they were approached by a little person who stood no more than 4'5".

"My name is Mau. Can I help you?" asked the little man.

"This is the archivist," said Nichols. "He can help you find what you want."

"You see," said Mau, "there is virtually an infinite amount of raw footage here. I would assume that you would be more interested in some of the summarized work that has been done. Most of it is in that far aisle in the back. We've pretty much got anything you could ask for."

"I'm primarily interested in one thing," said Wilson.

"What's that?" asked the little man.

"The book," replied Wilson.

"What book?" asked Mau.

"Surely, you must know the book!" said Wilson. "It's a book about all the inventions of Mankind and the mysterious characters who virtually fostered every major technological breakthrough Mankind has had over the last hundred years or so."

# RESOLUTION...................

"Oh! That book!" said Mau. "How do you know about that book?"

"You know something," said Wilson. "I'm not even sure of what I just said or why I said it. I'm beginning to feel a little woozy."

Wilson began to feel severe disorientation. Holding his stomach, he barely noticed a man in the far aisle in the back of the archives. The man wore black and seemed to be studiously taking tapes and placing them on a cart, but he who was too far away to see any distinguishing characteristics or features. Wilson became feint, however, and lost his bearings to the point where he was having a hard time standing.

"So, you want the book?" asked Mau.

Wilson no longer heard what the man was saying because he suddenly froze as the man spoke. The man named Mau continued to talk, but there was nothing Wilson could do to respond. His will was paralyzed as he collapsed.

"I'm afraid we don't have that book," said Mau. "It's been on my wish list for a very long time."

## CHAPTER THIRTY-FOUR

## ALONE

Heidi looked into Ali Bey's eyes. Together, they were a contrasting pair. He was older and of swarthy complexion while she was fair and still young enough to pass for the age of thirty.

"I have never felt so alone," she said to Ali.

Ali, who was still contemplating the perplexity of the mysterious electronics that were being shipped to him, looked at her with concern. This woman, who for all intents and appearances was investigating him, was opening up to him in order to be consoled.

"I have more to tell you," said Heidi. "There has not only been a great tragedy in terms of this investigation but a human tragedy as well."

"Is there more bad news about the general?" asked Ali.

"No, that is a tragedy, too. I have sent Gretchen to look after him as well as guard him. I think he will recover all right, but there is something else. It is Colonel Mack."

"What is it?"

"He survived the accident relatively OK. Together, we reviewed all of the information. We both deemed it prudent that he would investigate the gypsy as our next step. You know, the one who was in Konrad's office."

"Investigate?" asked Ali.

"Yes," said Heidi, "she had done a tarot card reading for me just before all of these incidents took place. With pinpoint accuracy, the Hanged-Man card came up. It resonated so much with the death of Hess and the consequent events that I couldn't believe it. The Hanged-Man is also all about opposites. When you see something, the opposite just might be true. The Hanged-Man is upside down because that is the opposite of how you would normally perceive something. It encourages you to look at the hidden inner meaning which is opposite the apparent meaning. This is particularly true in the case of the gypsy lady. Always appearing gentile and rather charming, she suddenly and inexplicably shows up looking like a slut when you saw her."

"I noticed!" said Ali with a wry smile. "What does this have to do with Colonel Mack?"

"He went to see her to get a reading for purposes of the investigation. In the process, he hoped to question her without giving away his position — at least not yet. Up to that point, she had not seen him and didn't know who he was.

"I'm afraid to say," continued Heidi, "that he was consumed in the most terrible way by her wanton sexuality. What is most odd, however, is that I never could have imagined her acting that way before. It seemed out of character."

"Where is Colonel Mack now?" asked Ali Bey.

"He is in a hospital himself, but he has become more of a psychiatric case."

"How did this happen?" asked Ali Bey.

"He went in to see her, just bird-dogging her to see what information he might glean, but it was as if she was already ahead of him and waiting for him. I have been able to talk to him and find out something of what happened, but he is no longer fit for duty and he has the shakes.

"When he entered her establishment, she was wearing a very risque see-through, and he admittedly could not help but succumb to her alluring behavior. She is a rather attractive lady, but with a potentially hard edge that I could easily see transmuting into something rather ominous."

"Exactly!" said Ali-Bey in agreement.

"But I wouldn't have said that about her based upon my own earlier encounters," said Heidi. "She turned into the exact opposite. Giving a reading to Mack, she quickly steered him into sexuality and he completely succumbed to her. Besides being a lousy case of investigation, the sexuality would not have been so bad in and of itself. Unfortunately, it somehow short-circuited him. It was as if he was drugged."

"Was he drugged?" asked Ali.

"The medicos have found no evidence of that. It is as if she blanketed him with a highly potent type of voodoo or occult sexuality. I think they call it macumba. I've heard about this sort of thing, but I have never actually seen or known anyone who experienced it. This poor man has been wrapped around a telephone pole and it is questionable as to whether he will recover. I have never seen anything like it."

"What is his current state like?" asked Ali.

"At first, right after his first encounter with her, he was just excited to see her again. Soon after, however, he became completely obsessed about seeing her and right away. When she said she could not see him, he began to press the issue and finally just fell apart. It was as if he could not wait another minute to see her. When she then indicated she could not see him again at all, it made him go bananas. He soon became catatonic and also screamed and hallucinated at times. We got him to the doctor and he is on medication, but it is a very nasty situation. The doctors do not fully know what I know. I got that out of him before and after his psychotic break, but he trusts me. I have told him to lay low about the investigation if he can, and I feel that he might comply. As it is, he's half-in and half-out of consciousness. Mostly, I am worried about him. Of equal importance, however, is that the investigation has been compromised. I am now the only investigator left, and here I am talking to a civilian."

"This is highly irregular, isn't it — for you to be talking to a civilian over such matters?" asked Ali.

"Look it," she said. "I am a female, and I have feminine intuition. I know you're a good person, and I trust you. I know you are on the level."

"You know, there are some herbs that could help your friend," said Ali Bey.

"Oh?" asked Heidi.

"Yes, and I will give you a card of a botanica where some friends of mine work. I'm sure Colonel Mack can be helped. From what you say, however, it might not be too easy."

"Ali," said Heidi, almost in tears, "I don't know what to do. I may be a strong woman and a capable soldier, but this entire investigation was a little over the top from the beginning. Hugh was obsessed with Hess and all of that has gotten us involved in a deep pile of dung."

"We can only go on what we know," said Ali. "What I find most intriguing in this entire equation is that shipment of goods that is coming to me."

"You mean the electronic gear?" asked Heidi.

"Yes!" replied Ali. "I have no idea what it is. Where is it now?"

"It should be in the Lion's Paw truck," replied Heidi. "It was carted away and would have been taken to a junk yard of some sort. It would be up to Lion's Paw to go and recover the shipment. They might have done that already."

"Perhaps we should check out Lion's Paw," said Ali Bey. "I am interested in getting my lamps, but I'd also like to know what that gear is intended for and why it's coming to me."

"The book!" exclaimed Heidi.

"The book?" asked Ali. "What do you mean about the book?"

"It's that book!" replied Heidi. "That material is being forwarded to you because you have the book."

"How do you figure that?" asked Ali.

"I just remembered something," said Heidi. "Before he freaked out, Colonel Mack gave me some details from the bill of lading conveyed by Lion's Paw. It originally had "Konrad" on it, but his name was scratched out and yours was put in."

"How could that be?" asked Ali. "Who did it?"

"It was done by whoever was filling out the order." said Heidi. "Konrad is the rightful owner of the book, and he is the original recipient. When he died, it was somehow concluded that the shipment must go to the new owner of the book and that is you; or at least it was at the time the order was made out."

"Now it's you!" exclaimed Ali Bey.

"What do you mean?" asked Heidi.

"I mean that if your theory is correct," answered Ali, "the equipment will be redirected to you."

"Oh my God!" said Heidi. "You are right! The book is now in my possession."

"Where is it now?" asked Ali. "Is it safe?"

"I left it in my office which has been compromised before by shrinks. We better get back there fast. Can you come with me?"

"Sure," said Ali. "It'll just take me a couple of minutes to close up the shop."

Heidi and Ali Bey then hurried to her car so that they could get back to the base as soon as was humanly possible.

......CHAPTER THIRTY-FIVE......

## LITTLE PEOPLE

Entering the Montauk underground, Chewey, Gibby and the Dropa doctor all looked for Crowley's steps in order that they could trace him. With their own special sensitivities to such matters, they could readily tell he had entered this portal, but they knew their tiny legs would not assist them in catching him if he tried to elude them in a foot race.

Making their way to a corridor, they saw Mau, the archivist. He was standing over a slumped Wilson whose head was resting on a desk. The general had not yet recovered from his feinting spell.

"Hello," said Mau to his fellow little men. "What brings you here?"

"There is a large man that we're looking for. He is wearing black and has eyes that are rather stone cold. Have you seen him?" asked Chewey.

"I certainly have," replied Mau. "He was back in the archives looking for some things. Unfortunately, this man over here at the desk had feinted and I was tending to him. At that exact point, the man you describe lurched out and ran away with a bag full of archival tapes. My legs are not quick enough to catch him. I pushed a security button, but there is no way they could have gotten to him in time. I think he headed for a portal."

"Sure!" said Chewey. "I'll bet he was watching this portal as we came into this realm and then escaped as we entered. He's not like the usual dim-witted humans. Besides being clever, he's very good about not advertizing the fact."

"Are you going to track him down and help me retrieve the archives?" asked Mau.

"I can track him down all right," said Chewey, "but only to his own realm. Once he gets there, I will be somewhat at a disadvantage. It's my realm, too, but I don't quite have the necessary pull in the big people's world. I can try and pull some strings though."

"What's going on over there?" asked the Dropa doctor who was looking at Wilson. "What is his malady?"

# LITTLE PEOPLE................

"He was asking for *the book*," said the archivist. "He began to get woozy and eventually feinted."

"You mean *the* book?" said the Dropa doctor. "I've heard legends about that, but I never knew it actually existed."

"Well," said Mau, "there are different books for different dimensions. The one he is referring to is a fabled book that lists a history of the major technical developments and scientific breakthroughs in his world. All of them were preceded by the help of the Wilson Brothers."

"The Wilson Brothers?" asked the Dropa.

"Indeed!" said Mau. "Have you heard of them?"

"Certainly I've heard of the Wilson Brothers," said the doctor, "but I'd better tend to this patient right now."

The Dropa doctor walked over to Wilson and felt his pulse. He then placed his hands on various points on the body. After a short while, he removed the general's shoes and began massaging his feet meticulously. The general soon responded by waking up.

"I feel much better. What is going on now?" asked General Wilson. "I remember feinting, but I do not remember seeing all of you."

"You just asked for *the book*," said the doctor.

"What book?" asked Wilson.

"You know, *the* book, the one about technology."

"I'm sorry," said Wilson. "I do not remember and have no idea why I would have said such a thing. Who are these people?"

"These are some of my friends," said Mau, "but this doctor I am meeting for the first time. It is a good thing he came along, otherwise I wouldn't have known what to do for you except to call for security and get some help."

"I don't know if that would have been a good idea," said Chewey.

"Why not?" asked Mau.

"Because he is not one of 'them.' He doesn't belong here," said Chewey.

"Oh?" asked Mau. "Perhaps I should call security after all."

"No," said Chewey. "Don't do that. It will only be a bother to all of us or perhaps worse."

"He comes from another world," said Gibby.

"The people you work with in this underground," said

Chewey to Mau, "are of an entirely different order than General Wilson."

"I'm afraid I don't understand," said General Wilson. "It's clear to all of you that I do not belong her. This is most certainly true."

"Except for the fact," said Chewey, "that you are here."

"If that is the case, perhaps you could explain it all to me," said Wilson.

"You are in a different world indeed," said Chewey.

"As I said, that is clear to me," replied Wilson. "That's why I am asking you what sort of world I am in. Can you tell me? Can you explain?"

"Where we are now is sacred space," said Chewey, "but all of these materials and installations here are an interface between our world and all other worlds."

"What do you mean?" asked Wilson. "Where do you come from?"

"Actually, I live in another world that is not much different from yours," said Chewey, "but it is different. The entire cosmos consists of many universes and many different time lines. You are alive in only one and I am alive in another. The difference with me, however, is that I know how to slip between worlds. My lineage is of the Mackiowi, the Little People. We are the original settlers of the locale here that is known as Montauk in both your world and in my world. You have no idea of the complexities and behind the scenes activities required to prop up a world such as you live in. Besides living in a world such as yours, I have a role where I serve as a conduit to other worlds. That is how I was selected and arrived here."

"If you come from another world," said Wilson, "why are you here with me now in this one?"

"I am actually in pursuit of the man who was in here earlier and made off with some critical video tapes. By the way Mau, what did this intruder take?"

"My cursory inspection indicates that he took the entirety of the life of Christ, including the missing years," said Mau. "What did you say his name was?"

"It is Crowley, Aleister Crowley," said Chewey.

"My God!" exclaimed Wilson.

"You know him?" asked Chewey.

LITTLE PEOPLE . . . . . . . . . . . . . . . . . .

"Do I know him? Indeed! Well, not personally, but he lived as a notorious occultist in my world. As a matter of fact, he fashioned himself as the Antichrist. It would therefore make perfect sense that he would take videos of the missing years of Christ and strip it from the records."

"He came to me in my own world" said Chewey. "He asked for a paid tour of the underground and crossed Gibby's palm with silver. He was worked over pretty good by some of our little friends, but he was allowed a look into another world. We will offer that to anyone for the asking. Being the mischievous characters we are, however, Gibby and I played games with him and left him to his own devices. That is sometimes how you test someone's mettle. He, however, turned out to be a little more to handle than we expected. He caught up with our doctor friend here. Now, he's lost on his tour and is deliberately evading us. We have to take him back to whence he came. If not, he might create some trouble."

"Perhaps he already has," said Wilson.

"Don't worry," said Chewey. "We'll track him down all right. First, however, I think there are some tapes that you should look at?"

"Why is that?" asked Wilson.

"As I said earlier, by good fortune or otherwise, you have stumbled upon sacred ground underneath Montauk Point. There is more to this world than meets the eye and there are more to these other worlds as well."

Chewey then went back to the archives and retrieved some tapes that were summaries of important historical incidents. He gave them to Wilson to review.

"Have him watch these," he said to the archivist. "I think he'll find them instructive and useful in understanding what is going on. In the meantime, we'd better go find our client before he creates too much more of a ruckus."

"You mean that you are going to hunt down the beast?" asked Wilson.

"Something like that," said Chewey as he turned and ran back towards the portal with his two comrades.

·······CHAPTER THIRTY-SIX········

## LION'S PAW REVISITED

When Heidi arrived with Ali Bey at Lion's Paw, she arranged to speak to the same manager they had seen before. She was careful to remind him that this was a formal military investigation of a crime and that now, as a result of the accident with General Wilson, it was crucial that Lion's Paw be as informative as possible under the circumstances.

"Gee, I'm sorry that this happened to the general," said the manager. "Our driver seems to be OK."

"Crowley, right?" asked Heidi.

"Yes, that is his name," said the manager.

"I understand that the goods aboard the truck were to be delivered to Ali Bey here, right?" asked Heidi.

"If this man is Ali Bey, you are quite right. The goods are now in our warehouse and waiting to be delivered. There's something funny here though ma'am," said the manager who was perusing the work order for the shipment. "We received a fax that part of the delivery was to be redirected to yourself. The lamps were and still are scheduled to be delivered to Ali Bey, but the equipment in back was changed. We received an order correction instructing us to deliver it to you. You are the same Heidi that is listed on this address here — it is to a military base in Virginia, right?"

"This is too much!" exclaimed Heidi. "Where on earth did this fax come from? Who sent it?"

"The origin of the shipment as well as the correction came from Montauk."

"Who?" insisted Heidi.

"Tom Hailey," stated the manager.

"The cop?" asked Heidi incredulously.

"I don't know him as a cop. He's just the name who sent the original order so it is in order that he was the one who changed it," said the manager.

"I can't believe it!" said Heidi. Let me explain something to both of you. This is the same name used by a man impersonating a cop at Montauk. He not only answered the general's 911 call to the crime scene where Konrad was killed

253

but is now on the other end of this strange shipment. You see, when the general went to follow up on the police investigation the next day, the police claimed there was no Tom Hailey. There was a policeman on the force by that name a year or two before, but he had died."

"I'm afraid I don't understand how this all fits together," said the manager.

"I don't understand either, but I am beginning to understand," said Heidi. "Someone is playing some kind of very strange game and they are using this name, 'Tom Hailey,' as a decoy. The person who was involved with the murder of your client, Konrad, has changed the direction of the shipment from Ali Bey to me."

"I don't know what to say, ma'am, but it seems that many orders we have from Montauk are strange."

"How so?" asked Heidi.

"I could keep you up all night telling strange tales about that place; but frankly, I don't think you have the time for it."

"You're right," she said, "but I might need to come back to you. Just arrange for the shipments as-is and please be available if I need to talk to you again."

"Sure thing," said the manager.

Heidi then escorted Ali Bey out of the building as rapidly as possible. They soon found a nearby park where they could sit down and not be heard. When they were alone and comfortable that there was no surveillance, Heidi spoke.

"It's obvious what happened here," she stated to Ali. "The order was changed because the book shifted from you to me. Somehow or another, the name used to change the order was the same one used to obscure the murder of Konrad."

"It's all rather unbelievable for a story we already seem compelled to believe," replied Ali Bey. "First and foremost, I must apprise you that you are dealing with an agent of illusion."

"You mean the name of this man and whoever is behind it?" asked Heidi.

"Exactly!" replied Ali. "It is a magician."

"Agreed," said Heidi. "Crowley?"

"I don't know," said Ali, "You are dealing with a magician or the realm of the dead. Did not this character, Tom Hailey, die?"

"Yes," said Heidi.

"OK," said Ali. "You have to consider the prospect that it really might be Tom Hailey but from the other side."

"Good point," said Heidi. "Now, let me run some stuff by you, just as a thinking exercise."

"Sure, go ahead," said Ali.

"We attracted the psychiatrists because of the investigation Wilson was conducting on Hess. We traced the shrinks back to Konrad, and he was killed. Perhaps he was killed for losing the book. In any event, the shipment that is now coming to me was originally supposed to come to him."

"Do you think," interrupted Ali, "that you could be in danger just as Konrad was? That is a logical assumption."

"It is a distinct possibility," said Heidi. "On the other hand, it seems that they want to deliver it to me. The shipment was only redirected when Konrad was wiped out. The redirection might have to do with him being no longer relevant to the shipment. On the other hand, there could be another reason at work that I have not suspected."

"If you ask me," said Ali, "I think Konrad was wiped out because someone was afraid the general would get to him and find out things that were not meant to be known."

"That would be the most apparent explanation," said Heidi, "but it all occurred at the same time that Konrad lost the book."

"I agree," said Ali.

"Now," said Heidi, "let me continue with the facts. Konrad was killed for some reason, possibly as just mentioned. In the pursuit of this investigation, the general and colonel discovered all sorts of strange time anomalies and mind control concerning the town of Montauk."

"That should not surprise us," said Ali.

"I wish you wouldn't interrupt me until I state all the facts, but I have to ask you — why do you say that? You are sounding just like the manager of Lion's Paw."

"Because," said Ali, "that place has a very strange tradition and history."

"Oh?" asked Heidi.

"Yes, it does. In ancient times, it was a pass-through point for ancient knowledge. The Egyptians and so-called lost tribes of Israel migrated to that point. Some tribes went to Europe and then migrated to the East Coast. Montauk was a central point of reference, sort of a way station. Other tribes migrated to Latin America via the Caribbean.

"Many others came straight through to Montauk before settling in other places across the United States. It was a pivotal headquarters. There is even a location in Missouri named Montauk. It was named after the homeland in New York. This was from mound builders who came many centuries ago. Besides migrating to Missouri, these mound builders travelled all the way from Montauk to Ohio and as far as Wisconsin. They built mounds, left mummies and were known as Pharaohs. There are many Egyptian plates that have been found in archeological digs in these areas."

"Egyptian plates?" asked Heidi. "You're kidding!"

"No, I am not," said Ali. "These are verifiable and there are many reliable accounts. If you look in the Smithsonian basement, you might find some. My people have recorded this sacred knowledge, but there has been a large counter-force seeking to destroy our history."

"OK," said Heidi, "I will take it for granted that Montauk is not only a strange place but a locale replete with great historical significance and even that it was a conduit for sacred energy. For now, however, let me continue with stating the facts of our case."

"Fair enough," said Ali. "Continue."

"Hess leads to the psychiatrists who lead to Konrad. Next, we get a very strange shipment of goods that is following Konrad until he is dead. Then, the goods are slated for you until you give the book to me whereupon they are slated for me. This book is an attractor in terms of energy."

"Like attracts like," said Ali. "Now, continue before your thoughts are interrupted any further."

"Thank you," said Heidi. "According to Colonel Mack, the whole police force at Montauk seems to be in on the conspiracy, and they are further backed by some sort of military presence. Whatever is going on there is classified to the point that we do not have access. It is a great puzzle, Ali. Tell me what you think."

"You have the shipment coming to you," said Ali. "It is apparently tied to the book that was originally intended for Konrad. Konrad is apparently tied to the psychiatrists coming after the general. It is Konrad himself that is tied to the two biggest mysteries here: the assault by the shrinks and the mysterious book. Don't forget that the whole intrigue began when the general got hot on the trail of Hess. The doctor seemed to be caught in the interference and is liquidated as a result. It is as if the equipment was perhaps chasing Konrad."

"Did you consider that the book and Konrad might represent opposing forces?" asked Heidi. "Perhaps the book represents real truth and Konrad's faction is the oppression of that truth."

"If that is true," said Ali, "it does not explain why the shipment was sent to him."

"It just occurred to me, Ali, that whoever killed Konrad could have been the guardian of that equipment."

"Or the book," said Ali.

"Or both," said Heidi, "The book and equipment are inextricably linked together."

"Yes, it's like a jinn who is directing or orchestrating the movement of the book and the technical equipment that goes with it," said Ali.

"And it's all likely tied to the technology in that book and the Wilson Brothers," responded Heidi.

"Yes," said Ali, "and don't forget that the general is also named Wilson. The last names are the same."

"I never thought of that," said Heidi, "but you're right."

"If it is a jinn," said Ali, "keep in mind that they can be ruthless in accomplishing their purpose. Konrad could have been wasted as simply being in the way."

"That puts a positive spin on it from my view," said Heidi, "because Konrad was behind the shrinks. You experienced some sort of divine guidance and that is what eventually put the book in my hands. Maybe that was meant to be."

"Excellent point," said Ali. "As we speak, the equipment is almost in the hands of the general himself because you are his secretary — all as a result of him getting in the way of their concealment of the Hess issues. I think whatever is going on has a lot to do with Hess. As soon as the general stuck his neck out of the rabbit hole, he unwittingly became a competitor to something in the supernatural realm. It was a collision course and ended up being a literal collision with the truck from Lion's Paw. Let me tell you something, Heidi. There is far more going on here than meets our eyes or other perceptions. It has to do with the name Lion's Paw. It is already a symbolic and suggestive name in and of itself."

"How is that?" asked Heidi.

"In Freemasonry, a lion's paw is the symbol of the potential resurrection of Mankind. As per the doctrines of Masonry, the builder of Solomon's Temple was Hiram Abiff. He was killed for not revealing the secret of the Temple. After Hiram's death, King Solomon ordered his fellow Masons to resurrect the slain builder but none could do the job. The task was finally relegated to Solomon himself who used the Lion's Grip to perform the resurrection of Hiram. It worked. The Lion's Grip is a secret code of resurrection."

"If that is all so, I find it quite odd that this company somehow acquired the name Lion's Paw," asked Heidi. "There must be an interesting story behind that, don't you think?"

"It could also be a mundane story. I have no idea. You can ask the manager, but it is not important. What is important is the symbolism involved here. Like attracts like. Somehow or another, Wilson's keen interest in the Hess affair inculcated the theme of the Lion's Paw into his life, but this fits in very nicely with what I told you about the jinn controlling or influencing the book."

"How is that?" asked Heidi.

"Because," said Ali, "Solomon was the master of the jinn. They did his bidding. A jinn is at work here!"

"This is all too bizarre!" said Heidi, "but I can also see that it is true. In any event this influence damn near killed him!"

"Perhaps," said Ali, "but you yourself said that he should be all right. What doesn't kill him might also prove to be the source of solving these riddles and mysteries. I feel that there are bigger implications here."

"I've seen enough of these secrets in action to understand now," said Heidi. "If this Lion's Grip is their big secret, it is more than ironic that Lion's Paw would come into his life in such a way. There is a principle at work here."

"True," said Ali. "That is the way things work. When you penetrate occult secrets, you open up caverns and corridors of a labyrinth. In our culture, there are many secret societies as well as different factions of Freemasonry. The players in these organizations occupy the corridors within the catacombs of these secrets. There are problems with most of these factions though. Many of them are derivatives of an ancient order. The original Masons are said to have derived from King Solomon himself. The York Rite of Freemasonry derives from the Jewish tradition. The Scottish, which is called Speculative Freemasonry, is a version embraced by Catholics and an attempt to rival the York Rite. All of these, however, are impostors from the original. We had Masonry in American long before Columbus. But, let us get back to the investigation."

"The background is fascinating and relevant, but we need to stick to the facts of the case," said Heidi.

"You're right," said Ali.

"The Hess affair," said Heidi, "inculcated interference from a quarter that traces back to both mind control and time travel. No matter what else we say or think, it is really that simple. Both of these come from or are associated with Montauk Point. Remember, Konrad was fleeing to Montauk Point, apparently as a result of our scrutiny. The duplicity employed there over his murder scene is a further example of mind control. Now, we are also baited with the proposition of equipment following the book."

"That is only because we took the book," said Ali.

"And remember," said Heidi, "you only took the book because you were moved by a unique experience to grab it. It was as if a spirit was watching over you."

"True," agreed Ali.

"When you told me the story about the book originally, I had a feeling that it was a good spirit and perhaps a life-opening experience," said Heidi.

"It has indeed been a life-opening experience," said Ali, "but I believe it is wrong to judge the spirit at work as being either good or bad."

"Why is that?" asked Heidi.

"Because there is always a good side and a bad side to anything — a dark side and a light side. An angel is only one side of a two-sided coin with a demon being on the other."

"Are you saying that maybe all of these characters connected to Montauk are not all that bad?" asked Heidi. "After all I've seen, they seem pretty sinister to me."

"I would not say they are good," said Ali, "except for perhaps with regard to one particular point. By their actions they have expanded our horizons not only of what is but what else might be possible in this world. That is not a bad thing."

"I agree," said Heidi.

"Traditionally," said Ali, "a two-headed coin with an angel and demon on it represents a gateway to heaven. In Rome, there was a coin for the god Janus who looked two ways, forwards and backwards. He was a god to time. After that, when the Christians came along, the angel represented the entrance to heaven. The demon meant you had to pay a price before you could pass. The symbolism in this tradition is very rich. The literalness of it being represented on a coin is suggestive that an aspirant to heaven might have to pay for his karmic baggage. The demon made you look at your past. If you were clean, the angel greeted you."

"I don't know what my past is to deserve this!" said Heidi.

"Up to now," said Ali, "the general and the colonel have suffered most of the fallout. You, however, are now facing the proposition of being greeted with a strange shipment that appears as neither a demon nor an angel, just strange. I look forward to seeing it."

"It may not be an angel or demon," said Heidi, "but I strongly believe it represents a gateway of some sort."

"An excellent supposition!" said Ali. "You will always find a jinn at a gateway. It is also traditional to see lions at a gateway. The Chinese use this symbolism a lot."

"I agree that there are gate-keepers involved," said Heidi. "It is a very strange gate. The gate-keeper, however, seems to be one Tom Hailey who is quite invisible. His appearance thus far seems more like a demon."

"I agree," said Ali. "The only thing I have to say about him, however, is that he comes from the realm of the dead."

"True," said Heidi.

"How about we check out that equipment?" said Ali.

"We have to see General Wilson first. The equipment is not likely to arrive until tomorrow at the soonest."

The two left the park bench and headed for the hospital.

## CHAPTER THIRTY-SEVEN

### R.E.M.

When it finally occurred to Wilson that he could open his eyes, he looked up and saw the naked chest of a very beautiful lady. This caused him disorientation as he was not quite sure where he was; and further, he had absolutely no recognition of any memory that might place him in such a unique and questionably favorable position. As he continued to look, he saw the woman moving in some sort of strange rhythm. She appeared to be self-absorbed as she did not seem to notice that he had now awoken from his coma.

"Did I die and go to heaven?" he thought to himself. "If this is heaven, I have gotten off to a very good start!"

"General!" said Gretchen who was laying straddled over him as she went through her strange motions. "You're awake!"

Gretchen reached down and hugged him with her completely naked body.

"Wow!" thought Wilson to himself, "this gets better and better."

He now recognized that the beautiful girl was Gretchen.

"What did I do to deserve all this?" he asked her.

"Oh!" she said, now reflecting on the fact that she was completely naked and out-of-context with anything society might consider to be normal or acceptable behavior. "I've been doing some procedures on you."

"That's quite evident," said Wilson with a wry smile. "I have to admit, Gretchen, if I were to wake up in a hospital after an accident, I can't imagine a better welcoming committee."

"Do you remember the accident?" said Gretchen, seemingly oblivious to her own nakedness.

"I remember blanking out as we hit a truck. I also remember an ambulance and an EMT saying my body functions looked OK. Then I went out again."

"Do you remember anything else?" she asked.

"Oh yeah," he said with a big smile. "I remember more than anyone would expect."

"What do you mean?" she asked.

"You might say I had a huge revelation while I was 'sleeping,'" said Wilson. "I don't know exactly what happened, but you might say I've arrived at about every answer I could ever imagine. Except for one thing."

"What's that?" asked Gretchen.

"Perhaps I shouldn't spoil it by asking."

"Asking what?"

"Why you are naked and sitting on me?"

"Oh!" she said, "I forgot. There are a lot of things I have to tell you."

"I sure hope so," said Wilson who was highly amused and entertained by these sensuous surroundings.

"I am trained in some very arcane tantric disciplines. Heidi authorized me to ensure your safety. There are guards outside for your own security, but I am the only one allowed inside besides the doctors and nurses."

"I hope you have a good explanation if they walk in on you," Wilson laughed.

"Oh, no — I know their schedule and they are aware I am doing an R.E.M. therapy with you," she said.

"R.E.M.?"

"Yes, R.E.M. stands for rapid-eye-movement and refers to the way a person's eyes move when he is in the dream state. When you first came in here, you were not looking too good. It seemed like you were a million miles away."

"I was," said Wilson.

"Yes, but it looked we might lose you, at least according to my calculations that is. But as I said, I am trained in some very obscure and arcane tantric arts that I learned from one of my aunts in Germany. She learned them in Tibet as part of her training as a Vril medium."

"I had no idea, Gretchen. Tell me more," said Wilson.

"There is so much more to tell you, and I haven't had the opportunity until now. This is admittedly a strange time to tell you, but perhaps it is appropriate now."

"I'm ready and waiting. I have a lot of things to say myself, but I think you'd better go first."

"I am the granddaughter of Rudolph Hess," said Gretchen.

Up until now, Wilson's face had betrayed a certain bemusement over the circumstances of this naked woman lying atop him. This bemusement was mixed with a countenance of earnest sobriety that was clearly reflective of his intense and proven survival instincts. When Gretchen uttered that she was the granddaughter of Hess, however, his expression turned to one of being completely flabbergasted. He was in ontological shock.

"Don't worry," she tried to reassure him, "I am telling you the God's honest truth. Rudolph Hess was the father of my mother, but it was out of wedlock. You see, my grandfather was one of the most powerful men in the world at his peak. Some people can convincingly argue that he was even more powerful than Hitler. His influence required an entire prison to hold him and hold him alone; and that lasted some forty years after the Nazi empire was subdued.

"There is more to the entire story," she said, "and no one deserves to hear it more than you."

"I wish you would have told me this earlier," he said.

"Oh no you don't," she said. "I might have been singled out for eradication so I had to wait until I saw you in person. Up to now, you have been too busy and this is really my first opportunity to talk to you alone."

"Keep talking," said Wilson whose expression had now changed to being clearly inquisitive.

"My grandfather had a harem of women. They were outside of his marriage and hidden from his family, but he loved each and every one of them. He took excellent care of them, too, at least while he was in power. My mother was one of them, and she was one of the Vril Society mediums. They were not really part of the Vril Society however. They were their own group sort of within the Vril Society. All of them were psychically adept and I share this lineage. I hope you understand that this is where my nakedness fits in.

"As I said, I was trained in tantra and was sent to Tibet when I reached adulthood. I learned some very advanced and powerful techniques that include R.E.M. or rapid-eye-movement during sleep. I can control or influence dreams."

Wilson's eyes perked up. He was keenly aware that the incredible experiences he had just gone through in the underground of Montauk were something akin to a dream. He remembered them in great detail and this was an advantage because it was very clear to him that what he had experienced was virtually true if not absolutely true in a so-called objective sense. In other words, he was certain he could apply the data and experiences of his dream to the real world with success.

"I had many remarkable experiences while I was out," said Wilson. "Was I dreaming?"

"It is not that simple," she said. "The actual prospect of what was going on with you while you were unconscious is far more exotic. There is a factor which makes up what we know as dreaming. People think of dreams and let them go as that. They are most often viewed as replications of unresolved issues, often on a deep level, or as dramatizations of deep emotions and archetypes inside of us that are longing to be expressed. There is another component as to what makes up dreams though and that is what I work with.

"When the dreamer goes into dream land, he is accessing a part of his brain that is not only tied to his deeper emotions and archetypes but is also tied to what Jung called the collective unconscious. In other words, all morphogenetic beings share a common thread of consciousness of the ecosystem that is reflected in the brain which is acting like an antenna. That is where the equation becomes extremely interesting to an astute observer. There are also spirits from various factions that can or might seek to influence various individuals. It is this part of the brain apparatus that is being used when these spirits make their inroads. Quite obviously, different individuals attract different spirits from various places."

"The brain is an antenna for spirits?" asked Wilson.

"Yes, I learned this in a Tibetan monastery where they have a myriad of techniques directed at this sort of thing. It is something they have obviously practiced for thousands of years. When I trained with them though, I was aghast at the propensity of the monks to misuse this energy. Some were very kind and Buddha-like, but I saw too many that were using these techniques to accrue energy like a spiritual vampire. Some used it clearly for sexual ecstasy. Sexual ecstacy is a part of the technique, but it is not really the same type of sexual energy that people normally think of. It uses the same channels as reproduction but it is designed to heal, transmute energy or to accomplish something more concrete than just ordinary sex would be expected to do. What I am doing is a highly esoteric technique and one that is jealously and sometimes viciously guarded. It is all closely related to that part of your dream state that is accompanied by rapid-eye-movement or R.E.M."

"Was I dreaming when I had all those wild experiences I just had at Montauk?" asked Wilson.

"Yes and no," said Gretchen.

"When I first came in, you weren't doing much of anything. There was virtually no R.E.M. going on. As I hung around, I could see you were glad to have somebody here even if you were not too consciously aware of it. I can sort of read minds. Finally, I began to see a flicker, just a flicker of eye movement in your body. I was then able to zone in and start cultivating it. That's when I got naked. I not only like to work that way as a tantrika, but my nakedness also made your closed eyeballs run kind of wild."

"I don't remember having any sexual dreams or experiences," said Wilson.

"You wouldn't necessarily have had any. I was using my mind far more than my body in all of this. Watching and increasing your rapid-eye-movement, I was able to guide and direct you. Mostly, but not exclusively, I was encouraging you towards more and more rapid-eye-movement. It got very intense. In fact, I've never seen anyone have such intense rapid-eye-movement. If this state can be prolonged and guided correctly, it results in an individual being able to work out the most difficult problems."

"I was travelling in time," said Wilson. "Well...no...that's not exactly correct. I was watching people back in time. It was as if I had a view into the past and was watching actual events. What made it so incredible is that it not only played off of real events and people but gave me great insights into what was or is really going on. I haven't tested it yet — after all, I'm still in the hospital — but I know that what I've experienced is on the mark for the most part. It all makes sense."

"Your soul was in shock and disconnected when I came in," said Gretchen. "The first source of connection to your body is through your eyes. I had to get those moving. The eyes are the window to the soul. I don't know that much about you, but I know enough to know that you are extremely interested in the mysteries surrounding my grandfather. I am, too, and perhaps that helped a lot with the rapport I was able to develop with you. It was obvious that your soul, once it got balanced and referenced with the rapid-eye-movement, was going a mile a minute trying to work out the same goals you would have been working on had you been awake. The mind is a miraculous vehicle. When you have it in a raw and unbridled state, you can tap right into the powers of the psychic realm."

"So, were you making me psychic while I was out?" asked Wilson.

"Sort of, but it can get very tricky," she said. "That's where my training comes in handy. You were ready, but you needed me to open the door for you a little bit and then hold it open. Serendipitously, I think the accident helped me access you on a deeper level than I would have been able to otherwise. You have been putting all the effort of a commando into getting to the bottom of my grandfather's situation. When you put in that much effort, it is as good as a magical ritual. You're going to get some sort of result. In your near-death or out-of-body state, you were able to tap right into all the astral accoutrements surrounding my father, and we both know those run pretty deep."

"I'll say," said Wilson.

The door knob then turned. Wilson had no idea who would be entering, but he was wondering how in the hell Gretchen was going to explain her unclothed condition, let alone the fact that she was still straddling him as they talked.

...... CHAPTER THIRTY-EIGHT ......

## MEN-A-TOL

Ian Fleming is most famous in popular culture for his authoring of the James Bond novels. To historians, however, he is most well known for his cunning role in inducing Rudolph Hess to fly to Scotland in order to conduct peace negotiations with the British.

Peace could easily have been arranged from the German perspective as they were willing to make considerable concessions to both France and England. The British, however, had an entirely different agenda. Their intelligence network was deliberately engaging Hess in duplicity so as to lure him to England and then use him as an instrument of propaganda against the Germans. This is usually the most agreed upon account of what happened by historians. In the final measure, however, the propaganda coup does not add up. Other than obvious and dutiful reporting of Hess flying to Scotland and being incarcerated, there was never any propaganda campaign in the press. Hess was not involved in military operations so his knowledge of troop movements would have been scant at best. History is therefore forced to ask why the top minds of British intelligence dedicated so much time to him.

History is quite clear that most of the negotiations to induce Hess were centered around two noteworthy individuals: Ian Fleming and Albrecht Haushofer, the Jewish son of Karl Haushofer (whose wife was half Jewish). Albrecht, who was officially "Aryanized" by Hess, worked in the German diplomatic corps but was never a Nazi. He and Fleming indulged in frequent correspondence via Viola Roberts in Lisbon. Meetings were also held in that city between Haushofer and Fleming, but Hess's English contacts never agreed to meet the Deputy Fuhrer in Lisbon. It is also true, that by reason of their occult ties, Albrecht and Karl Haushofer met with Crowley in an attempt to secure the meeting between Hess and the English duplicitors.

After a series of involved meetings, Crowley was paid by intelligence to concoct an elaborate ceremony in the Ashdown Forest which included several participating occultists. Several

## MEN-A-TOL . . . . . . . . . . . . . . . . . . . .

people of the military and intelligence communities witnessed this as well. A dummy of Rudolph Hess was put together and inserted into a plane of crude construction. This set-up was rigged so that at the end of the ceremony, the dummy plane and pilot would "fly" across an open space while harnessed to a line that was tied to the top of a tree and staked to the ground in a representation of their desire for Hess to fly to Great Britain. Although it is impossible to prove that the occult ritual enabled the flight to take place, it is quite certain that the occultists believed themselves responsible for bringing Hess to the British Isles. Crowley was the orchestra leader who waved the wand, but Ian Fleming was his employer.

While no one has ever denied the association between Crowley and Fleming, history offers only scant reports of their association with virtually all of it being centered upon the Hess affair. The association between Crowley and Fleming, however, runs far deeper.

Both were serious students of the Enochian language recorded by John Dee as well as all of the magical associations that went with him. As the founder of what became the British Empire, John Dee and his work sit at the fulcrum of power in the Western world. Whether the temporal powers of the world are aware of it or not, informed students of the occult are keenly aware of this principle and why it is so.

The Enochian language Dee transcribed has not only been recognized to conform to a logical structure and syntax, but it is in fact the language itself that Solomon used to consolidate the state of Israel. History (which conforms more to legend that what is commonly considered history) claims that the language was taught to Enoch by Adam, the original man. It is a language designed to communicate with the angelic realm and thereby enlist their efforts in earthly affairs.

John Dee's code number was 007, and it was for this reason that Ian Fleming utilized this number in his James Bond novels and identified himself with it. Ian Fleming also got his idea of collecting rare manuscripts and books from John Dee. Both of them referred to their specific collections as an *Incunabula*.

It was against such a background of mystery that Aleister Crowley, Ian Fleming and a third man sat in a pub in Morvah on August 12th of 1943. As a result of his earlier success with the Hess ritual, or at least the apparent success, Fleming was in Cornwall to see that Crowley would conduct another.

"Have you arranged for the payment?" asked Crowley.

"Yes," smiled Fleming in his most nonchalant manner. "It is the least point of my concern. I saw to it myself that it was wired into your account this morning. The money is insignificant compared to what we are to do today."

"I do not always ask for money, you know," said Crowley, "but I feel it is most appropriate for myself and Mr. Nichols."

Crowley was referring to the third person present, Michael Nichols, the Arch Druid of Great Britain.

"Not that it matters to me — you know I can get any amount I want," said Fleming, "but why?"

"I am old and there are many sides to me, but I am beginning to distrust more and more the people you are working for," said Crowley.

"Why?" asked Fleming.

"Long ago I had some friends...the Wilsons...they warned me about all of this," answered Crowley. "As I recall, it was at your christening. *The Book of the Law* foresaw these times. It referred to the warrior lord of the forties. Haushofer recognized this as Hitler, at least for a while, but the warrior lord is far bigger than Hitler. Hitler is now like a marionette. The Hess ritual proved that, but it is not the only proof."

"I must admit that I have had my own doubts, too," said Fleming. "I was charged with overseeing the liquidation of an entire Dutch crew in the Pacific. They had seen the Japanese fleet on their way to Hawaii and notified us. I was ordered to have them eliminated, otherwise the Americans would have been prepared for the attack. Command wanted the Japanese to pull off the Pearl Harbor attack so it would put the Americans on our side for good."

"Typical," said Crowley, "all too typical in war. I am tired of all this now. I am too old, but it is never too late to change. Now — what in the hell are we doing here?"

"A ritual," said Fleming.

"Yes, a ritual. I almost forgot," said Crowley.

"If you keep this up, you're going to make me forget, too," said Fleming.

"OK," said Crowley. "I'll behave and try not to stir up any more trouble for you, but I have one question."

**MEN-A-TOL. . . . . . . . . . . . . . . . . . . .**

"What is that?" asked Fleming.
"Why today?" asked Crowley.
"*That,*" said Fleming, "is an excellent question."
"It is an excellent question indeed," said the Arch Druid.

## CHAPTER THIRTY-NINE

## THE LION'S MOUTH

Heidi and Ali Bey entered Wilson's hospital room only to see a naked Gretchen on top of him. Approaching the bed, Heidi was completely nonplused by Gretchen's naked state. Ali Bey said nothing, but his eyes betrayed surprise and interest.

"Hello," said Heidi to the general. "How are you feeling?"

"Not too bad under the circumstances," smiled Wilson. "Care to join us?" he asked with a smirk on his face.

"Very funny," answered Heidi. "How did you do, Gretchen?"

"We made excellent progress and far beyond what I could have hoped for. He is a gifted subject," said Gretchen.

"Excellent," said Heidi. "I want to hear everything."

"Would somebody mind explaining to me exactly what is going on?" asked Ali Bey.

"I am sorry," said Heidi. "I should have explained to you, but I did not realize we were going to come in upon them this way. Gretchen is specifically trained in esoteric tantric procedures. She was only helping him to regain consciousness and work some things out. I know it looks bizarre. Personally, I am kind of immune to strange behavior myself."

"Why is that?" asked Ali Bey.

"When I hit puberty, my parents died. My uncle was overseas so I became I foster child for a good while and was under the care of Mormon families, some of them being cults apart from the main church. I never bought into the religion, but I was exposed to some very strange things before my uncle came back. What Gretchen is doing neither surprises me nor shocks me. When she told me of her abilities, I encouraged her to use them on the general. He needed help and was out like a light. I never expected to catch her in the act though."

"So, you're not upset?" smirked Wilson.

"Very funny, Hugh," she replied. "Let's get down to business now."

"Where would you like to start?" asked Gretchen.

"Maybe I'd better talk first," said Heidi. "We've got some very serious occurrences happening."

"Like what?" he asked in the most casual of tones. He seemed only barely interested — as if he did not have a care in the world.

"Remember the book?" asked Heidi.

"What book?" asked Wilson.

"The book — you know, the book that Ali Bey found in Dr. Konrad's office. Remember, you sent Gretchen and myself to retrieve it on the day you went to Montauk. We did. It is now in our possession," said Heidi.

"Oh, yes!" said Wilson. "I forgot. You know, I've been rather preoccupied."

"Anyway, we found something very interesting about the book. It was originally in the possession of Konrad and mysteriously went into the hands of Ali Bey. At that exact point, a very odd shipment was redirected from Konrad to Ali by a mysterious source at Montauk, supposedly by a certain Tom Hailey. Quite oddly, it was transported in the very same vehicle from Lion's Paw that struck you. The shipment contained lamps that Ali ordered for his shop, but it also included mysterious electronic equipment, at least four items of which were large coils."

"No kidding?" asked Wilson. "This is getting interesting."

Wilson had the expression of someone who was watching an entertaining show. He no longer was playing the role of an astute intelligence officer but betrayed the expression of an entertained audience. Watching his expression, Heidi showed a puzzlement and irritation but said nothing.

"Something very strange happened after that," continued Heidi. "When Ali gave me the book — and he actually did so — it was is if somebody else knew that it came into my possession. At that exact time, the electrical equipment, but not the lamps, was mysteriously redirected in transit and addressed to me. It is a very long and involved story, but someone all of a sudden knew who I was and my address. I have since determined that whoever possesses this book is designed to receive this mysterious equipment."

"You are being set up for something," said the naked Gretchen.

"A time machine," said Wilson very calmly. He then closed his eyes as if he was going to fall asleep.

"A time machine?" asked Heidi. "You think so?"

"Sure," said Wilson with his eyes closed. "What else could it be? You really shouldn't be so surprised."

A very tired Wilson then fell asleep.

As Wilson slept, Gretchen got Heidi up-to-date on what she had missed during her sessions with the general. When she finished talking, Wilson open his eyes.

"Would you like to hear my story now?" he asked.

Gretchen, who was still naked, listened intently with Ali Bey and Heidi as they all heard the adventures of his visits to Fritz Kraemer, Barry Goldwater and Preston Nichols. He then told them about his witnessing of the drug-induced interrogations of Rudolph Hess.

"Well," said Heidi, "are you going to talk to Kraemer and Goldwater?"

"I already have," said Wilson. "What do you mean?"

"That was in your subconscious or altered state," said Heidi.

"I am quite certain," said Wilson, "that if you contact them, entirely independent of me, they will admit to you that they spoke to me."

"That's impossible," said Heidi. "You've been here all the time. Gretchen can testify to that."

"I have been with him," said Gretchen, "but I can't testify that they have not been with him"

"Why is that?" said Heidi. "Did they come here to visit?"

"Because," said Gretchen, "it is quite possible, and the general seems to intuitively know it, that he could have materialized right before their eyes. He was in a very deep trance state, and we were not only working with a part of the brain that is related to deep visualization but to one that can precipitate into actual manifestation. I was not thinking about it when I was working. I was just trying to guide his energy to resolve the deep issues he has been engrossed with. In other words, his experiences were so real that it was as if the characters he was meeting were indeed before his eyes. On the other hand, the part of the brain that is related to manifestation could have similarly triggered him to have actually manifested before their eyes. The work I do is very potent."

"Like Jesus manifesting before people?" asked Heidi.

"Something like that," responded Gretchen. "You might want to call these characters and find out."

Heidi picked up the phone and spoke directly into it.

"Please give me Fritz Kraemer at the Pentagon," she barked into the phone. "This is an emergency!"

After a few minutes, Heidi heard a voice on the other end of the phone.

"Dr. Kraemer?" she asked. "This is General Hugh Wilson's secretary. Did you hear what happened to him?"

"No," said Kraemer. "Did something go wrong? Is he all right?"

"He suffered an accident, but he seems to be recovering," answered Heidi. "He thought I should let you know."

"Thank you for telling me," said Kraemer. "He was just here the other day. Is it possible that I could talk to him?"

"Sure, he is right here," replied Heidi as she handed the phone to the General.

"Hello, Fritz, my old friend," said Wilson. "I got a little messed up."

"Did you make your trip to Montauk?" asked Fritz.

"Yes! And it nearly finished me off upon my return," said Wilson.

"What injuries did you sustain?"

"Just a concussion as far as I know. I seem to be OK," answered Wilson.

"Very good," replied Kraemer. "Let me know if you need anything whether it is on your investigation or not. I would like to help you if I possibly can."

At that point, there was an unexpected knock at the door. Heidi immediately went to the door as Wilson finished up his conversation with Kraemer. To her utter astonishment, it was Colonel Mack. He was in uniform but barely. He looked disheveled as if he were on the run. Obviously puzzled about how he had gotten out of the sanatarium, Heidi spoke to him.

"How did you end up here, Colonel? Are you OK?"

"I escaped and managed to get home and found this uniform to wear out of the dirty laundry. I hope I don't look too bad, but I had to leave the house quick because that is the first place they would look for me," replied Mack.

"How come you left the hospital?" asked Heidi.

"I was in bad shape, I must admit," said Mack, "but I overheard the doctors talking. I was pretty crazy but not as crazy as they thought. They sometimes talk and think crazy people don't hear them. Believe me, crazy people hear *every* word. I've talked to plenty of crazy people and I know."

"Listen, Colonel Mack," said Heidi, "you're not crazy. You just had a rather severe problem."

"An attack from that voodoo woman if you ask me," interjected Gretchen with a very sympathetic expression.

Colonel Mack's eyes suddenly turned to the naked Gretchen. A very pleasant smile came to his face. He could not believe what he was looking at.

"How the hell are you?" asked Wilson as he looked up at Colonel Mack. "I hear you've been in for a very rough time. I do not look very powerful here in this bed, but I want you to know that I will do anything I can to help you. You are still one of my most dependable men."

"Even now?" asked Mack.

"Let me put in this way," said Wilson. "If I gave you an order, I wouldn't believe for a minute that you would not execute it."

A sudden look of pride waxed across Mack's face.

"Maybe all is not lost after all," he said.

"Why did you leave the hospital?" asked Heidi.

"As I was saying," said Mack, "I was listening to the doctors. They were visited by a psychiatrist who wanted to do some exploratory work on me. It was just talk, but this guy reminded me so much of those idiots we have under lockup that it sort of woke me up. I've been despondent, but I knew these guys would make chopped cabbage out of me. I knew I had to escape and do it fast. Fortunately for me, I had given no prior indication that I wanted to leave. I surprised them."

"They might not even come looking for you," said Heidi.

"True," said Wilson, "not if he was not on a watch list. On the other hand, the shrink might've wanted to get to the bottom of his involvement in our investigation. Good work on getting the hell out of there, Mack."

"Thank you, sir," replied Mack proudly.

"Wait a second," said Heidi, "how did you find us here?"

"You are forgetting that I do police work and intel. That wasn't hard at all," replied Mack.

"Yes, I forgot," said Heidi. "We've got to get you into safety, and we can protect you with our intelligence umbrella. I'll send over someone to get your clothes and have them washed."

# THE LION'S MOUTH . . . . . . . . . . . . . . . . .

"I would like to help him with his other problem," interjected Gretchen.

Hearing this, Mack's face beamed with joy. "I do not know what you have in mind," he said, "but I think I am going to like it."

Ali Bey had a bemused smile on his face.

"How in the name of Allah did I ever end up this situation?" he said as he laughed and shook his head.

"It's simple," said Wilson. "You were looking for that document about your people. You know, the one that spelled out the capitulation of the Moors and the land grant to the Spanish Crown. It goes back to ancient Egypt."

"How do you know about all that?" asked Ali.

"I have a lot more to tell you," said Wilson.

"Me?" said Ali.

"Yes, but now is not the right time," answered Wilson.

At that point, there was another knock on the door. Mack began to bolt for the window but Heidi lightly restrained him with her arm.

"Don't worry," she said to the colonel. "You are protected by my orders. They cannot get to you here."

Mack relaxed a bit as Heidi went to the door once more. She was gone for a short minute and returned.

"Was it for me?" asked Mack.

"No," said Heidi, "it was a nurse. General, they did some blood work on you for precautionary reasons and said that you look fine except that there is an ergot mold in your system."

"Ergot mold?" said Mack, "What on earth is that?"

"Ergot mold is a fungus that grows on wheat. It can be hallucinogenic. LSD is derived from it," said Gretchen.

"Oh my god!" said Heidi. "That might explain some of those experiences the general was having. I guess it can go to the brain from wherever it is in your system."

"Of course," said Gretchen.

"But it still doesn't explain Fritz Kraemer remembering his interaction with the general," said Ali. "There is still some sort of magic voodoo at work here."

"LSD is a mind amplifier," said Gretchen.

"That's exactly right," chimed in Wilson.

"It might've made my work easier or more potent," Gretchen said.

"If it had anything to do with it at all," said Ali.

"True," said Gretchen, "if you want to be clinical, but I think he's been under its influence most of his life."

"Why is that?" asked Heidi.

"Because he's a Wilson," said Gretchen.

"Why is that significant?" asked Colonel Mack.

"The Wilsons are a unique and special clan," answered Gretchen. "In fact, I am a Wilson."

"But I thought you were Rudolph Hess's granddaughter?" asked Wilson.

"You're kidding!" exclaimed Mack.

"No, it's true," said Gretchen. "My grandfather had a harem who were, in fact, mediums for the Vril Society. According to patriarchal society, I am a bastard, but I have no regard for their rules. My mother's surname was Wiligut."

"Wiligut," said Wilson. "That name is familiar. Wasn't there a Wiligut involved with the SS?"

"Yes," said Gretchen. "That was Karl Wiligut, Himmler's rune master. He was an expert on runes and the indigenous people of Europe. My grandmother was a cousin of his."

"How exactly does that make you a Wilson?" asked General Wilson.

"Same family but we have different names in different countries," she said. "Wiligut means 'will of god.' God and the sun have long been associated with each other. They are synonyms from the days of Mithras. The Christians took it one step further and made the sun 'the son.'"

"So, then," spoke Wilson, "my name means 'will of the son, the same as 'the will of God?'"

"It sure does," said Heidi. "It is the same as the Vril."

"Like the film about Hitler, *Triumph of the Will*," he said. "It could just as well have been called '*Triumph of the Vril.*'"

"Exactly," said Gretchen. "That was the esoteric way to say it but they did not put that before the masses."

"Where does Hess fit in?" asked Wilson.

"It was a long established secret tradition for a Wilson to mix with a Hess. It was supposed to make a magic baby," said Gretchen. "Both of these families lived in northwest Europe. They were royal and important families. The Hesses are mostly known for Orange-Nassau and the Wilsons are often identified with Belgium, but that is only a sliver of the story."

"What do you mean?" asked Wilson.

"Wilson is just one name that derived from a larger group of our ancestors who are sometimes known as the Walloons. They also thrived in Germany and in Romania. In the British Isles, they are known as the Welsh."

"Is that why Hess had such a passion for the English people?" asked Wilson.

"Yes, it was in his blood," replied Gretchen. "To the rest of Britain, the Welsh are known as outsiders themselves. People think of them as 'foreigners or aliens.' In fact, etymologists will tell you that the name *Wales* is derived from a term meaning 'stranger.' It really has more to do with an ancient will that absorbed a name like Wilson into its tradition."

"What are you getting at, Gretchen?" asked Wilson. "You are making it sound like the name *Wilson* is another name for aliens."

"The Walloons were known for the tradition of ergot mold. With it, they could pierce the veil of perception. It gave them an ability to be seers. Eventually, it cost them their crown. They became too powerful and found it absolutely necessary to create a secret tradition of going underground. As a result, they were some of the first people to come to America. They settled in the area now known as Brooklyn and became a powerful force to be reckoned with.

"On the other hand, the Hess family migrated to a place called Stone Arabia in upstate New York. This eventually became the capital of that state. The area is near Albany."

"Why was it called Stone Arabia?" asked Heidi.

"There is another secret tradition in these families and that is that the Hess and Wilson families both come from Egypt," continued Gretchen. "Egypt and Arabia were once synonymous terms for each other; hence, the name of Stone Arabia. The Welsh, however, refer to their country as 'Kymru'. Only outsiders refer to it as Wales."

"Kymru?" said Ali Bey. "That is the same as Khemet, the name that Egyptians use for their homeland."

"You are correct," said Gretchen. "Wales was once known as 'Khemet North.' *Khem* or *Kheme* is Egyptian for black. This is how the name *Kymru* evolved. *Kheme* refers to black earth, but it is also related to the black virgin and her escorts."

"What escorts?" asked Wilson.

"Sometimes known as Olivers or Paladins, they are also known, in a far more secret tradition, as the Camrunes or Camerons. They were the escorts of the Black Virgin. The name *Cameron* evolved from *Kymru*. It goes very deep."

"I've heard that name Cameron before," said Heidi.

"Sure you have," replied Wilson. "Dr. Ewen Cameron — he's the shrink who wiped out Hess's memory."

"Yes," said Gretchen, "He also had a cousin who used to visit my grandfather. He would help plant Nazi spies in the American government. This man worked with the Thulists and knew Hitler and Haushofer, too. He was a Cameron."

"These characters are an abomination as far as the Black Virgin is concerned," said Ali Bey.

"Sometimes the guardians have to be dark," said Gretchen, "but there is more to the story and how it all relates to Stone Arabia in New York. The Welsh *Kymru* goes back to Qumran, the name of a locale in ancient Arabia. It's where the Dead Sea Scrolls were found. The name *Qumran* means 'two moons.'\* It is called 'two moons' because when you are there at nightfall, you can see the moon plus its reflection in the water. The two moons are symbolic. They are not only associated with the dark of night but with the concept of duality itself. You'll find a representation of two moons in Crowley's Tarot deck. It's the Ace of Swords and shows two crescent moons. One faces up and one faces down. In other words, the Ace of Swords is the root spirit of Air and it can go either way. There is a dark side and a light side. My family and their allies have been very dark. They can, however, also represent the other side. Sacred things are always guarded by dual spirits."

"Where are we going with this, Gretchen?" asked Heidi.

"It has everything to do with the General and his genetic heritage," she replied.

"We have already determined," said Heidi, "that he became sandwiched between Hess and this so-called electronic time machine. It is like a baloney sandwich with cheese. Hess and the machine were the bread. The general was the cheese and Konrad was the baloney. That is why the general caught the attention of Dr. Konrad and the shrinks in the first place. There is a connection between them and Hess. The general

---

\*Qumran is derived from an Arabic word meaning "two moons." [*qum* = moon, *ra* = two and *n* = ruins]

## THE LION'S MOUTH . . . . . . . . . . . . . . . .

was bird-dogging Hess and, unbeknownst to him, he was on a collision course with their operation."

"But," said Colonel Mack, "We don't know exactly what their connection to Hess was though."

"They were part of the containment program," said Gretchen. "Hess knew far more than he could say or anyone would let him say. There were political problems — that is true, but there is much more esoteric phenomena going on here. While my grandfather was alive, they would mine him for information. They would ask him about space ships and all sorts of things, even stuff he did not know anything about. It was always under truth serum. They were very cruel. Any cursory examination by General Wilson would have tipped him off to Dr. Konrad's crew and his superiors."

"There is more going on than that though. Konrad was connected to this time machine and he was connected by the book," said Heidi. "The book, however, is becoming a bigger and bigger mystery. We know too little about it and don't even have much time to study it."

"Do you know what's in the book?" asked Wilson.

"It's a book about how all of the major technological breakthroughs in the history of the world, at least many or most of them, were the result of two brothers with the last name of Wilson," said Heidi.

"There you have it," said Colonel Mack, "the Wilson name again."

"There is, however, one other mystery about the book that no one has yet to bring up," said Ali.

"Are you referring to who made up the cheese and baloney sandwich in order to eat it?" asked Mack as everyone had a short laugh.

"No," said Ali, " I am referring to the author of that book."

"Is there an author or name on the book?" asked Heidi.

"Medici," said Ali.

"Lorenzo the Magnificent?" asked Heidi.

"No, just Medici," said Ali. "It is the only name on it."

"What about the title page?" asked Heidi. "Is there one? Does it say where it was printed?"

"Good questions!" said Ali. "There is indeed a title page. It says 'The Arise Leo Press, PO Box 72, London, England, the British Isles.' That is exactly what is says. There is also a depiction of two Chaldean signs for the constellations Aries and Leo. I did not understand it at first but eventually figured it out. It looks like this."

Ali then drew symbols, side by side, on a piece of paper. As he drew, General Wilson's eyes opened wide and, for the first time, he sat straight up.

"The book is implying a direct relationship between the signs of Aries and Leo," said Ali. "Both are fire signs, but if you look closely at the sign for Leo, you will see that the sign of Aries has been superimposed upon the puss or mouth of Leo. Aries is supposed to represent a ram, but it fits into the mouth of a lion. I eventually realized that 'Arise Leo' was an anagram for 'Aries Leo.' The publishers were sending a message."

To the amazement of all, a magnificent light began to shine around Wilson. He no longer seemed the same. The light seemed to be shining from his inner being. It was clear he had changed, but it was a change no one understood.

"I see now," said Wilson. "Everything makes sense. I think I have finally figured everything out."

"What on earth do you mean by that?" asked Heidi.

"This is a major illumination for me. Ali is so right about Aries representing a lion's mouth. It is the voice of the lion, just as Solomon used the Lion's Grip to heal. It has touched me. I now know what to do. Heidi, I am all better."

"Better?" she asked. "You look different all right, but I think we still first need to get you a clean bill of health from the doctor. We need to make sure you have enough rest, too."

"Don't worry," said Wilson. "I'll be all right. I've been walking around the room and getting exercise."

"No you haven't," said Gretchen. "I've been with you."

"Well," said Wilson, "at least in my head I have been walking around. I'm operating on pure manifestation. Watch me get out of this bed and walk with no problem."

"Are you kidding?" asked Heidi. "You might be confident, but I am scared half to death that you're going to fall flat on your face."

"I understand your concern, but don't worry," said Wilson. "I've gone through a very profound change. My energy has been completely transmuted from an ordinary human being into something else. I can get up walk."

"Please explain," said Heidi.

"It's that symbol for Aries. Like any good symbol, it did exactly what it was supposed to do. It reached into the deepest level of my pyche and told me about something I've been wrestling with most of my life. I never understood it until Ali showed me that symbol."

"Continue," said Heidi.

"That symbol is the voice of the lion. In some strange way, I've been listening to that voice all of my life. It is the voice of healing, just like in the fable of Solomon. It is all linked to that aspect of the brain which heals. That is what the Lion's Paw represents. I've already been in touch with it, but the work with Gretchen amplified it. There are so many things I haven't told you yet, but seeing that symbol for Aries has catalyzed a full realization of who I am and what I am here to do. You know, it is as if the symbol from that publisher was rendered just for me. Aries is really a lion and not a ram at all."

"Actually, it's both," said Ali. "The ram is an overlay. Ram is a part of the code."

"What code?" asked Heidi. "I do not understand."

"The code of the cat," said Ali. "Aries means *ram* in Latin, but *ram* spelled backwards is *mar*, a virtual synonym for my people, the Moors. *Moor* and *mar* are the same sounds, but all of these words mean 'cat.'

"You see, the word *Moor* derives from *Maurus* in Latin which is from the old Greek word *Mauresh*. This word is a synthesis of *mau* and *resh*. *Mau* is the Egyptian word for cat while *resh* is Hebrew for 'head' or 'king.'"

"Yes," agreed General Wilson. "Don't you also see that the book is authored by Medici, a name which is a direct phoneme for *mau de chi*. That is the chi or life energy of the lion or cat. The word *medicine* evolved, directly or indirectly, from the healing power of the lion as illustrated by Solomon."

"I had never noticed that before," said Ali, "but there is more. Although *Aries* means ram in Latin, the Greeks use *Ares*, virtually the same word, for *Mars*. Mars is not only the planet that rules the constellation Aries in astrology, but it is also the home of the lion. You see, Cairo is the home of the lion known as the Sphinx. In Egyptian, the word for Cairo is *Al Kahira* and that means Mars."

"I didn't know that!" exclaimed Heidi.

"There is more," continued Ali. "Aries is virtually the same word that you know as *Erie*. That is named after the Erie Indians who well tell you that *Erie* means "cat." This is also where the Iroquois derive their name, from the *Ir*."

"This all makes perfect sense to me," said Wilson. "As I said, I've been wrestling with a lion in my head ever since I was a kid reading H.P. Lovecraft. There was this strange character mentioned in his work, a lion-headed Ong. That is what he was called. Only scant mention was made of him, but I started having dreams about him. God! He was the ruler of the pits of hell, but I used to have dialogues with him in my sleep. Now, I finally understand it all. The sleeping lion in me has awoken! I am truly healed."

"But I see another factor at work here," said Ali. "This mysterious book also represents the healing energy of the lion and so, evidently, does this electronic gear from Montauk."

"You are right," said Wilson. "It is more than my personal awakening. It is a universal awakening. Each one needs to wake up to the cat. Now, I have some work to do."

"Before you start giving any orders, we need to make sure that you can even walk," said Heidi. "Let's see how you do."

"I'll be just fine," said Wilson as he gestured her away with his hand. "Everyone quiet. Let me breathe first."

Wilson slowly sat up and started breathing. Then, he augmented the breathing with the stretching of his limbs, not unlike a lion. After five minutes of this, he got up from the bed and held onto the headboard.

"I'm all right," he said. "Don't come toward me. I need to breathe a little more."

Standing up for the first time in several days, Wilson began another round of breathing. He kept stretching and breathing until he gestured that he was ready to walk. As everyone stood looking, Heidi came over but he motioned her away. General Wilson then walked across the room with no difficulty. Everyone gave a small applause.

"Well," said Heidi, "I'm convinced you could walk out of here, but how can I be sure you could do a round of shopping, let alone do combat with a rogue spy who might be coming after you?"

Wilson then went into a martial arts pose.

"Try me — anyone," he said. "See if you can throw me."

"OK," said Heidi as she lunged towards him, trying to push him back on the bed.

Wilson deflected her adeptly. She was not hurt, but he had demonstrated his ability to take care of himself.

"OK," said Heidi, "but I'd still like more explanation."

"With the work I've been doing with him," said Gretchen, "it doesn't surprise me too much. His brain is working at full tilt. He can amplify his will and bypass what might be termed normal brain procedures. Remember, the normal brain of an ordinary human being is quite demented, at least if you consider the full potential it is capable of."

"She's right," said Wilson. "I figured out the breathing on my own. I'm a changed man, but I'm still the same person. This whole damn experience has changed me, but that's not for now. There are some things we all need to do."

"I already have a clean and pressed uniform waiting for you," said Heidi. "I knew that having it here would encourage you to a quicker recovery."

"I saw that, and I appreciate it," said Wilson. "Now, we've all got work to do. Gretchen, the first thing I want you to do is to heal Colonel Mack. He's been through the ringer worse than any of us, even me. Ali, it's not my place to give you orders, but would you be kind enough to come with me?"

"Certainly," said Ali. "I would be happy to, even if I do not know where you are going."

"Look it, friends," said Wilson, "I am operating at full tilt as a result of Gretchen, but I'm not so stupid as to think I am infallible. I need Ali with me for some special details as well as backup. I'm sure I'll be OK. Gretchen, I hope you can do half as good a job on Mack as you did with me."

"I hope so, too," said Gretchen, "and maybe Heidi can assist me."

"That would be an excellent idea!" said Wilson.

Wilson then put on his uniform and walked out the door with Ali Bey.

"I'll be in touch but not for several days, Don't worry about me," said Wilson as he turned and strode down the hall.

## CHAPTER FORTY

### AUGUST 12TH, 1943

"We have picked today, August 12th," said Ian Fleming, "as a consequence of our sessions with Hess."
"The sacrificial lamb!" said Crowley.
"It is based upon his occult sources," said Fleming.
"Yes?" asked Crowley.
"It is what I have learned from Mr. Nichols," said Fleming.
"Mr. Nichols has taught me well himself," said Crowley. "As a matter of fact, I was his very first pupil."
"I didn't realize that," said Fleming, "but I'm glad you sent me to him. I have learned a lot from him."
"You didn't dare tell the Crown about him did you?" asked Crowley.
"If I had," said Fleming, "I do not think Old Nick would be sitting with us right now."
Crowley and Fleming stopped talking and both turned their heads toward Michael Nichols, the Arch Druid who was known affectionately as Old Nick. After a lengthy pause, Nichols looked straight ahead, neither at Fleming nor Hess. Intently concentrating, he was in a trance of his own making.
"The planet once had an orbit of 360 days," said Nichols.
"I know," said Crowley.
"Yes," said Fleming, "but it came up in the Hess reading."
"A massive cataclysm changed the orbit to 365 1/4 days," continued Nichols, "but the collision is recorded as having occurred ten days after the winter solstice. This eventually contributed to the changing of the calendar beginning on January 1st. This is just ten days after the solstice."
"According to the Vril mediums," said Fleming, "the energy of the Earth was profoundly different before the cataclysm. We learned this from Hess. There was once simultaneous menstruation for all the goddesses of Earth."
"Virtually all women menstruated in unison prior to that time," said the Arch Druid. "It complemented the natural rhythms; but the cataclysm threw everything off. The calendar only emphasized the trauma. The reverence for the moon shifted to that of the sun."

# AUGUST !2TH, 1943..............

"Why is this important to what we are doing today?" asked Crowley.

"This was the very same energy — the female energy — that the Atlanteans were tapping into. They harnessed this energy for their flying craft. It is a psychic energy and it is said that there is no more psychic energy than a female at the time of her menstruation," said Fleming.

"The endocrine glands — you know, the ductless glands — are streaming at full strength during that time," said Crowley. "It is a cascading of emotions, all the emotions of life itself. They are all carried in the blood. That is why the Christians drank blood. It is life; not from Jesus you understand but from the fountain of life itself. It comes from the women. I understand this. What else did Hess say?"

"All of this simultaneous menstruation created an electromagnetic bubble around the planet itself," said Fleming.

"And this powered the flying craft of ancient times?" asked Crowley.

"That is what we were told," said Fleming.

"Yes," said Nichols. "It was not only a real current of electromagnetic energy, but an energy that was directly plugged into the Amygdala gland. With the cataclysmic disaster and the resultant disunity of consciousness, the proper functioning of the amygdala gland began to atrophy in everyone. Human speech started to change at that point. Those who were more able to maintain the function of their amygdala became the bluebloods. They were more in tune with the natural order of things, but the natural order of things was slowly becoming less and less natural.

"In addition to being a literal current of power, the electromagnetic current of universal menstruation was an excellent template for creating. It was pliable to ideas and the strength of ideas. This is the truth of the ancient legend of Solomon. His name, *Sulayman,* is "sal mon" or "sal men." It is a salutation of recognition with regard to the menses and the power thereof. The stories of him building pagan temples had much more to do with harnessing female power than it did with an appeasing of their gods for public relations sake. The seventy-two jinn were functionaries of the Mon which became Ammon-Ra. This term was originally represented by the term "men" which means menses. The original word for women was "men" and it changed after the cataclysm. All of these energies became convoluted and dispersed. Only a fragment survives in the Bible and the Koran."

"Yes," said Fleming, "and there was the electromagnetic bubble of the Southern Cross Project. This refers to an electromagnetic bubble the Nazis discovered beneath the Atlantic Ocean, not far off the coast of South America. The bubble is ancient and was engineered by an ancient class of elders in subterranean tunnels beneath what is called the City of the Golden Gates. These elders are connected to the Tuareg of the Ahaggar in southern Algeria. The Germans, through the Vril mediums, penetrated this secret to a significant degree. The Germans who were actually able to enter this realm underwent very profound changes. They were no longer who they had been, but a new and mysterious association with the German high command came about as a result of these Germans who penetrated the bubble. The returning Germans were supposed to be functionaries who would reestablish mon or men, the universal energy."

"The Vril!" stated Crowley.

"Yes," continued Fleming. "These are the people who Hitler referred to when he was heard to have said, 'I have seen the Ubermensch and he is terrible!' The mediums in the Vril Society, however, neither trusted nor liked what was going on in Germany. They became uncooperative."

"I can hardly say I blame them," said Crowley. "So again, I must ask you 'why this day in August?'"

"Through our intelligence network, we have sought to create our own bubble in Philadelphia on this day," said Fleming. "Today, there is a biorhythm that is tied to the ancient cataclysm which is tied to the original stream of menstruation as it originally occurred on this planet."

"The body is a biorhythmic machine that menstruates every 28 days in a woman," said the Arch Druid. "Today, August 12th, is 225 days from the last day of the Gregorian year. That is not only the equivalent of eight menses cycles or 28 day months, it is the length of a Venutian year. The coincidence of the biorhythm actually fluctuates from year to year with the lunar calendar."

"I still do not understand exactly why I am here," said Crowley.

## AUGUST !2TH, 1943...............

"You are being called upon to activate the jinn by sending a virgin boy through a feminine stone here at Men-a-Tol," said Fleming. "As you once taught me, these stones carry a telluric current — one that runs right through Men-a-Tol."

"We have to direct the current," said Crowley.

"Yes," said Fleming, "toward Philadelphia in the United States."

"No," said Crowley, "to Montauk."

"Why?" asked Fleming.

"I have experience in these matters," said Crowley. "Montauk is a place I've been to before and in the strangest of ways. As you know, the stone-placers placed these stones along the telluric currents of the Earth. They ran like a grapevine of primal communications. The whole world was in touch. It still is — the collective consciousness is always in touch with itself — but the connections are far more complex in today's world. People, even the priests, are far more removed from it as a conscious process than they once were. Only a few know what is really going on."

"What can we expect if you do this?" asked Fleming.

"At best, we can penetrate the bubble you spoke of," said Crowley, "but the one at Montauk. It is more powerful."

"To what end?" asked Fleming.

"You and I will soon outlive our usefulness to our masters in the British government. The war will be over in a year or two. I am old and your power will change after the war. I dare say to you in confidence that our so-called masters will undermine themselves and civilization as well. Something tells me that this experiment they are doing in Philadelphia will be a breakthrough in terms of science but a disaster in terms of humanity."

"Why is that?" asked Fleming.

"The same people who are making the concentration camps are the ones utilizing this technology. It can only be used to make a prison planet," said Crowley.

"And?" asked Fleming.

"A part of me, and you as well, should send a thought of reform into this whole mess. A ray of hope into the future that this entire occult government that is wrapping itself around humanity will trip itself up," said Crowley.

"Do you agree?" asked Crowley as he looked at Nichols.

"You have learned well from me," said the Arch Druid. "For all of your travails, and there have been many, you have maintained the seed of redemption."

"I have lived my life in such a way," said Crowley, "that I have invited people to view me as the opposite of redemption, but within the sea of darkness is the sea of light. Hitler is no different."

"One might argue that he is a more powerful magician," said Nichols, "but Hitler has sowed the seeds for the destruction of Germany."

"He's had a lot of help, too," said Crowley.

"As much as I am a part of the occult and have learned so much from you and others, there is still that rational part of me that considers all of this so much hocus-pocus," said Fleming.

"It is all hocus-pocus," said Crowley. "Hocus-pocus is a word that is a corruption of the Latin mass because the ritual of the priests was never really understood by the people. The role of the priest is to stand between humanity and the infinite divine. Whether the people understand the infinite divine or not, the people and the infinite divine are both still there. Sometimes the infinite divine does not understand the people. It goes both ways, but the priest is always in the middle whether he is a Catholic, a Muslim or a pagan. There is understanding in a priest that goes both ways."

Crowley sipped his ale and looked out the window. It was a dreary day in Cornwall and the weather was beginning to look even drearier. He bent his head down and closed his eyes.

"As I said, I am old. My time is coming, the end of it that is. Inwardly, I have always revolted against established authority. Even so, I have not always been right. My magick is potent, but it has not always achieved a result that I could be happy with. This government of ours is no better than any of the past, but it is not the government that is at fault. It is the rank above the government. As above, so below."

Looking out the window, they wondered if the weather would break so they could accomplish their ritual without getting wet.

AUGUST 12TH, 1943...............

## CHAPTER FORTY-ONE

## THE TIME MACHINE

Five days after Wilson left them, Heidi, Gretchen, and Colonel Mack stood before and marveled at the crate that had been shipped to Heidi from Lion's Paw.
"We'll need a crow bar to open that crate," said Mack. "I'll get one and be back in just a few minutes."
"What do you think will be in here, Gretchen?" asked Heidi.
"Coils, probably Tesla coils," said Gretchen.
"And what else?" asked Heidi.
"We will find out soon enough," said Gretchen. "I think you might find some instrumentation as well."
"Why do you say that?" asked Heidi.
"My work with the general. I have had a psychic rapport with him since then," said Gretchen. "I just have a feeling."
"I thought we would have heard from the general by now," said Heidi. "It has been five days already. Do you think he's all right?"
"Yes, I think he's all right," replied Gretchen. "I also think we will hear from him soon."
Colonel Mack then reappeared with a crow bar in his hand. Immediately, be began prying off the huge staples that fastened the wooden planks. He continued until two sides of the crate and the top came off. There were four conical coils about four feet high. In addition, there were other rods that appeared to be made of copper. They were of different sizes. The apparatus was reminiscent of tinker toys that needed to be assembled. There was also a copper ball that appeared to be the size of a punch ball.
"It is obvious that this needs to be assembled if it is going to do anything," said Heidi as she looked at Mack. "Any volunteers?"
"No," said Gretchen, "don't touch it."
As Gretchen finished her words, a very small person appeared. Everyone was too preoccupied to see where he came from. He was a "little person," no taller than four feet and was dressed in army fatigues.

"I can help you," said the little man.

No one said a word while the tiny man rapidly went about assembling the mysterious structure. He worked intently and quietly.

"Sir," said Heidi, trying to speak to the little man.

"Don't interrupt me," he said in a stern businesslike manner that was intimidating. "If you do, I cannot do this work. I will be done soon and you will understand."

The man continued his work. It was obvious he had done this before. When he finished, the four coils were in a square. The ball was extended over the coils and in the center. There was no instrumentation whatsoever, only a strange array of coils and copper.

As soon as the man completed his task, he stood underneath the copper ball.

"Don't come near me," he said. "If you do, there could be problems, especially for you."

The man then began to fade out of this reality until he was entirely gone.

"Should we be surprised?" asked Heidi. "I am ready for anything."

"I think you will be surprised very soon," said Gretchen.

About thirty seconds after the little man completely disappeared, a haze began to form in the center of the coils. This time, however, it was a larger man and he was sitting in a chair as he was gated into this reality. It was General Wilson.

"General!" said Heidi, "I can't believe it's you! I was just wondering when I'd hear from you."

Wilson nodded at Heidi and smiled.

"Yes, it's me," said Wilson. "And I mean to say that I am the same General Wilson who left the hospital more than a couple of days ago. Things have worked out for me, and I am indeed quite well."

"I was wondering if you were all right," said Heidi.

"I am all right, but I am no longer the same," said Wilson. "You won't be seeing much of me anymore, but don't worry. Everything will be taken care of, and I am here to complete business with all of you. You each have an important role to play in the future of this reality."

"We're all relieved that you are all right, but please tell us what the hell is going on," said Heidi.

"Remember, Heidi, do not be surprised at anything," said Wilson. "I have had a most illustrious experience. During the work with Gretchen, I had a complete transformation. Something was obviously working on me well before that, but the session with her catalyzed everything.

"I went to Montauk after I left the hospital, but this time the people there were completely different. Earlier, there had been a conspiracy to keep me from finding out anything at Montauk. Now, it all turned like a worm. The people seemed to recognize me. In fact, it wasn't much different than in my dream world visit to Montauk with Preston. But this was real life, no trance state or anything."

"What happened?" asked Heidi. "How did they recognize you?"

"It was funny until Ali Bey explained it to me," said Wilson. "He was with me the whole time. Ali said that through all of the various experiences I had been having, I was actually being initiated."

"Initiated into what?" asked Heidi.

"It is a little hard to explain," said Wilson, "but it is almost like an initiation into Freemasonry. I hate to use that analogy, but it is appropriate. Ali explained that Freemasonry is a series of degrees that mimics the evolution of life experience itself. He was quick to point out, however, that organized Freemasonry is corrupted and often serves a very convoluted purpose.

"The point is that the people at Montauk who guard the secrets are no different than the jinn that King Solomon commanded in the Bible. Solomon commanded the jinn. Normally, the jinn are representatives of this so-called continuum that we call the cosmos. It has its own divine order, rules and regulations. The time experiments that were conducted at Montauk reach out beyond the limits of the ordinary human mind. In such circumstances, human consciousness cuts off and the software inside of people's brains operates to a different tune than it might otherwise. These people at Montauk have become spokesmen for the jinn per se. This is only an analogy, you understand. In fact, it can go both ways. People can be bad or good, dark or light."

"I think I understand you pretty clearly," said Gretchen. "My question, however, is different. In this analogy, are you like King Solomon?"

"I never thought about that," said Wilson, "but I can certainly tell you that I am not in control of everything. I am, however, at the command of certain forces. That is why I was able to go there and now here. There is, however, a lot more of Solomon in me than I realized. Thanks for pointing that out."

"So you are not a god then?" asked Gretchen.

"No, not at all," said Wilson. "I'm not doing too badly though!"

"Very good," said Gretchen. "I was testing you. People in your position, and I have heard of them before, can become very arrogant."

"That characteristic was never one of my personality traits," said Wilson. "What is important here is that circumstances dictated that I travel the life path I was on. Finding out about Hess was key because it percolated my interest in these matters and enabled me to transcend my ordinary life."

"This is stupendous," said Heidi, "and I am tempted to endlessly wonder over it all, but I still have some relevant questions. If you have access to Montauk and the mystery of that locale, please tell me who the hell Konrad was and why he was on your tail? How does that fit in with your initiation?"

"An excellent question," said Wilson. "Konrad was an operative. Again, I must use the analogy of Solomon and the Jinn. Think of Konrad as a jinn. He was jamming the frequency."

"Can you explain further?" asked Heidi.

"My interest in the Hess affair was triggered by the circumstances under which I served in World War II. My association with Patton was a big part of it. Hess himself was in the middle of many currents when he was alive. There were Tibetan currents, Haushofer's Vril Society, the Thule Society, German industry and some ET currents, too. Besides all that, he was also Hitler's most trusted confidante. Hess stood at the crossroads of many secret societies and factions. He emerged not only as *the* financial power of the Nazi Party but the bastion of kindheartedness in a cold and cruel realm.

"Someone like this attracts attention from almost any realm you can imagine, at least more than the average ditch digger. I am talking about dimensional realms here. Although his power was vanquished when he flew to England, the strings he was tied to were like a highly powered electric cable that was not shielded. When I began investigating him, particularly when the opportunity of interviewing him was almost at hand, you might say I absorbed some of his electrons, like a cathode. Konrad was like a resistor. To the degree I was reactivating Hess, I was reactivating a current that Konrad had to jam. He was jamming the frequency."

"I understand much better," said Heidi, "even if I'm not used to electronic terms."

"I guess Preston Nichols is rubbing off on me just a bit," said Wilson.

"Preston Nichols?" asked Heidi. "You met him in your unconscious state, not in person. Did you ever call him to see if he had any recollection of you?"

"Actually," said Wilson, "I did meet him in person. On the way to Montauk, I thought it best to stop by and compare notes."

"What did he think of your experiences via Gretchen?" she asked.

"It might interest you to know that he recognized me," said Wilson. "He said this sort of thing happens to him all the time. Consciousness is being played out in many different realities and venues. When I was working with Gretchen, I was not only plugging into a much bigger picture than the average human is ever consciously aware of but I was also connecting up with Mr. Nichols. It is just one of his unique operating modes, at least according to him."

"Interesting," said Heidi. "You've explained Konrad, at least as far as him trying to stop you, but you haven't explained a few other things. For starters, what does he have to do with this time machine? It seemed like it was his province and now it is in our possession."

"You are quite right," said Wilson. "It is in our possession, and it is a rather stunning coup if you ask me. I now know why I was selected for this job. They needed someone who could pull it off."

"Wait!" said Heidi. "You are going too fast. Please explain who selected you."

"It's not quite like that," said Wilson. "The universe selects you and you select yourself, just like you have selected yourself to be involved in this moment. Ever since I was a kid,

THE TIME MACHINE. . . . . . . . . . . . . . . .

I knew I was different, but I was so able to get along with everyone that it didn't make much difference. You might say I had an angel looking over me."

"A guardian angel?" asked Heidi.

"Yes," said Wilson, "but be careful not to get carried away with analogies like angels or King Solomon. The universe runs on a system that is best likened to artificial intelligence. The religious analogies sometimes serve well, but the cosmos and life are too complex to be codified in a human system.

"In my case, I was visited by a Lion-headed creature," said Wilson.

"Yes," said Heidi, "you mentioned him in the hospital."

"You are right," said Wilson, "but I have only since realized how this whole new awakening was able to take place in me. The universe runs on something like artificial intelligence, but there is also a divine intelligence within it. It is not a perfect system but a system nevertheless. It seeks to correct its mistakes and that is what redemption is all about. Redemption is about fulfilling your original program which is sometimes the same as what people refer to as destiny."

"Redemption is also religious," interjected Heidi.

"Yes," said Wilson, "and that is why the Lion-headed creature named Ong fits in so well. Completely unknown to me in my youth, the lion is the symbol of resurrection. Solomon used the Lion's Grip to resurrect Hiram Abiff, the master craftsman who built the Temple. It is funny how the mind works, but it is also funny how the divine intelligence of the universe works. You see, I was hit by a truck from Lion's Paw, a name that is virtually the same as Lion's Grip. The lion, or Leo, is the King of the Zodiac."

"He is also the King of Beasts and it was Daniel who took the thorn out of the lion's paw in the Bible," interjected Heidi.

"Correct," said Wilson, "and Christ was the Lion of Judeah. It is all pointing to the lion as the symbol of resurrection and redemption. Things really started to make sense when I was in the hospital and remembered the lion-headed Ong. That tweaked my mind with the collective conscious and everything connected together. I realized that I was on a carnival ride of divine intelligence that was making all these connections through the lion. It was with me for a long time though, ever since I was a boy. I think the work that

Gretchen did, however, made the whole thing possible."

"You are damn right it did!" exclaimed Gretchen. "And I am also here to redeem whatever redeemable aspects there are of my grandfather and his work. The best work he did was with his women and my grandmother. Do not forget that the Sphinx is the oldest monument and that it is also a tribute to the lion. The Egyptians called her Sekhmet and Bast. She is female. It is this energy of the cat that the Church tried to destroy by killing cats. They called them familiars of witches and then burned both the cat and the woman. Ever since, the Church has killed the principle of resurrection."

"I think we all agree," said Heidi, "but I still don't understand how Konrad fits into this time machine."

"I was going to get to that," said Wilson. "Konrad belongs to an obscure and rarefied part of the universe. He is tied into the Lion-headed Ong who presides over a purgatory that reaches far beyond the concepts of our hell. Lovecraft described the heated and pitted landscapes with boiling lava. It is a wasteland of desolate and rejected spirits. Ong appears as the harshest taskmaster imaginable, but it is only out of necessity and in keeping with the desolation of the souls concerned. That job requires a terrifying soul to keep them in line. The lion can terrify. Yet within the seeds of this unimaginable hell is the seed of resurrection which is once again symbolized by the redeemable features of the lion-headed ruler. This is why the appellation of purgatory can be applied.

"The realm of the lion is the same as the realm contacted by magicians when they seek to invoke Tetragrammaton, the four-lettered name of God. Magicians who contact this realm too often end up as casualties. This is the realm of the root spirits of fire, water, air and earth and all of their imaginable depictions. These elements are at the core of our reality, and their assemblage is like a coprocessor in a computer. The 'computer' language is very ancient and far from our own.

"Even then, when I was young, the Lion-headed Ong ruled over his territory with an iron fist, but he found time to communicate to me in the strangest of ways. He did it through the dream state. These creatures, which you can call the representative of God if you want, are very far from the day-to-day realities we know. They relate to us no more than we can relate to the world of an amoeba. It is often through endocrine secretions and emotions that they make contact, but it is like an alien language.

"Anyway, in this sea of bizarreness, which I did not realize until after my work with Gretchen, I was being prepared all of my life for such an adventure. This force was often with me on the battlefield, but I did not know what it was, and I had to act on my own initiative in order to survive those horrifying times. The strange thing, however, is that I was never horrified. Only when I look back can I now see the horrible danger that I was able to navigate my way through. In a sense, I was being battle tested.

"Now, and at long last, I am working on a program of full-scale resurrection. But, it is an eternal program. I can only be with you for a short time longer as I have work to do."

"Could you please get back to Konrad?" asked Heidi.

"He's still a little hard to explain, but only a little," said Wilson. "If there is a reconstructive energy or resurrection program in the universe, he acted like a jinn. He was jamming the frequency, but he was a little more complex than all that. He was also a repository of information, and that is why he dealt in ancient antiquities, documents and the like. Konrad was a rarefied collector of such because they were loaded with clues. His job was to hide the clues. When he lost the book that Ali picked up, he had a temperamental fit and with good reason. His loss of that book was to be his own personal undoing. We wouldn't be here having this discussion if he still had the book."

"Yes," said Heidi, "but Ali was guided to have that book. It was meant for him."

"And you as well," said Wilson. "There was yet more to Konrad, however. When I visited Senator Goldwater, I was well aware he had been strongly supported by the John Birch Society. What I did not know at that time was that Konrad was involved with that society.

"The Birch Society has an interesting history, and I have been closely parallel to them since my early days with the Patton group," said Wilson.

"You mean the group that operated in secret after Patton's death?" asked Heidi.

"Exactly," answered Wilson. "Any historian knows that the John Birch Society was virulently anticommunist and their agents had meetings in the living room of William F. Buckley, Jr., a member of Skull and Bones. The Birch Society were Freemasons and were thereby linked to the Mormons, another outfit run by the Freemasons.

"What intrigued me about the John Birch Society, which I realized during my meeting with Goldwater, is that Ezra Taft Benson, the President and Prophet of the Mormons, is one of the biggest advocates of the John Birch Society. He is also a Freemason. Quite oddly, it was also this same namesake, 'Benson,' that acquired the land at Montauk from the Indians.

"There is, however, a secret history to the John Birch Society of which most historians are completely unaware and that has to do with John Birch himself.

"John Birch was a Freemason who lived in Macon, Georgia and devoted his life to the ministry with his parents. Having travelled to China, he was an expert in the language and knew all of the local folk tales as well. When World War II started, he became a natural fit for the U.S. Army who needed representation in China. When the famous Jimmy Doolittle landed his plane in China after bombing Tokyo, Birch singled-handedly rescued him. This earned him an immediate and permanent promotion as head of Army Intelligence in China. He also ran all of the OSS operations in that country as well. His assignment included the supervision of the famous, or infamous if you will, Flying Tigers. The latter day version of the Tigers became involved in drug scandals which you've all heard too much about.

"That is the official history of John Birch, but there is a far more secret side to his involvement in the Far East. He was tied to two very important entities. One was the Coca-cola Company of Atlanta and the other was George Patton's cousin, Larry McDonald."

"Yes!" exclaimed Heidi. "McDonald was the U.S. Congressman who was shot down while flying through Soviet air space about four years ago."

"You're exactly right," said Wilson. "He was shot down on Korean Air Lines Flight 007."

**THE TIME MACHINE** . . . . . . . . . . . . . . . .

"Oh my god!" said Heidi. "I just realized the significance of that. 007 is James Bond. You're talking about Ian Fleming here, aren't you?"

"Yes, I am," said Wilson.

"How does this connect to Hess?" asked Heidi.

"I'm just about to tell you," said Wilson.

...... **CHAPTER FORTY-TWO** ......

## ALBRECHT

After having stationed different people at specific locations around the doughnut-shaped stone at Men-a-Tol, Aleister Crowley took his wand and spoke an Enochian chant into the ear of a man he had positioned. He then continued, speaking a chant into the ears of the different people stationed a short distance apart. After this part of the ritual, he knelt down before the stone in deep concentration.

Crowley was well aware that both dark and light energies penetrated his physical and spiritual vehicles. Knowing he did not have too many years left to live, he knew this might be one of his last opportunities to conduct a ritual of this order. Reviewing his life, he thought of the good deeds and the bad deeds. In his eyes, they balanced each other, but these were not really his concern. His primary concern was about the people he was working for. He found it amusing that he despised them as a general rule yet here they were paying him for his occult services and trying to use them for their own advantage. Crowley then thought of his earlier travels to Montauk and directed his energy there as if he was surrendering to a higher power. In his own verbiage, he thought: somehow, some way, "release us all from the madness of these idiots." He was referring to the Allies and whoever their masters might be.

Crowley then rose and spoke Enochian words into his young son's ears. He then placed him on a board and placed him through the center of the whole. When it was all over, Crowley took Ian Fleming off to the side.

"By the way, Ian," said Crowley, "did you know that our contact in Lisbon was as queer as the guards in Buckingham Palace?"

"Do you mean Albrecht?" asked Fleming. He was referring to Albrecht Haushofer, the son of Karl Haushofer. "Should that last statement surprise me coming from your mouth?" Fleming was referring to the fact that Crowley was himself a homosexual.

"I don't know," said Crowley, "but I realize it may have

## ALBRECHT

gone past you. Albrecht was deeply involved with the Marquis de Clydesdale, the Duke of Hamilton. It is a shame when people's sexuality gets in the way of strategic planning. I almost regret to tell you that the whole English government, particularly during the conduct of this war, is at the behest of god damn fucking queers!" said Crowley. "And frustrated ones, too! Albrecht is not the only one."

"Again," said Ian, "should I be surprised that these words are coming from your mouth?"

"I cannot speak for them except to say that they are all idiots. What I have done personally in my life has often been called into question, even by myself. I cannot put my own deeds or misdeeds before the objective judgement of others. In other words, my own misdeeds do not prevent an objective observation. So be it. I thought you should know these things if you didn't already."

"I will keep it all under advisement," said Fleming, "and you can be sure I won't share the information with anyone."

Thus it was that Aleister Crowley, the so-called "King of the Queers," at least as far as he was described in certain British circles, implicated his own brethren to Ian Fleming, the dashing playboy who referred to himself as 007.

The seed of the Nazi's downfall had long since been planted by Albrecht Haushofer, a man who not only orchestrated the divestiture of Hess from Germany but who boldly engaged in a covert assassination plot upon Hitler himself. Himmler, who was a tacit partner in the plan, protected the imprisoned Haushofer until the last possible moment. When Himmler was forced to flee himself, he ordered Haushofer shot so that there was no possibility of implicating himself in the treachery.

Ian Fleming, who had been instrumental in all of Britain's negotiations with Haushofer and Hess, eventually participated in Operation James Bond, a mission into Berlin that rescued Martin Bormann and thereby facilitated the transfer of the Nazi's Swiss bank accounts into British control. Already having adopted John Dee's occult code name of 007, Fleming now united those infamous numerals with James Bond, the pseudonym he used on the Bormann mission. The novels he later wrote contained only fragments of a truth that was indeed too strange for fiction.

......CHAPTER FORTY-THREE......

## JOHN BIRCH

"Birch's family were evangelists," said Wilson as he continued his dialogue to his friends, "but they were much more than that. They were also Freemasons and their evangelism served as a perfect cover for their real work which included scoping out military potential in China during the thirties. Their son was an eager and quick learner, and he ended up playing a key role for our government. Besides the clandestine maneuvering, the Birch family helped the President and our overseas spy ring with all sorts of covert activity. The Coca-Cola Company, unwittingly or not, ended up playing a significant role in this covert activity.

"Dr. Konrad's family had strange and mysterious ties to the opium trade that had once flourished between Great Britain and China. As the Chinese Boxer Rebellion put a damper on the opium trade, a new illegal drug of choice was discovered: cocaine. Actually, cocaine had to be outlawed in the United States before it could become significantly profitable. This involved Coca-Cola both directly and indirectly. In those days, cocaine was an actual ingredient in Coca-Cola. Therefore, when the Coke Company processed their ingredients, they had to remove the outlawed ingredients. This left an abundance of cocoa leaves that had to be disposed of or used for some other purpose. An obvious asset to the underworld, these leaves found a new home. Konrad's family was involved with key politicians in Chicago, and a secret plant was created to produce cocaine from what the Coca-Cola Company no longer used. Crime syndicates became involved and an entire culture was created to protect this new fledgling industry, all backed by the old opium traders of Great Britain.

"With the money earned from these endeavors, Konrad's family became big stockholders in the Coca-Cola Company and were extremely influential. As time went forward, the Birch family was absorbed into these connections. I cannot tell you that the Birch's worked for Coca-Cola, but I can tell you that they worked with people who were using the company. You see, Coca-Cola is a world renowned trademark and it did not happen by accident. Konrad's people used the Coca-Cola Company as a beachhead in foreign countries. Eventually, the CIA used Coca-Cola as an entry way into political manipulations, but this was preceded by other interests acting first.

"The John Birch Society got its name because John Birch was considered the first casualty of the Cold War. The story told and generally believed is that, soon after the war ended, Birch and his soldiers were ordered to halt and surrender their weapons by some of Mao's communist–s. In what was essentially a misunderstanding by the Chinese, all of the soldiers gave up their guns but Birch. He refused. After all, the Americans were victors and Chinese troops should at least respect his rank as well as American sovereignty. This, however, was not the case. The Chinese showed him no respect. Instead of capitulating to the Chinese and trying to sort out matters with courtesy, Birch adamantly refused to surrender his gun on principle and was summarily executed on the spot. Even the John Birch Society itself presents Birch as a hothead who was neither diplomatic nor smart about his own self-preservation. His adamant and vehement stand on being an anti-communist is the virtue that is extolled in his obituary.

"The actual story is far different and is too bizarre to be believed. As I said, Birch was in command of the Flying Tigers who made constant runs into the western hills of China, an area which is a part of ancient Tibet. Here things become a little murky, especially to historians.

"Murky?!" said Gretchen. "If you think it is murky, I could tell you some things about that area."

"From the Vril girls?" said Wilson. "I'd like to hear it."

"This is where a famous Tibetan lama came from," said Gretchen. "He was known as the Man with Green Gloves."

"Please tell our friends who that is," said Wilson.

"Sure," said Gretchen. "He appeared in Berlin newspapers by reason of several meetings he had with Hitler. My grandfather knew him and arranged for his passage, but the contact was initially through Karl Haushofer who had met him in the Orient. There was a mysterious civilization in this area of the Western Hills that goes way back into antiquity. My grandfather learned about it from Haushofer."

"Shambalah?" asked Heidi.

"Yes and no," answered Gretchen. "This was a rather complete civilization in its own right, but from my understanding, it pointed the way to Shambalah."

"In other words," said Heidi, "travelers on their way to Shambalah would pass through this area in the western hills of China in order to get their 'passport' so to speak.

"Something like that — yes," answered Gretchen. "This is where it gets murky to me. It was this very region which created so much interest in the so-called peace plan between my grandfather and England. It was the Marquis de Clydesdale who made his famous over this remote area and clearly saw what was left of this ancient civilization from his airplane. The actual results of his mission were of the most sensitive nature, both politically and on religious grounds as well. When Karl Haushofer learned of this discovery by the Marquis, he used (his son) Albrecht as a go-between."

"You are talking about the Duke of Hamilton," said Wilson. "I just wanted to clarify that for everyone who is here. The Marquis de Clydesdale was the Duke of Hamilton."

"Exactly," said Gretchen. "After the Duke's flight, the English all of a sudden became very interested in what the Nazis had long since known about. This was some of the most steamy and highly charged political intrigue upon which many other issues were eventually based. In the end, it was completely obfuscated."

"Exactly," said Wilson, "but I actually saw films of this region when I viewed the Nazi expeditions into Tibet."

"You mean," said Mack, "that you also saw films of Tibet after the war? They were amongst the collection that Fritz Kraemer and the gang showed you?"

"Yes indeed!" said Wilson. "The Nazis had extensive films of this area, and they included many little people. The people from this area derived from the Dropa Civilization, a bizarre and unique civilization which claims to have come to Earth as the result of a crash landing from the stars. Their descendants eventually mixed with the local human beings and that incident has inspired many legends. They became a hybrid sort of race."

"What exactly did you see in the films, general?" asked Gretchen.

"Some very interesting things," said Wilson. "There was an entire city with walls made of hard clay or earth, and it was rather extensive. It was not a high wall like the one in Lhasa, but it was built on the top of a mountain. There were also huge cisterns that seemed to lead to an extensive underground. There were, however, no films that went into the underground, perhaps because of the lighting techniques of the day. The German generals did, however, say that this was a pathway into Shambalah. It was discovered, but with the turncoat behavior of the British — as they referred to it — their primary attention became riveted on Europe. They were unable to explore it to the extent they would have liked."

"Yes," said Gretchen, "the English knew the Germans had a hold on this area. The Brits, however, were in no position to go after this area themselves by reason of their own geographical situation. They therefore had to keep Germany occupied at all costs. This was the grand deception. I should also tell you, however, that the Germans had the lighting technology to take meaningful shots of the underground. There was a whole division dedicated to underground activities, and they would have filmed it. That division, however, is far more secret than the regular occult bureau operations."

"So," said Mack, "this was the real reason for World War II? It was a fight over Tibet and access to the Dropa Civilization and Shambalah?"

"One could look at it that way," said Wilson, "but there are many more complex issues that I have already discussed. It is more like this issue came to the surface with all of the chaos that was created by war. It does bring some very pertinent issues to light."

"I'm still not sure how Haushofer fits in," said Mack.

"Albrecht," said Gretchen, "was completely afraid of Hitler. He thought he was a nut. His father, Karl, had always thought he could keep Hitler under the control of the secret societies, but he learned that this was not the case. He knew he had miscalculated badly. Albrecht, who eventually participated in assassination plots against Hitler, sought out the Marquis de Clydesdale and enlisted his support. This was a disaster to the Germans because what he was really doing was telegraphing to the British that Hitler no longer had the support of his own secret societies. They no longer trusted him

— at least Albrecht's faction — and this was the most severe betrayal to Hitler imaginable. It was Albrecht Haushofer."

"Patton would have had a field day with what you just said," said Wilson. "It all goes back to the queers ruling the roost! The Duke and Haushofer had something in common besides their knowledge of the Dropas in Tibet. The two men were lovers. It was through them that the Nazi Party was brought down. A Brit and an Anglophile!"

"I thought," said Mack, "you said that it was the queers who did in Patton, too."

"I never said that," said Wilson, "but that was how he viewed it. I can tell you, however, that had he survived and acted on the films I saw and the other data he had seen, the world would be far different today. He wanted to go after the Russians because he knew they would also make a move on that area in old Tibet. Patton knew Tibet was a strategic area, and he wanted it for America. Years later, this was the basis for the CIA sneaking into Tibet and rescuing the Dalai Lama.

"Patton had no reason to fear Russians coming to the United States. They only took over a fraction of Germany and that was because it was due them by reason of their being members of the Allied Command. There were also other issues at stake. Patton was killed off by the OSS but at the behest of the British."

"How did this play out after the war?" asked Heidi. "This makes the whole chess board of world politics look quite different to me."

"FDR and Vice President Wallace had already sent Nicholas Roerich on a mission to find Shambalah, but they kept it very secret. This was part of Roosevelt's seeming duplicity and treachery when it came to the Germans. Historians know that Roosevelt engaged in despicable deceit against his fellow Americans when he pitted them against Germany, but there were other issues at stake that the public and even historians are still clueless about. Not even German apologists know the full story, let alone the true story, and so much of it has to do with Tibet.

"In some respects, the British had been working on these brush strokes for years. When they brought down the Ottoman Empire in World War I, this was the first stage in what has become almost a century old plan to return Palestine to the Jews. This was not done out of the goodness of their British hearts nor because they considered themselves good Christians. They were only trying to gain favor with the chosen people for their own selfish reasons.

"All of this goes back to the Chinese opium trade with Great Britain. The British had caused so much suffering in China as a result of their pushing opium that the Chinese government rebuked them. In their attempt to secure cooperation with the Chinese government through bribes and other persuasive means, they ended up discovering one of the harshest secrets and mysterious secrets of Chinese politics: the Jews had a remarkably strong influence in that country that went far back into antiquity.

"During the age of the silk trade route, the Jews controlled virtually all of the way stations, including the trade that went in and out of China. Controlling the area for centuries, the Jews became extremely wealthy merchants. Eventually, they worked their way into the merchant class of China and mixed their religion and genetics with the locals. This extended into political circle to the point where it became deeply imbedded in the Chinese culture. One of the most sacred traditions in the Chinese ruling class concerns the fact that the highest class is secretly Jewish. Chinese rulers are traditionally but secretly proud of their Jewish heritage and have kept true to their religion although it is a bit different than the Jewish religion we know today in the West.

"While the Americans supported Chiang Kai Shek and that faction, the British were busy cultivating their Jewish connections and secretly helped to fund Mao Tse Tung who hid out in the caves that are in the very region of where the ruins of this ancient civilization once existed.

"From the very early days of Communist China, you can see that they even had a Jewish person on their advisory committee. His name was Shapiro and before he went to China, he used to make bagels in the Bronx."

"No shit!" said Mack as the girls laughed.

"Just as the British secretly cultivated Jewish Bolshevik Communism in Russia, they did a similar turn in China. The Jews have always been the breeders of communism but with the British standing happily behind them. If you do not believe what I say about the Jews, check out the communist flags that are often flown over kibbutzes in Israel. Cultivating communism in China, however, was extremely strategic. It kept the Russians out of Tibet. Believe me, the Russians were ready and willing to invade Tibet at any time. As for the Brits, they felt shortchanged by the Russians. After having helped set up communist Russia, they ended up on the short end of the stick when Stalin took over and cleaned house. He slaughtered Jews as revenge.

"After the war, the British immediately acted to secure the ancient civilization of the Dropa and to capture all artifacts and destroy any evidence of a city having been there. The Chinese soon took over as custodians of this area. If you care to study history, you will often find that, willingly or not, historians are more dedicated to obfuscation and subversion than they are in finding out the truth about archaeology.

"But to get back to our original subject of John Birch, his team of Flying Tigers was making forays into the same area. Remember, he was operating both Army Intelligence and the OSS in China. Brooke Dolan was an OSS member who, with Ilya Tolstoy, undertook an OSS mission into Tibet during this period. It was on behalf of FDR, but the President wanted Tolstoy to command the mission. This did not make too much sense because Dolan was a Tibetan explorer long before that and had also led a German team into the area. Dolan was friendly with all the Germans. Besides that, Tolstoy had also been humiliated by his fellow soldiers at the OSS camp in Canada and was not a true leader of men. FDR, however, saw Tolstoy playing a crucial role as the leader. First, Roosevelt did not fully trust Dolan because of his German connections. More importantly, Tolstoy spoke Russian. This was essential to pursuing and dealing with any Russian influence in Tibet.

FDR had also seen films of Dolan's earlier missions and was most interested. He subsequently ordered the Nicholas Roerich mission into the Far East in an attempt to find Shambalah. Remember, this was the time of the movie *Lost Horizon* which excited everyone about Shangri La. FDR even named his retreat Shangri-La, but it was later changed to Camp David in order to stave off attention about these highly charged and very secretive political issues.

"Birch was representing the American faction as far as these Tibetan interests were concerned. This was the real reason the commies killed him. It was a turf battle, pure and simple; but it was never about a petty issue such as who had seniority. It was about this ancient locale. Remember, Birch was the head of intelligence and he knew more about the area than any Westerner. Although most people do not know it, the Birch Society still hides these facts."

"What about the Man with Green Gloves?" asked Mack. "Let's get back to him."

"OK, Gretchen," said General Wilson, "I think you'd best take it from here."

Everyone's ears were perked as they readied themselves to listen to the story about one of the biggest mysteries of Nazi Germany, the enigmatic Tibetan who was known only as the Man with Green Gloves.

## CHAPTER FORTY-FOUR

### RENDEZVOUS

It was just before Christmas in 1949 when Arch-Druid Michael Nichols had a happenstance with fate. Bustling along a busy London street, he found himself coming face to face serendipitously with Ian Lancaster Fleming.

"Good day, old man!" exclaimed Fleming. "How are you doing these days?"

"I could be better," answered Nichols, "but it is most refreshing to see you. How have you been?"

"Not too bad," answered Fleming. "Could I buy you a drink?"

The two men went into a nearby pub and engaged in a very lively discussion as they caught up on the past few years. Eventually, the discussion turned to their association with Aleister Crowley.

"What happened in the end?" asked Fleming. "I couldn't attend the memorial service, mostly due to security reasons. The Admiralty did want me to be publicly associated with him, especially with regard to the Hess affair."

"His life did not end as everyone has thought," said Nichols. "Had I had your contact information, I would have consulted you. Then again, perhaps not. Crowley had asked me to invoke complete silence concerning the operation. Exactly what happened in the end is that he came to me in 1947 sometime. He was quite sure a psychic "hit" had been put out on him. Of this he had no doubt. A man by the name of Israel Regardie had appeared in England, and Crowley was quite certain this man was either behind the hit or an agent thereof. Crowley was not sure which, but he sought out my protection from this force."

"I remember Regardie," said Fleming. "He was a rather effeminate man and became quite bitter when Crowley could no longer afford his secretarial services. A most bitter man with an inferiority complex. Highly intelligent though."

"Whatever the case," said Nichols, "I helped Crowley fake his own death. People do not realize that when you have the right contacts, faking a death is a very easy thing to do."

"I had no idea about the staged death. It is easy to stage such though," said Fleming. "What became of the old man?"

"He thought it would be quite funny if he could go to Regardie's home country. By that, I am referring to the United States, but Crowley also had someone he wanted to see very badly. Her name was Eva Tanguay, and I understand she passed away last year. Her passing was not long after Crowley's visit to her in Los Angeles. It was as if the two needed to consummate some sort of business or connection because Crowley passed not too long afterwards himself."

"What happened?" asked Fleming.

"For his safety, I had two of my druids accompany him to the United States. Together, they flew to New York and took a train to Los Angeles. Once there, he met with Tanguay, an actress from vaudeville who once had top billing wherever she performed. Exactly what was between the two of them remains unknown. They had been lovers many years ago, and Crowley remembered her quite fondly but also as an instrument he had used in the days before he went out to the end of Long Island. He was unhappy, however, about his ritualistic activity with her. What he remembered most about her, he said to my druids, was her remarkable performance in doing the Dance of the Seven Veils. He said nothing had ever moved him so much and that it was enough to make him completely heterosexual. Fortunately or unfortunately, life did not work that way for him. He did, however, share with my druids part of his conversation with Tanguay.

Apparently, by reason of her association with Crowley, she had been assaulted from many different sides, particularly from her Theosophical friends. When he visited her, she presented him with a memento she had kept. It was a playbill from her days with the Ziegfield Follies and had been framed. One of her Theosophical friends had given it to her, sort of as an amulet of protection from him. When Crowley came to visit her in Los Angeles, she told him, quite amusingly, of all the protection that had been invoked on her behalf with regard to her relations with him. She told him that she had never taken it all too seriously, but she wanted to present him with the memento. Behind the playbill, the Theosophist had apparently placed two pictures of Christ on the Mount of Olives. It was apparently symbolic.

"How so?" asked Fleming.

"The Mount of Olives, as you may recall, is symbolic of the end of the Temple. It is from this vantage point that Christ foresaw the destruction of Jerusalem. It is also where he ascended to heaven from. It also represents the bridge from heaven to earth.

"As Crowley and Tanguay were each at the end of their lives," continued Nichols, "she thought it would be a most appropriate memento to give him under the circumstances."

"Lammas bread..." muttered Fleming.

"What?" asked Nichols.

"I said 'lammas bread'," answered Fleming. "I just realized something. When the old man had told me about the entity Lam..."

"Lam?" asked Nichols. "Who is Lam?"

"Excuse me," said Fleming. "I apologize for muttering to myself. Something just occurred to me. It is about Lam. He is a very strange character Crowley used to talk about. Lam was an entity he contacted in New York. This had to have been around the time he knew Tanguay in America. You see, Lam was part of a working he did just prior to going out to Montauk. That was the place he directed the energy to during that ritual in Cornwall."

"Oh, yes," said Nichols. "I remember that all very well."

"Prior to now, I was not aware that Miss Tanguay was involved in that time period" said Fleming. "When you mentioned her a little while back, something occurred to me. I understand now."

"What's that?" asked Nichols.

"Lam is not only the name of the magical entity he contracted..." said Fleming.

"You mean contacted, right?" asked Nichols.

"Yes, that's right," said Fleming, "contacted. It's Lam. That's the entity that he contacted just before his initial trip to Montauk. What occurred to me, and why I stopped, is that I just realized that "lam" is the root of lammas and lammas bread is the Celtic people's pagan equivalent of the Christian Eucharist. You mentioned the olive and the olive is the bridge between heaven and earth. So is the bread and so is Lam, at least in theory."

"Interesting," said Nichols, "very interesting."

### RENDEVEAUX . . . . . . . . . . . . . . . . . . .

"So what became of our friend?" asked Fleming. "Did he ever return to England?"

"No. After his meeting with Tanguay in Los Angeles, he said that he wanted to repeat a bit of history and insisted my two druids take him back to New York. He wanted to visit Montauk one last time."

"Really?" asked Fleming.

"I remember that he was quite obsessed during that ritual. He wanted to direct all the energy to Montauk," said Nichols.

"Oh, by the way, I just remembered something," said Fleming. "I remember when we were at the ritual. I told him that if he ever made it back to the States to look up one John von Neumann."

"I'm glad you reminded me of that," said Nichols. "I know who you are talking about. Crowley told my druids about him, and they accompanied him to a meeting with him. How did you know about von Neumann?"

"I met him when I was visiting Colonel Donovan and helping him set up the template for the OSS," answered Fleming. John von Neumann was one of their top scientists and was working on an invisibility program. I had relayed some information to him about what had come up in the Hess interrogations, stuff about the electromagnetic bottle off of South America. His response was that it all made perfect sense but that there were a lot of technical details that had to be worked out. He said it was a complex proposition."

"To say the least," said Nichols. "It all makes sense, too. Anyway, by that time, von Neumann was working for an outfit called RAND in the town of Santa Monica. Crowley and von Neumann had a nice lunch together. They spoke quite freely in front of the druids. When von Neumann realized who Crowley actually was, he gave him quite an earful. He also considered it an honor to meet him. Von Neumann said he was trying to approach with science what Crowley had done with occultism. He told Crowley about his efforts to make a ship invisible but said it resulted in mental and physical casualties for the sailors aboard. Crowley had quite a bit to say, but neither myself nor the druids could begin to explain it all. They said that Crowley and von Neumann had a rapport with each other that was uncanny. They seemed to understand each other quite well.

"The two men met up again shortly after that. Von Neumann invited Crowley to his house on Long Island and even arranged for him to perform a ritual at one of the initial meetings of the United Nations at a place called Lake Success. I remember the name. It was at the headquarters of Sperry.

"But, the impetus of Crowley on Long Island was for him to go to Montauk Point. He wanted to go there one last time."

"Yes, you said that" said Fleming. "Continue."

"He shared his experiences at Montauk with von Neumann," said Nichols. "It was all very interesting and was certainly an intriguing way to pass out of this life."

"How did it happen exactly?" asked Fleming.

"Crowley went out to Montauk Point and visited his old haunts. He lamented the loss of the pyramids due to a hurricane in the thirties. I can't tell you how much that disappointed him. Sitting on the beach, he propped himself up against a cliff and looked out to sea. He was within a short distance of the lighthouse and he simply passed.

"His body was too awkward to carry without a stretcher so the druids called an ambulance. There was no question that he died of natural causes, but there was one problem. Crowley had a very strange last request. He wanted his body to be severed at the waist with the upper part being buried and the lower part being cremated. It was very odd.

"I cannot tell you what an unusual problem this created for the druids. They learned real fast that the protocol of morticians would not easily allow any part of such an endeavour. Besides professional standards, they have taboos about such things. It created the potential of a messy legal situation as well. The druids were not too keen about the situation anyway. Between themselves, they decided on a compromise. Crowley had originally asked for his upper torso to be buried at Montauk and that the ashes of his lower half be sent to his brethren in New Jersey. The compromise was that they had the entire body cremated on Long Island. They took half of the ashes and spread them out over Montauk Point. The other half were sent to New Jersey. That is how it ended."

"Thank you," said Fleming. "I finally have closure."

"But it's not all over," said Nichols. "There are far too many factors involved here for it to be all over. It is a kinetic situation if you ask me."

## RENDEVEAUX

"Indeed!" said Fleming. "As for myself, I'm going into private life. The intrigue has been fun, but it's time for me to enjoy the fruits of my labors. I have some travelling in mind and might even settle in Jamaica someday."

"I understand," said Nichols, "but be sure that you don't turn your back on the people you once worked for. Anything you left behind with them is no longer yours."

"I'm going to write fiction," said Fleming. "It's just a lot of made up stories as far as anyone is concerned."

"If you write it as fiction," said Nichols, "nobody will care. Just be sure not to spill the real beans on them. That way you'll be safe."

"I don't know," said Fleming.

"What's that?" asked Nichols.

"There's something I can't forget."

"What?" repeated Nichols.

"I have been responsible for a lot of deaths, and it is something I will never be able to escape," answered Fleming. "The Crown gave me a license to kill. I plan to be writing about that in my novels. In some way though, I will have to make up for it some day. I will do what I can. My safety is not as important to me as you might think. In my own way, I will try to find a way to correct the matter."

"That was just what Aleister said when we did that ritual in Cornwall," said Nichols.

"Exactly," said Fleming. "I now feel the same way myself."

True to his word, Ian Fleming withdrew into private life and achieved considerable fame as a prolific writer. In 1962, when his MI6 colleague, Ivan Sanderson, was conducting his own personal investigation into the death of Morris Jessup and the mysterious Philadelphia Experiment, Fleming vowed to fly to America and share what he could with his old friend. Forgetting that he was no longer so important to the Crown, Fleming's life became cheap. Before he could travel to New Jersey, he suffered a mysterious heart attack and was pronounced dead on August 12, 1962.

Few men ever know the power and intrigue that Ian Fleming enjoyed as a trusted officer of the Crown. All of that power and protection he enjoyed, however, was never really his. It belonged to him only as a functionary of the Crown.

...... CHAPTER FORTY-FIVE ......

## LAM

"The Man with Green Gloves?" asked Gretchen. "He was a man of great mystery and was sort like a Pope in the Orient. Haushofer had met him in Tibet."

"Was he connected to the Dalai Lama?" asked Heidi.

"Yes and no," answered Gretchen. "He was recognized as a spiritual head of a string of many monasteries which extended to Mongolia in the north and all the way to Manchuria in the west. The modern Dalai Lama ruled primarily over modern Tibet which was much smaller. The Empire of the Green Dragon extended far beyond those borders. Today, it is the Chinese who rule Tibet."

"What was he doing in Germany?" asked Mack.

"The lama with green gloves came to Germany because he trusted the Germans to carry out his plans."

"Which were?" asked Heidi.

"His plan was to open up a conduit between the two worlds. By that," said Gretchen, "I am talking about the inner world of man and the outer world of man."

"Do you mean the world between aliens and humans?" asked Heidi.

"You could say that if you want to," replied Gretchen, "but it is a little more complex than that. I am talking about a gateway between the ordinary human condition and all the elemental creatures or identities. In a sense, we are talking about the various hierarchies of all sentient beings."

"Yes," said Wilson, "but these various spots on the totem pole of evolutionary consciousness are only reached or achieved through initiations. What I have just gone through with my sojourn to Montauk is a prime example. It has been a remarkable experience, but it is a path each individual has to tread for themselves."

"Yes," said Gretchen, "but some of these creatures work on behalf of the collective consciousness and try to break it all open for everyone. Sometimes, however, it creates more chaos, but a character like the Man with Green Gloves was not working on just an individual template for himself. He was working on a grander scale. To his people, he was considered a representative of Shamabalah."

"Or the King of Shambalah," interjected Wilson.

"Some say that, yes," agreed Gretchen, "and one who came to this world to save Mankind. Whether he was divine, of this world, or fit somewhere in between, his program suffered from fatal flaws."

"He trusted Hitler to carry out his plans, right?" asked Wilson.

"According to his calculations, Germany was the top of the civilized world. Tibet was the geographic top of the world. He chose Germany long before they chose him. Haushofer recognized this and facilitated his journey to Germany. When Haushofer recognized Hitler and decided to sponsor him, it was all on behalf of the Man with Green Gloves. Hitler, who came later, respected the Tibetan and listened to him. He did not order the death of the Man with Green Gloves."

"I read that he died by ritual suicide," said Heidi. "There was a circle of dead lamas with him in the center."

"Yes," answered Gretchen. "He and his adjutants did commit ritual suicide, if you believe the story. I'm not sure that he really died the way they said or that he even died at all. I have also heard that the Russians preserved his body and that it is still in the hands of the KGB to this very day."

"How did he influence Hitler?" asked Mack.

He told Hitler about the Lamanites," said Gretchen.

"Excuse me," said Mack. "Who are the Lamanites?"

"They appear in Mormon doctrine," chimed in Heidi. "They were ancestors of the Native Americans but not the only ones. They are like bad guys in *The Book of Mormon*."

"That's correct," said Gretchen. "Hitler was always very interested in Native Americans. Although the Mormons believe that the Lamanites descended from the Mideast, the Man with Green Gloves taught that they traveled to America from the Mideast but that they had originated in Tibet and the Dropa Civilization. They derived their name from an ancient elder of this alien race whose name was Lam. This was the ancestor of the Man with Green Gloves. The Lamanites knew the passage ways to Shambalah in America.

"At one point, Hitler even had a mad plan to invade America through underground caverns in Arizona. Had he ever had the access to transport his troops from one location to another, he might even have pulled it off, but it was a very mad plan."

"You mentioned Lam," said Heidi. "That is very interesting because I have read that Lam is the name of an entity contacted by Aleister Crowley in 1918. Is it the same one?"

"I am familiar with what you are talking about," said Gretchen. "Lam is what Crowley called a praetor-human intelligence. This intelligence he contacted identified himself as a Tibetan elder. It is reasonable to assume that Crowley's Lam is either one and the same or an imitation. His students try to use the portrait of Lam that he drew in order to contact the other side."

"Are they successful?" asked Mack.

"Hah!" laughed Wilson, "They are successful to the degree that a host is successful when they have the life sucked out of them by a vampire!"

"Well put," said Gretchen.

"Lam," said Wilson, "is a bridge between the two worlds, but it is a damn narrow bridge. As a matter of fact, Crowley defined *Lam* as a Tibetan word for 'way.' Having just come back from the nether world myself, I can tell you that any of those jokers who call themselves disciples of Crowley are going to be consumed real fast. There are so many predators waiting at the gateway to consume the unworthy."

"This is the same problem with the remote viewers," interjected Heidi. "They are so messed up."

"God, yes!" said Wilson. "They become consumed and start propagating the agenda of a predator which is usually the harvesting of souls."

"Isn't that what happened in Germany?" asked Heidi.

"Exactly!" answered Wilson. "The Nazis came so close to bridging the gap that they became consumed by the predator in the harshest of manners. It is just like one of these athletes making it to the Super Bowl or World Series and blowing the big play in the last minute or last at bat. The humiliation is unbearable when they fail."

"The higher they go, the harder they fall," said Mack.

"Yes," said Wilson. "For many, they wish they would have never even reached into that rarefied area in the first place. The Nazis were smashed and smashed hard."

"They still survive though," said Heidi.

"Very true," said Wilson, "but the bridge that they sought has been relegated to the underworld."

"That is the realm of Pluto," said Gretchen. "The bridge has taken on a new contour. It is no longer in the realm or hands of Nazis. As priests, they were a failure," said Gretchen.

"Then," said Heidi, "if Lam is the bridge between the worlds, what does it all mean to us and this investigation?"

"I saw Crowley when I was in the Montauk underground," said Wilson.

"You did!" exclaimed Heidi.

"Sure," said Wilson, "I still haven't had time to explain everything."

"What did he say?" asked Heidi. "I'm fascinated."

"He didn't say anything," answered Wilson, "at least not to me. I didn't know who he was until after he was gone, but he had stolen videos of the lost of years of Christ."

"That is very interesting," said Gretchen. "But there is still more I need to explain to you about Lam. General, you were only partially correct when you quote Crowley as saying *lam* is a Tibetan word for 'way.' He got that from Madame Blavatsky, but the original word and etymology in Tibetan are much more interesting and help to explain how Crowley would be so wrapped up with Christ in your R.E.M state."

"Continue, Gretchen," said Wilson.

"If you transliterate the Tibetan word Lam into English, it is actually spelled *l-a-m-h*. The word is spelled with an *h*, but it was originally a silent *h*. The word *lamh* eventually evolved into *lama* where the *h* was pronounced as an *a* and became *lama*. In today's Tibetan, *lama* means 'teacher.' In the original indigenous language of Tibet, the word *lamh* means 'cross.' To be more technically correct, however, this cross really refers to a whorling vortex and is symbolized by the swastika. This symbol was imported to Germany from Tibet, in no small part by Karl Haushofer, and was used as the center of their movement.

"Interestingly enough, *lam* is also used in the Orient as the vocal intonation for opening up the first wheel or vortex of the chakra system. It is moving from the initial state to the more progressed state. The fact that one is using the intonation 'lam' to move from the first chakra to the second chakra is also symbolic of Aleister Crowley's magical working. The awareness of Lam had them working in a primal and primary manner. Crowley was being used as a vehicle himself."

"By Lam?" asked Mack.

"It's hard to say who was doing what, but it is the same bridge Lam was trying to build," said Gretchen. "My sources say yes. Lam is a very very old concept and word.

"It is important to point out here," continued Gretchen, "that there is a very deep association between this Tibetan tradition I've been talking about and some of the original concepts of Christianity. You see, the Biblical Christ spoke a language that shared a common denominator with Tibetan. He spoke Aramaic which was, like Tibetan, also a Persian language. Is it not ironic that when Christ said 'I am the way,' he was also being symbolized by the cross? You see, the concept of "the way" and "the cross" are inextricably linked in the very language Christ spoke, all through the word *lamh*. But, a swastika is a much better translation because it implies whirling, moving and evolving. It is the opening of the kingdom of heaven as opposed to a stationary cross or the concepts that go with it.

"All of this," continued Gretchen, "goes hand-in-hand with what Tibetans call the Mon-Lam Festival. In Tibet, this is the grandest and most sacred festival of the year. In Chinese, *mon* means gate and it represents the ancient gate-keepers who were later called Mongols. Mon-Lam refers to the gateway through the whirling vortex of the swastika. Although its literal meaning is diluted, this festival represents the gateway to Shambalah. You see, both Crowley and Hitler shared a common denominator. They were both being worked by an entity known as Lam."

"Gretchen," said General Wilson, "I should add something here. If you consider the Celtic holiday of Lammas, you will find another Christian concept. Lammas refers to 'consecrated bread.' This is a pagan tradition which parallels the Christian ceremony of consuming bread as the body of Christ. Lammas refers to pagan bread but it's the same concept."

"OK," said Heidi. "This all fits together pretty nicely but how do you compare Christ with the alien looking entity that Crowley drew? Is Lam the same as Christ or his shadow?"

"Consider that Christ is like a bridge foreman," said Wilson. "His job was to construct a bridge so that you could negotiate either side of the equation, earth or heaven so to

## LAM

speak. Lam is a more distant prehuman form that has something more to do with making the blueprints for the bridge. The concept of the whirling vortex is also suggestive of a pathway back to the creator. The swastika is like a bridge in that sense.

"If you want to compare Lam to little gray aliens, consider that they are essentially entities from his realm, or the 'other side,' who are trying to do a job. While they have been used for evil at times, their main problem is that they are so far afield from this dimensionality that they do not understand the human condition. Their inability to empathize results in human abuse and projects that lack virtue, to say the least. All of this stems from the lack of understanding that both sides have with each other. There is a lack of communication in terms of transferring data from one side to the other. You therefore have what is known as evil. This analogy is not much different from the human body. When chi energy flows within it, disease cannot arise. When there is little or no communication between the meridians, malignancy ensues.

"Lam, as well as the creatures which spring forth from him, often come to this dimension; but they are often frustrated and cut short in their attempt to communicate with us, just as we are with them. There are other guardians and safeguards in place, but it is a complex subject."

"So," said Heidi, "we are talking about a bridge between this world and the other world."

"Other worlds, to be more precise," said Wilson.

"Where do you fit in, Hugh?" asked Heidi.

"I'm in the middle of it all now," said the General. "In fact, I'm coming and going at the same time. All of this other phenomena, this paranormal phenomena, is all about the in-between state. There are lots of names for it. Through your association with me, you've all been introduced to it or it has taken you a bit further into it than you already were."

"OK," said Heidi. "Between you and Gretchen, you've said a lot. I don't know about the rest of you, but I've got to sit on what's been said and process it all."

"That only leaves me with one question," said Mack.

"What's that?" asked Wilson.

"Ali Bey," said Mack. "Whatever happened to him?"

"Ali Bey has passed through to the other side," said

Wilson. "Actually, what happened with him is not much different than myself. You know, it is a time-honored stunt of adepts to fake their own deaths. We have both moved to the other side and have abandoned our regular lives. I am currently here only by reason of this electronic apparatus and am really only able to maneuver here in an abbreviated fashion. I must remind you all not to touch me or to get too close. It might create problems, more so for you than for me.

"In the 1920s, Ali Bey was a contemporary of a man known as Noble Drew Ali. Noble Drew Ali brought Moorish Science to America and taught the true heritage of the Moors. In his own way, he was a representative of this same bridge of consciousness between one world and another.

"As a young man, Ali Bey was a part of the Moorish Science Temple run by Noble Drew. When Noble Drew left this world, Ali Bey saw the ravaging of his Sacred Temple and was unwilling to participate in what eventually became the Black Muslim movement. Instead, he went to Egypt and sought out the same masters that Ali Bey had once known and learned from them. Through their influence and other circumstances, he acquired a business in importing so-called magic lamps. Now, he is working on the other side. He is trying to sort out the Moorish situation. Originally, he came to Dr. Konrad looking for a mandate stating the true ownership of the Americas. This has proven very hard to find. Just as we have had obstacles and counter-intentions in this world, I should tell you that it is no different on the other side. That is one of the reasons I have had to pass. They need my mentality and bravado. It is a whole new hornet's nest I have to deal with, and I will be helping him as well."

"I hope this answers all of your questions," said Wilson, "at least for now. It is now time for me to go. I know you will all be scratching your heads and have a lot to talk about amongst yourselves. That is fine. Just hold the fort until I return. I can't tell you how soon I will be back, but it won't be too long. I am talking about days though, not hours. Do not try to follow me. I will be back."

Wilson then walked out the door to head for his car.

LAM........................

## CHAPTER FORTY-SIX

## THE RECKONING

"It's about time you got here!" exclaimed Heidi as Colonel Mack walked into the door of General Wilson's office. "General Wilson said to make sure that you were here above anyone else."

"It's not a big deal, Heidi," said Mack. "I'm only a short walk away when I'm on duty. The worse I could be is a few minutes late. Where's the general?"

"He will be here any minute," said Gretchen.

"So, it's just the three of us?" asked Mack.

"For now," said Heidi. "Frankly, I thought you'd be here earlier just out of eagerness to see the general. After all, he said this would be our last visit with him."

"I've been very antsy actually," said Mack. "He said it would be a matter of days, but as the days rolled by, I began to wonder if we would see him again. Did he give you any idea of what he's been up to."

"No," said Heidi. "Wait, I hear someone coming down the hall."

Going to the door, Heidi opened it and saw the general at the end of the hall. He was accompanied by Morgan, the beautiful gypsy lady who was wearing an evening dress.

"I can't believe this!" Heidi muttered under her breath.

"What?" said Mack.

"Quick, I've got to close the door," said Heidi. "He's with the gypsy. I don't know what the hell is going on."

After Heidi backed away from the door, she sat on the couch with Gretchen. Colonel Mack remained standing as General Wilson and Morgan came through the door.

"General Wilson — hello!" said Colonel Mack. "Great to see you again."

Morgan looked shocked to see Mack in the office. A look of betrayal and surprise overtook her face as she also noticed Gretchen and Heidi. She looked like a cornered cat and her beautiful face began to turn as ugly as it could possibly appear.

"You damned bastard!" said Morgan to Wilson. "You tricked me you bastard!"

# THE RECKONING

"If you resist, you're going to be cuffed," said Wilson to the gypsy. "Best to calm down and talk to us."

"Do you mind me asking what is going on here?" asked Heidi.

After calming down a bit, Morgan made a sudden bolt for the door so as to escape. Wilson grabbed her and she responded by clawing at him as she tried to break his grip.

"Get the cuffs, Heidi. You and Gretchen should be able to take care of her," said Wilson.

Having already touched her without incident, Wilson did not want to tempt fate. Knowing he should avoid touching anyone, he directed Mack to grip Morgan from the back as Gretchen restrained her arms and Heidi put cuffs on the prisoner. As Morgan was seated in a chair, Wilson got out some duct tape and secured her to the chair so that she could not even get up.

"I still need to know what is going on," said Heidi. "Are you ready to explain?"

"Sure," said Wilson, "now that she is finally subdued for the moment. By the way, Colonel Mack, I'm glad to see you smiling over this."

"This has got to be good!" said Mack, who had a big smile on his face.

"OK," said Wilson. "Just so you know, I haven't spent the whole week on this little project. I'll brief you later on what else I was up to later, but this woman is unfinished business. Heidi, get me the sodium-pentothal in my office."

As Heidi went to retrieve the truth serum, Wilson continued. "I sought her out for two reasons. First and foremost, I wanted to make sure that the energy is cleaned up between her and the colonel. What went on between them is very nonkosher. Second, there are some questions I have for her.

"After taking care of some business for all of you, I went and looked her up. She came on to me just the way that she did with Colonel Mack. I had a big advantage, however. I not only knew what she did to Colonel Mack, I am not particularly attracted to the woman. I pretended to be taken in by her, but instead of falling for her on the spot, I arranged a dinner date. Next, I told her I would take her to my secret office."

"Here is the serum," said Heidi as she handed Wilson a hypodermic needle.

"Thank you, Heidi," said Wilson as he took the hypodermic and flexed his fingers so that he could make an insertion. As he did, Morgan began to squirm and became as violent as possible for one who is tied to a chair.

"Steady her arm please, Heidi," said the general. "I shouldn't really be touching her but no harm so far."

As Heidi held Morgan's arm, Wilson made the injection.

"Now," said Wilson, "we'll wait for it to take hold and then ask her some questions she wouldn't answer right now."

"You bastards," said Morgan as she squirmed. "I'll get even with all of you — you bastards."

"My, my," said Wilson, "you should be glad we're not trying to get even with you for what you have done. You have quite a slate to clear, my dear. I'm talking about karma, you know."

At that statement, Morgan's face went pale.

"If you apologize for what you said right now," said Wilson, "I promise that we'll take it easy on you and give you a chance to make good."

"OK," said Morgan, as her eyes began to relax. "I'm sorry," she said as she slumped down. For the first time, she looked submissive. After a short while, she went out.

"Heidi, take the drip unit in the closet and bring it out. We might need it," said Wilson.

As Wilson and the others waited for the drip unit to be set up, he went and made coffee for everyone except himself.

"None for yourself, General Wilson?" asked Gretchen.

"I think you know better. I'm not quite suitable for digestion. Not now anyway," he answered.

When everything was in place, Wilson took Morgan by the hand and felt her pulse.

"Shouldn't you avoid touching her?" asked Heidi.

"It's not so critical when she's in a state like this," he said.

"Relax, Morgan," said Wilson to the sleeping lady. "We are here because we love you and there have been others who have caused you great harm. We are here to help you and to keep you from being harmed. Nod or blink and let me know that you hear me."

Under the influence of the truth serum, Morgan nodded her head slightly.

"Tell me," said Wilson, "the circumstances of your birth and exactly how you came into this world."

**THE RECKONING** . . . . . . . . . . . . . . . . .

Morgan's body jolted. The question clearly made her uncomfortable. When he repeated the question two more times, she went into a violent convulsion until she threw up.

"God!" said Heidi, as she ran to the bathroom and quickly returned with a towel. She cleaned up the woman as rapidly as possible.

"You'll be OK, Morgan. Don't worry. You'll be OK as soon as you tell me the truth about all that."

"I was..." she mumbled, "I was...."

"OK, go ahead," Wilson encouraged her.

"I was orphaned," she said, followed by a long pause. After a while, everything began to flow out of her. She began crying hysterically. Finally calming down, she began to speak.

"I was from a gypsy family," she said. "They sold me. They sold me because I was born in the veil. That means I was born with a film of skin over my face. It is an indication that one is clairvoyant and has special abilities. Instead of a gift, however, it has been like a horrible curse. My life has been terrible. It began before I was even born. My birth had been predicted by the gypsies for centuries. I was from the line of the black virgin. I never should have been taken from my family. They were gypsies, too."

"Where were your parents from?" asked Wilson.

"From the south of France, not far from Marseilles," she answered.

"Why did your parents sell you?" asked Wilson.

Morgan began to cry once again. Her crying increased until it shook her entire body. This was clearly a deeply traumatic incident for her. When she finished, Wilson spoke.

"I understand, Morgan. What was done to you was not right. We will try to make up for it, but you must help us. Why did your parents sell you?"

This question made her jolt. She spit out a black substance that looked like bile.

"Fuck you! Fuck you all!" she said as she began to writhe in an attempt to escape. She cursed and writhed again and again until finally she belched long and hard. After several more belches, she executed another exaggerated burp which was this time accompanied by a dark mist.

"She's fucking possessed!" said Gretchen. "Everyone stand back. Get out of the room, quick!"

Gretchen went straight to Mack and began to escort him out the door.

"Wait a second," said Wilson very calmly. "Give this a while. I know what I'm doing. She'll be OK. The bad has to leave before we can restore her. You are right, Gretchen. She has been possessed. We're going to clear that up now. Burn some sage, Heidi. That will help."

Morgan was now relaxed after the continuous and deep belching. There were no longer any signs of turmoil.

"Has it left you?" Wilson asked her.

"I think so," she said. "What has taken place with me is horrible. I am truly sorry if I have caused anyone any harm. When I said it before, I was just PRing you. I mean it now."

"OK, Morgan," said Wilson. "I want you to know that I was quite serious when I said we would try to help you."

"Thank you," said Morgan. "I want you to know that although I am under serum, I can still see and think as the clairvoyant I am. I am not completely in the dark as other subjects might be. I recognize you are here to help. I will try and comply."

"Excellent," said Wilson. "Where did Konrad come from and how did you get involved with him?"

"He was the one who bought me from my parents!" she exclaimed. "It was during World War II. He was stationed in the Alsace-Lorraine mountains and then moved to Marseilles when he learned of me. He was a Nazi doctor and had a team which had spies in the gypsy camp. They had been monitoring our legends for many years. Finally, when I was born, they knew it was me they were waiting for."

"How old were you when they took you?" asked Wilson.

"I was a young baby. They wanted to wait until I was older, but they took me when I was still young because the war was beginning to turn against them."

"When were you born and how do you know all this?" asked Wilson.

"Partly because I am psychic and partly because Konrad filled me in on the details. In some ways, he was a very nice man, but a very disturbed one. To answer your question, I was born on August 12, 1943. They had paid for me before I was born, but they only took me after the failed assassination attempt on Hitler in July of 1944. They were afraid that they

might lose the opportunity if they did not take me then."
"Wait — you were born on August 12th, 1943?" asked Wilson. "You are sure?"
"That's what I said," answered Morgan.
"OK," inquired Wilson, "why did Konrad want you?"
"He wanted me because I was foretold by gypsy legends," answered Morgan. "My family on my father's side was Romanian. My mother was a Sephardic Jew, but both of my parents had Moorish blood as well. The gypsies speak a language known as Romany and the name has always mystified scholars. The name 'Roma' is really a code word because, if you spell it backwards, you will have *a-m-o-r* or *a-m-o-u-r*, a word which means 'love' but a word that also signifies "Moor" when you drop the *a*.

"The gypsy legends about me were in anticipation of what is referred to as a magical child, sometimes called the black virgin. There are many more tales behind my birth than even I know. All I know is that these legends told them they needed certain genetics to produce this child. The missing ingredient was a Pharaoh. They needed someone of the Pharaonic line with Egyptian heritage. At long last, they finally found a Pharaoh but not one from Egypt. They were from the United States. My maternal grandmother was a Pharaoh."

"What was her name and where was she from?" asked Wilson.

"Her name was Fowler and she was from Montauk," answered Morgan. "The genetic Pharaoh was supposed to come from my mother's side and this woman fit the bill."

"Thank you very much, Morgan," said Wilson. "That is very important information and is much appreciated. I want to assure you once again that my friends and I will take good care of you, but I have some more questions first.

"Morgan, I want you to understand that Montauk is significant," continued Wilson, "because it is where Dr. Konrad moved to before he was assassinated. How does Konrad tie in to your bloodline being from Montauk?"

"It was the original tracing of the gypsies and their lineage that interested the Germans in Montauk in the first place," said Morgan. "In the years preceding my grandmother, nobody was quite sure how to find a Pharaoh. At long last, they found an old gypsy woman. Her name was Mahleva and she was Romanian. She told a story which no one had ever heard before. She claimed that the Pharaohs of Egypt had not originated there. Instead, they had come from a far off land. Everyone knows, of course, that Egyptians are believed to have come from Atlantis, but Mahleva had a different twist on it. She talked about a land that was a part of the United States that was also once a piece of Egypt that fit into where the Nile is now. It was a center of culture and contained sacred tombs, all underground. This is the land we know of today as Montauk. In ancient history, we know that the Pharaoh was at Montauk long before Egypt. Montauk has served as a relay point for the culture of Egypt and other areas."

"Can you be more specific how this plays into Dr. Konrad and what he was doing here?" asked Wilson.

"Yes," answered Morgan. "He had suddenly gone to Montauk because you were on his trail. I went after Colonel Mack in an effort to stop you. Montauk was a place he had resided in before, and he was returning to what he considered to be safe ground. What he didn't know, however, was that his masters now considered him a liability. They were cutting him off."

"How do you know all of this?" asked Wilson. "Does it not compromise you to share this?"

"I do not have masters in the sense that he did," said Morgan. "I was only subject to the entity which is now released. The entity worked on both me and Konrad, but he also had masters in the physical sense. By that, I mean he had people that he reported to. They were at the Montauk base."

"What do you know about the base?" asked Wilson.

"It is a strange admixture of different echelons of government strata. The Germans have been there the longest. There are also Americans and British and even French. It is a U.N. in its own right and it is run by secret societies: Freemasons, the Vatican, the Knights of Malta, Illuminati and you name it. It is a multiplex of different nationalities, even from different times," said Morgan.

"Is that true, Hugh?" asked Heidi.

"All I saw was U.S. military insignia," answered Wilson. "Can you explain that, Morgan?"

"It depends on what level you are looking at and at what time," she answered. "You can penetrate these various areas

## THE RECKONING...............

I am talking about as you expand in your own life. Do not discount what I say just because you have not seen it nor because it is not as close to this realm as you might like."

"Earlier, in the car, you mentioned to me that there were Tibetans at Montauk. Does this tie in to the so-called 'Man With Green Gloves' and if so, how?" asked Wilson.

"Konrad was actually part Tibetan himself," she said. "The Tibetans have a special role to play. Konrad explained to me that part of my lineage was Tibetan but did not come from Orientals per se. I am related to an ancient Romanian count whose name was St. Germaine. You may know of him already. He lived in different time periods. He was a friend of Marie Antoinette and even popped up in America. There are consistent historical records of him appearing throughout history, but he is originally from Transylvania and is not a corporeal entity like the people on this planet. In fact, you are very close to him in your current state. His last known appearance in 'regular reality' was with the Prince of Hesse."

"That is my relative!" interjected Gretchen.

"Yes," replied Morgan, "the Prince of Hesse is from a very secretive family that is tied to Rudolph Hess as well. After he departed from the Prince, St. Germaine is known to have retreated to the Himalayas. There, he is said to have resided with the Ascended Masters. It is from his namesake and inspiration, all directed from the Himalayas, that Deutschland came to be known as Germany. This name was fostered upon the Germans and held sway over them."

"According to Theosophical threads, St. Germaine did indeed retreat to the Himalayas. Are you also aware that St. Germaine is adored by many romantics and people of many different persuasions?" asked Wilson. "He is an object of literal worship, inspiration and higher ideals."

"That is not untrue," said Morgan, "but there is a dark side as well. Who better than myself to see that? I was born into the light but the arrangements of my family and the oppression against them quickly turned me to the dark. Only through you, Hugh Wilson, am I beginning to return to the light — at long last. Thank you so much."

"Can you tell us more about St. Germaine?" asked Wilson.

"It is hard to explain. Let me think for a bit so I can compose it for you," said Morgan.

"I can add something while you wait," interjected Gretchen.
"What is it?" asked Wilson.
"All of those Ascended Masters that ended up in the Himalayas — did you ever notice that they are all men?" said Gretchen. "They are always depicted as men. That also applies to most of the great religious leaders of our planet."
"You've made a hell of a point," said Wilson.
"Yes, Gretchen," said Morgan. "You have made an excellent point. The desecration of the female is very relevant in this regard. During the time of Atlantis, crafts were powered by the energy on the planet. This included the female energy. As the energy became compromised, transmuted and convoluted, all of the female energy became vampirized and started to drain. It has been receding for many millenniums. Only upon my return is it supposed to change. These characters in the Himalayas siphoned off the energy. There have been different devices and contraptions over the years to accomplish this end. One of their methods was to create myths and legends of vampires. This is Bram Stoker's *Dracula*. These characters cannot become corporeal but can indulge in a psychic drain of energy that affects the collective. Satellites have also been put up to this end. In ancient times, satellites were put up to formulate and propagate opinions and ideas that would serve this feeding frenzy. They could even direct people like Konrad. He was an early explorer of Tibet, and he claimed to have had a personal dialogue with St. Germaine. Most of the people who think they have a dialogue with St. Germaine are communicating with astral thought forms often generated by beat up old satellites and what not."
"I am sensing that this has something to do with time travel," said Wilson. "Am I right?"
"It has everything to do with time travel," she answered. "Time travel is a technology that is designed to transfer people or things from one place to another. It is a perfect device for siphoning off energy. In fact, sometimes the energy can be siphoned off without moving the actual physical properties. This means that the energy is taken without anyone noticing it too visibly."
"The problem with time travel is the same problem with economics, politics, religion and most any situation common

THE RECKONING................

to Mankind. There is exploitation by a few at the top of the pyramid. On the other hand, all these things can be used positively as well. Each of us has to tread their own path, and I have a lot of karma to make up for."

"Well said, Morgan," said Wilson. "I think you have answered all of my questions. "Now, I want to make sure that everything is OK with Colonel Mack and your involvement with him. Colonel?"

"Thank you, sir," said Mack. "I am quite OK with all of this. The healing that Heidi and Gretchen did on me is more than adequate. This is just icing on the cake."

"I have something to say about this," said Morgan. "I was directed at Colonel Mack like a predatory vampire. I had to stop him at all costs, but that was only because I was being driven by the entity. I can tell you that I am truly remorseful and am now a different person."

"I could not be happier about the way things have worked out here," said Wilson. "I could not be happier. My work is done here."

"Thank you very much, General," said Morgan.

"You are welcome and free to go," said Wilson, "I know I said that this was the last time I was supposed to see you all, but I've still got a few more errands to run and will see you once again in a day or so."

Wilson then got up and walked out the door.

## ......CHAPTER FORTY-SEVEN......

## THE FUTURE

General Wilson was beaming as he returned to the office. He had a package from Fedex in his hands.

"You're back!" said Heidi excitedly. "What's the big smile all about?"

"Just another remarkable coincidence," said Wilson. "Just as I arrived at the guard booth, a Fedex truck arrived. They had an international Fedex package for me. We both got here at the same time!"

"Did you get everything else done?" asked Mack.

"Yes, and then some!" answered Wilson. "And just when I thought I was all through, I now have a Fedex."

"Where is it from?" asked Heidi.

"It is from Switzerland," said Wilson.

"Yes," said Gretchen. "Just before I left Berlin, a colleague of Agent T gave me a video, but I never had the time to watch it. He wanted to give it to Agent T, but he had already left. The contact said I should pass it on. With all of the activities going on here, I completely forgot about it. In Europe, I placed it in the hands of a trusted solicitor who was supposed to send it after a certain number of days passed if he did not hear from me. I had him wait as I wanted to ensure there were no mess ups on your end or with me getting here."

"Let's look at the tape," said Colonel Mack.

Putting the tape into a European PAL video player, they saw that it came with a coded note which General Wilson soon deciphered.

"What does the note say?" asked Heidi.

"It is just a short note," he said. "It says that these are some short splices of the Hess crime scene taken from the video surveillance system at the prison. There is no sound and it is only a few minutes long. It should prove of great interest."

Watching the video, they saw a dwarf-sized person entering the crime scene. He was carefully placing tarot cards at the garden house where Hess was said to have killed himself. The little man also placed cards in the cell and in the garden. It only took a few minutes or two to see the entire video.

# THE FUTURE........................

"It's bizarre," said Heidi.

"Yes," said General Wilson, "but it explains a lot."

"But not who put the cards in his car," said Heidi.

"I think it gives you a pretty good idea. It looks like it's the little people who scared off Agent T," said Wilson.

"Agent T is a very good man," said Gretchen, "but he doesn't have your occult acumen."

"Nor your battlefield acumen," said Mack. "Getting scared of little people is kind of amusing."

"He was being threatened by a force he didn't understand," said Wilson. "That is understandable, but you are right. It is amusing — a dwarf at the crime scene leaving clues."

"Well," said Heidi, "I guess the little people would have a much easier time slipping in and out of the all the nooks and crannies of the prison."

"I don't get it" said Mack.

"I thought I was all through, but I realize now that I have a lot more explaining to do," said Wilson. "As I told you all before, we are standing in a crack between the worlds. The little people are the stewards of this twilight realm. With regard to Hess, and I am not referring to his physicality, his spirit and the forces he represented were always a part of that twilight world. This is why they showed up after his death. They are, in their own way, attempting to repair a crack between the worlds. It is as if they were waiting there and hovering for years. When he died, they took advantage of the situation as if to signal me. It was a somewhat rocky ride, but I experienced far worse during the war."

"General, you've been battle-tested. Now you've gotten your cake and will soon be able to eat it," said Heidi.

"It's not as easy as you think," said Wilson. "My hardest work is before me. On the other hand, you people might find yourself eating a lot of cake very soon."

"What do you mean by that?" asked Heidi.

"I told you I had some things to take care of," said Wilson. "I've been working on your future as well as various legalities."

"Legalities?" asked Heidi. "Please explain."

"I have had to make arrangements for my own death certificate as well as the dissolution of this unit," said Wilson.

"Oh no!" said Mack. "I'll be reassigned. After working with you, it will be a hard pill to swallow and far too routine."

"Don't worry," said Wilson, "I've taken care of that for you, too. Colonel, you and Heidi are going to be mustered out of the military. Don't worry about the time you put in. You'll be getting a retirement package to die for. Gretchen, you'll be getting a similar package, too. I've transferred monies from many slush funds and black ops budgets that I have administered over the years. You'll all be set for life."

"What is this *really* all about?" asked Heidi.

"Suffice it to say," said Wilson, "that a trust fund has been set up so that you'll each be making more in interest than a doctor and lawyer put together. There will be plenty of room for luxuries if you want them, too. In addition to that, there is a sizable operating budget for looking into other matters.

"The only caveat in all of this," continued General Wilson, "is that I can no longer guarantee you the same military support we enjoy now. As I pass, that is beyond my control. Believe it or not, that might prove to be your biggest obstacle. But, you'll have plenty of time to eat cake!"

"I can't believe this, Hugh," said Heidi. "I don't know if this is too bizarre to be true or too good to be true."

"Just look at it as one more initiation," said Wilson.

"Before you give us an idea of what matters you want us to look into, can you give us an idea of what we should do with the prisoners?" asked Heidi.

"The shrinks?" asked Wilson. "As a matter of fact, yes. I've set aside an account for them, but not too much. They don't deserve too much. I've put aside ten thousand for each one. I will give them a bus ticket to Montauk. My directions to you are to trace them and find out where they go and what they do. I'll start them off with a thousand dollars each. After that, each one will have nine more moneygrams waiting for them at any Western Union depot over the next six months. After that, they are on their own. That is their problem, but you might be able to find out a bit if you watch what they do and where they go."

"What about their old jobs?" asked Mack.

"I don't think they'll be returning to their former masters, if they can even find them. Their former masters won't want to have anything to do with them. They are small fry in my opinion. As for you, Gretchen, you might have the most interesting task of all," said Wilson.

# THE FUTURE . . . . . . . . . . . . . . . . . . . . .

"I have no reason to doubt you, and I know you are telling me the truth," said Gretchen. "I can't imagine any reason why I would resist your suggestions. What do you have in mind?"

"I would like you to head to Cape Town, South Africa," said the Wilson. "That is the location where Agent T went to. I am the only one who knows his address, and I can guarantee you that he is quite safe from the wrath of the little people. If anything, he did them a favor."

They all laughed at this last remark.

"Once you get there, Gretchen, you had better believe you will be in for some interesting times," said Wilson. "Agent T will be up to something."

"What will that be?" asked Gretchen.

"I can only give you a hint because I actually don't know," answered Wilson. "The one thing I can tell you is that Agent T has a very active mind. The reason we picked Cape Town as a hiding place was that it is remote, but it is also a source of great intrigue for the both of us. It is a depot for submarines that travel to the Antarctic."

"Oh, the Nazi's Antarctic connection!" exclaimed Heidi. "That should present a wonderful bowl of mysteries to you, Gretchen. He's right, you do have a most interesting job."

"I can't imagine anyone who is more suited for it than Gretchen," said Wilson.

"What about us?" asked Mack.

"What about you?" asked Wilson. "I see wedding bells for the two of you."

Heidi's mouth opened with a gasp of surprise and shock. Mack just smiled.

"I can't believe it!" said Heidi. "Morgan just gave me another one of her card readings yesterday. She said I would be getting married very soon. I had no thoughts about Colonel Mack though."

"You always told me how much you admired Colonel Mack," said Wilson. "Now's your chance. I wish I could be around long enough to be the best man."

"Or give away the bride," said Heidi sarcastically.

"This is a shock to me as well," said Mack, "but I'm not doing any complaining. We're obviously going to have to process all of this. But, what do you have in mind for us as far as the work you were referring to?"

"Your first assignment is to get everything out of this office and basically destroy all of the sensitive records. There are certain ones you can send to the National Archives. Heidi, you can keep all of the files on the past investigation of Hess. It might come in handy with what you have to do later."

Wilson then handed each of his three friends large envelopes.

"In each envelope, you will find accounts with various instructions on how you can access them. Your first job will be to make your own banking arrangements tomorrow, just to make sure everything works out. You will have no problem. Gretchen also has personal instructions on where to go in South Africa and where to make contact. As for you two, you'll be the ones taking care of wrapping things up here. I'll take care of the shrinks myself and you won't have to worry about them. Trace them if you can though. That will possibly prove useful."

"Is that it?" asked Heidi. "Is it just good-byes from here?"

"Well," said Wilson, "I guess it is unless there is something else you want to ask."

"Let me understand correctly," said Colonel Mack. "Are you saying all we have to do is just evaporate this unit of military intelligence and that all of the bureaucratic paperwork is taken care of already? What do we do then? Go out and find a job or just start loafing?"

"Your instructions are inside of the envelopes. I do have some work for you to do, but it is not something I can enforce upon you. I know you will both give it your best shot though," said Wilson. "Besides providing for your future, I know that I have selected something for you that will not only prove useful but will also interest you. I would not have picked you had I believed otherwise."

"I guess we shouldn't really shake hands or hug, right?" asked Heidi.

"It really would not be a good idea," said Wilson. "Emotions are particularly sensitive with regard to this sort of thing, but I wanted to extend my love to all of you, and I have a feeling we will all be in touch in the future."

"There's one thing you haven't mentioned," said Heidi, "unless you mentioned it in the envelope.

"What's that?" asked Wilson.

## THE FUTURE . . . . . . . . . . . . . . . . . . . .

"The time travel device. That is highly sensitive. Do you want us to destroy that, too?" asked Heidi.

Wilson slapped his hand to his forehead. "How could I be so stupid?" he said. "For all of my recent enlightenment, I have neglected to tell you that I need that in order to make my return trip. I forgot the most important part of my getting back to my new home."

"You also forgot to mention something else," said Gretchen.

"What is that?" asked Wilson.

"When you were talking about the little people, everyone forgot to mention that it was a little person who set up the time machine so that you could come through," said Gretchen.

"Gee," said Wilson, "I didn't know that. I didn't see any little person when I arrived."

"We were all so glad to see you that we forgot to take notice of the little person disappearing. He was wearing army fatigues!" said Heidi.

"That's how those people are. They move at their own pace and in their own time," said Gretchen. "They are very mysterious."

"Maybe it is out of our hands," said Heidi, "but are you or is anyone planning to take the time machine?"

"You have the book, Heidi," said Wilson. "As far as I know, the device will stay with you as long as you have that book. If you lose the book, however, it is going to move towards its new owner."

"Boy," said Heidi, "this sounds like risky business. What if I were to send this book to the bottom of the ocean?"

"Let's not find that out," said Wilson. "Whether or not it's risky, I will say that it creates the potential for chaos. Do keep in mind that I am new to this realm myself and there are no safe bets. Chaos will always be a factor."

"And interest as well!" said Gretchen.

"True," said Heidi. "Don't worry. We won't throw out the machine nor the book."

"You know," said Colonel Mack, "for what might amount to the saddest of good-byes, this sounds like a splendid beginning for all of us."

"Indeed!" said Wilson.

## CHAPTER FORTY-EIGHT

### ATLANTIS RISING

After his friends read their instructions, General Wilson sat in the time machine and spoke.
"You all know what to do. Any questions?" he asked.
"No, sir," said Mack and Heidi in unison.
"Gretchen?" he asked.
"I'm fine," she said.
"Excellent," he said as he sat between the coils.
"Does anybody need to do anything?" asked Mack.
"Don't worry about a thing," said Wilson. "There's somebody on the other side, sort of like Scottie on *Star Trek*."
As Wilson prepared to depart this dimension, a small green haze suddenly appeared in front of him. He looked puzzled, as if something was not quite right. Everyone's eyes became fixated on this green light until it slowly materialized into a large-sized envelope.
"My goodness," said Wilson as he looked at the envelope that had virtually manifested on his lap. "It's for you, Heidi. Looks like you've got mail from the other side!"
Wilson tossed the envelope in her direction as a new green light began to envelop his entire body. After a short while, he disappeared completely.
"Never a dull moment!" said Mack as he picked up the envelope and handed it to Heidi. Her name was on it but there was no return address.
"It's from Ali Bey!" exclaimed Heidi as she opened the envelope. "I recognize his handwriting."
She shuffled through several handwritten pages and verified that it was indeed his signature that was at the end of the very long message.
"This is from Ali all right," said Heidi. "This is something of a surprise."
"I never quite understood how he went over to the other side with General Wilson," said Mack.
"Maybe it says in here," said Heidi. "I'll read it to you all."
Heidi then began to read the lengthy letter from Ali Bey. It read as follows.

"To my dear friends (Heidi, Gretchen and Colonel Mack),

I can't believe what has happened to all of us! In so many ways, it is as if all of my prayers have been answered. It seems that I have at long last reached a stage in evolutionary development that past searchers on the path have only dreamed of but either seldomly or never dared experience.

I never believed that death was anything more than a natural process of being in-between lives. It is just something one passes through. Now, even though I never "died" in a so-called "normal" manner, I have a full taste of what it is like to operate with a spirit and no body.

Surprise and disorientation are an understatement to what I have experienced here. Although I can obviously still relate to the entity which you knew as Ali Bey, there is an inherent inertia in this realm for me to drop that identity altogether and adopt a new frequency and assignation. I still intend to work for those principles I believed in on Earth, but my vehicle and methods will be different.

The most unsettling thing in this realm, and I feel that it is my sincere responsibility to warn you all for your own sake, is that the resistance to truth in your world is only amplified and intensified in this realm. The pain and emotions that go with this are even more heartfelt and dramatic on this side. This is hard to explain. The best I can do is give you the old saw, 'As above, so below,' but that is also an understatement.

My people, the Moors, were suppressed on Earth, almost to the point where they have been forgotten. In this world, the bias and virulent activity against them is even more pronounced, perhaps because it is so clearly visible.

In any event, I have learned a few things which I will pass on to you. I sincerely hope that you can look further into the information I present. It is important because it contains keys that can open more doors. Do with it what you can.

The 'other side' is far stranger than I ever imagined. No matter how I try to communicate it, this cannot be considered other than a garbled transmission when I put it into a form such as a letter. Please try to understand this. I will do my best.

The first thing I would like to impart is how precisely accurate the practice of astrology is when it assigns Neptune as the planet and Pisces as the sign that rules the spiritual realm. The reason for this is that everything over here is like a big ocean. It seems that I am approached by many life forms that are akin to schools of fish. They move in patterns like fish. Some are predatory and some are benign or even pro-life. There are various other factions as well. There is also a factor here that reminds me of binary digits. You know, the zero's and one's that computers are made of. You can also call them yins and yangs if you want to.

In this world, you do not have a body. Instead, you attract an assembly or assortment of characteristics. The best way I can describe this phenomena is as I have said above: binary digits. Here, you attract and hold things to you so you can be recognized for what you want to be represented by. Who you *really* are is truly invisible. Without a body or eyes and ears, you have to invent your own characteristics.

If I had died by normal means, I might not be as on top of things as I am now. I have seen many people, if they can even be thought of as people (it is hard to explain), who passed over and have been taken advantage of. Those who have recently passed are usually deluded as to what is going on, and they tend to run their new 'lives' by associating too much with what they 'knew' in your world. Too often, they are at the bottom of the 'food chain' here.

I am trying to be as brief as possible so that I can arrive at the major thrust of my communication, but you should know that General Wilson and I have had very different experiences. We 'ascended' together, but we have gone in two different directions. It is hard to hold onto the identity of my old body-self, but I can hold onto it to some degree because I have a very specific purpose. For all of the wisdom that I had acquired, particularly in the esoteric realm, I am surprised at how difficult it has been for me to negotiate the other side. To the contrary, General Wilson seems far more able and fit for the job ahead of him. This is noteworthy because he does not possess my background of esoteric study nor did he ever meet with the masters I knew. I suppose it can be chalked up to us both being unique individuals with different roles to play.

I can only attribute his agility over here to two things. First is that he is one tough son-of-a-bitch. His ability on the battlefield really was a psychic ability and that seems to have served him well here. Second is the work that Gretchen did.

She primed the recesses of his mind in such a way that he is extremely fluid with whatever he encounters. He sees beyond many veils and moves without hesitation.

I will now begin the import of my message to you with the following. I have had several experiences over here but only one that I feel is representative of how things operate — not only over here where I am but where you are as well. As I said earlier, 'As above, so below.'

This experience began after I decided to find out who was in charge in this new continuum that I was in. Not much longer after putting forth this question, I came across what I can only describe as a resplendent pyramid that was surrounded in primordial slime. It was as if it was bubbling in toxic liquid. The pyramid, shining and beautiful, seemed to represent the answer to my question with regard to who was controlling things. It was at least presented before me.

When I came to the pyramid, it spoke to me and identified itself as Aiwass. He said he was the eye of the triangle which was the same as the Eye of Horus. These were familiar concepts that I had learned about in life. Aiwass was not only a character in Aleister Crowley's *The Book of the Law* but can be equated to the jinn master who controls so much of organized consciousness. No sooner had I heard his voice than I saw him in a more personalized form. He looked like an Egyptian priest. Many sacrifices, all of them men, were brought before him. He promptly slit the throat of each one with a knife as a resplendent joy shined within him. The sacrifices kept coming, one after another. With continual repetition, things became boring and the joy lessened in intensity overall, but there would still be a vestige of joy each time he saw the look of fright upon his victim's face. This was disconcerting, particularly if you consider that he might be the controlling force over here. When I approached, however, his countenance changed completely. It was very clear that I was not meant to be one of his victims, at least not now. In some strange way, he treated me as if I were an equal.

'Aiwass is my name,' is what he said as he produced a large black obelisk that was made of pure obsidian. Placing his hands across it and looking very proud, he said that this implement was the source of his magick. He then told me that he controlled the world. This time, however, he was referring to the world you live in; nevertheless, it also applies here. As above, so below. He said that he had consolidated his power in the United States which was not only the New Atlantis but part of the old Atlantis, too.

He said that George Washington was his key in the initial struggle for power in the United States. I personally found this intriguing because native tradition has long recognized Washington as an indigenous person. I am referring not only to the Indians but to the Moors. The tribal chiefs always recognized Washington as having Moorish blood. Did you ever notice that there are no white people named Washington? They all seem to be black because the name Washington derives from the Moorish Washitaw Empire who are recognized as the oldest indigenous people of the Earth. Place names like Wichita are also named after them.

Besides the above, there is another interesting etymology to his name that sheds so much light on what I have already told you. According to common history, George Washington's family came from a locale in England that was once known as the de Wessington Estate. The name Washington is believed to have derived from Wessington. George, however, was not of de Wessington lineage but his family had acquired the estate and took on the name. The truth of Washington's family is that they originally came from America and went to England. The currents of the Atlantic made travel to the British Isles considerably easy and there were many migrations of natives. His family's migration went way back and they re-migrated back to America. He was also of a Masonic heritage that derived from the original masons of America, the Moors.

There was an esoteric energy template that surrounded George Washington as well as the estate of the de Wessingtons. It was a template that not only included his family and the people of the estate, but it also included the connections he would make in life with the American natives. He was carrying a heritage that was much more than his family name and genetic line. It derived from Aiwass. The de Wessington Estate had actually derived its name from Hwaes, a great Saxon general. Wessington derived from *Hwaes* + *inga* (family) + *tuni* (estate); hence, Hwaes-ing-tun = Wessington. It was this general, Hwaes, who carried the magic energy of Aiwass, their names being virtually identical.

The colonies were quite ready to crown George Washington as a king. They even contemplated this on the basis of using Native American titles. Eventually, it was decided to relegate these names for use in secret societies. He was, however, clearly a royal man who inherited the mantle of this new republic. The best way I can describe his ascendancy to this 'throne' of power is as a compromise between God and the jinn. It does not make Washington either bad or good. It makes him a vehicle of convenience or a gateway. In this respect, he was something of a doorman for Aiwass. All of this comes to light when you consider the magical fiber of Washington and his involvement in Freemasonry.

George Washington was a surveyor by trade. Surveying, however, is really more of a name for the laymen. As you well know, Freemasonry evolved from the building trade. The most important and fundamental aspect of building, particularly from a Freemason's point of view, concerns where to build. This is where the surveyor comes in; but to the Freemasons, these surveyors were known as measurers of the Earth. This included ley lines and most every imaginable measuring that one could do. The term surveying, however, had been degraded in modern usage where it refers to a task. The word *survey* is a compound of *sur* and *vey* which means a superior view. The Latin word it comes from refers to the same. In time, the word *sire* derived from the Latin *sur* and *sire* is a word which means majesty or magus. A surveyor is a measurer, but he is much more than that. The word *measure* itself is interesting because it derives form *mensura* or *menses*. These words refers to menstruation, the original rhythm or beat of nature. Menstruation measures time. Historically, in its most exalted sense, the word *surveyor* refers to the "King's Rule," even if it does obscure the feminine principle upon which his rule is based. Measurements done by the Craft were always done on behalf of the Master Builder.

General George Washington learned the trade of surveying under the sponsorship of his relative, the Baron de Cameron, who owned the greatest tract of land in Virginia at that time. During the Revolution, the Baron remained a Loyalist which, in fact, made him an enemy of the state. His connection to Washington, however, enabled him to remain free from harm.

Washington's bloodline was very mysterious, but it also solved a great problem for his contemporaries that he served. Prior to the French and Indian War, Virginians (or any Europeans for that matter) were not allowed into Ohio and the sacred mound area. Washington's blood was a solution because the natives recognized him as having Moorish blood. He not only had the Khemetic blood from the indigenous clans of America but also from the Camerons of Britain. It was his indigenous or Moorish blood that made him acceptable to the people of the Ohio mounds, but it was not only his blood. Washington also possessed the Masonic passwords that the natives recognized. He was therefore afforded access to Ohio that neither the British nor other Virginians could avail themselves of.

These common passwords were a result of European Masons and indigenous masons of North America having originally derived from the same tradition of master builders that had once thrived in Egypt. The mound builder culture had originally migrated from Egypt and they were Masons themselves. They had come by way of Montauk, many with the great pharaoh known as Montauk Pharaoh. The mound builders taught Washington the importance of Montauk with regard to the history of the ancient people. It was not only a major port but a center for royalty. The more esoteric aspects of Montauk, however, had to do with its depiction on ancient treasure maps and as a capital of Atlantis. When it came to the role of 'surveyor,' a word which means 'overview,' Montauk reigned supreme. All of this, believe it or not, led to the Montauk Lighthouse becoming the first official public construction project of the United States of America, commissioned by President Washington. The lighthouse was his obelisk. In order that you understand, I will explain further.

One of the original forms of magic from Africa is called obeah. It is another word for magic or sorcery. The Masons stylized this word for their own use and it was known as the magic of the secret light. It is from this word *obeah* that the word *obelisk* is derived from. The Greek etymology that is usually given for this word refers to a sharp writing instrument, the *obelus*, but the Greeks actually derived that from the original word *obeah*. The obelus is a magical instrument in itself because writing is the highest form of magic.

As a Freemason, Washington realized that the pyramids at Montauk needed an obelisk if they were going to wield magic. When he built the lighthouse, this magic became the province of the imposing Freemasons rather than that of the indigenous people. Most of the Montauks had been moved off of the land by that time. It was thus that the Montauk Lighthouse became the magic of the secret light.

The original lighthouse at Montauk doubled as a secret entrance to the underground caverns that are abundant and still there to this day. The lighthouse keeper at Montauk was also a gate-keeper to the underworld. Do not underestimate the truth of this in your own world.

As I said earlier, Montauk appeared on ancient maps. The Freemasons' obsession with measurements and surveying had to do with ley lines but also had to do with ancient maps of gold. These maps represent the data on a computer hard disk that has crashed. To this day, secret societies fight to protect or secure the fragments or fruits of these ancient maps.

The Knights Templar who originated during the Middle Ages were custodians of these maps, but they were not the original knights. They are actually a reinvention of an earlier order that are somewhat accurately depicted in the legends of the Knights of the Holy Grail. Theses knights were of the original Merovignian bloodline or were protectors of that bloodline. The original bloodline arose in France, and that is the bloodline of the original King Arthur.

These knights had the original maps of Solomon's treasure and where it was taken from. The treasure needed to be returned. These maps contained routes to America. Years later, Francis Bacon, under the auspices of the Templar tradition, personally saw to the return of many caches of treasure to the New World. Treasure was sent to Montauk and Utah, both locations having suffered greatly in current times as a result of subsequent political manipulations.

These treasures and maps were the true inspiration behind the concept of El Dorado. The Spanish conquistadors, on behalf of the Vatican, were seeking known treasure and not just pursuing a folly or a pipe dream. In those days, the important secrets of the world were held by royalty. The original Merovignians held these secrets and had certain knowledge. As the Vatican wanted this knowledge, they targeted the Cathars of France for elimination. Their alleged heresy was a smaller factor than was the acquisition of their maps. These issues were also a part of the political rationale behind the Council of Nicea and their imperious decisions.

One of the earlier bearers of this knowledge was Prince Madoc, the brother of the real King Arthur. They lived at the beginning of the 6th Century and both were knights under their father, Meurig, a name which means "King of the Moors." In Welsh, it means "black." Arthur succeeded Meurig as king, but Prince Madoc had a colorful life, too. He travelled to America and inspired the name of that continent.*

Prince Madoc is known by historians to have come from Wales, but he is also known to have been inextricably linked to Egypt and America as well. Wales was known as Khemet North to ancient peoples. Khemet is, of course, the ancient name for Egypt. To the Indians, Madoc was known as Montauk or Montauk Pharaoh. Montauk and Madoc are transliterations of each other. To the natives, *Montauk* means "the highest expression of divinity."

The greatest secret of Montauk is that Madoc not only carried the royal lineage of the Egyptian Pharaoh but also that of the Christ. This was the significance of the Pharaoh. They were one and the same. It is also why they used someone of the Cameron lineage in the time experiments at Montauk. This divine lineage was the secret tradition of who should be the true "surveyor" or "overseer" but impostors have assumed the throne and carry emblems and regalia of the true heirs. This is who the Pharaoh actually is meant to be: the representative that stands between the heaven and the Earth.

The implications of what I have written here are not only fantastic and complex, they are a guideline to assist you with your future mission as delineated by General Wilson.

One thread I should share with you is that Prince Madoc not only took trips to South America (the Orinoco River in Venezuela is named after his gold exploits, *oro* meaning "gold"

---

* The word *America* can be derived from *Emir* or *Amir* (an Arabic word for "prince") + *ika* or *ica* (another word for "land.") In this sense, America is the "land of the Emir or Prince (Madoc)." *Amir* is also the same as "the Moor" and you see this in the namesake of Morocco which is "the land of the Moors." *America* is also believed to have derived from "Al Maurikanos," i.e. "El Morrocco" or the "Land of the Moors;" but it is also "The Land of the Prince "Madoc." Both are one and the same.

in Spanish) as well as up the Mississippi. His party reached as far as the caverns of Utah and the Great Salt Lake. The path of the Mormons is key here. Note that Joseph Smith's closest disciples, based upon his direct instructions, followed the path of the Montauk Indians and went to Wisconsin. It was Brigham Young, a Freemason, who altered the directives of Joseph Smith and took the majority of his brethren to what became Salt Lake City. It was in this locale that they enlisted the Ute Indians to help them find many treasures of old. There are still many Egyptian and Templar tombs and temples to be found in Utah to this day.

What we are coming to now is one of the most pivotal times in history. It applies to both your world and to mine. It is known as the Second Coming of the Pharaohs. So much of it centers upon Montauk Point and the Egyptian heritage which not only passed through that sacred location but extended into the center of America as well.

What George Washington knew in this regard was substantial. It is now time to put into perspective what I said about him earlier. Washington carried the magical energy of Aiwass, their names being virtually identical. One of his early initiations, under the tutelage of Baron Cameron and his agents, was the surveying and construction of the city of Alexandria, Virginia. This city was named for the Egyptian city of the same name, the very place where Rudolph Hess grew up. This was also the home of the famous Lighthouse of Pharos. Standing at the gateway to the Nile, Alexandria was the home of the greatest library the world has ever known. The vast number of scrolls were distributed amongst different locations, but the most valued manuscripts were secreted in hidden catacombs beneath the Lighthouse of Pharos. These included the maps I have referred to. The city of Alexandria, Virginia was built in the tradition of the great Egyptian city.

Compared to the Lighthouse of Alexandria, only a fraction of ancient knowledge was stored at the Masonic Lodge in Washington's Alexandria. Considerable in its import and potential, this knowledge was not all stored in one place.

While much negativity has been circulated about the Freemasons, some of it well deserved, one has to remember that they are (in their own image) keepers of sacred wisdom. They stand at the gateway to exalted knowledge that is deemed only accessible to the worthy. If they act like demons or gargoyles, understand that this is the function that they serve. Like a computer security code, most are unconscious of the data they unleash. This is why the Lighthouse of Pharos held the most sacred knowledge. It shines the secret light. The treasure maps I referred to earlier were hidden at Pharos, all in the tradition of the secret knowledge of the Pharaohs.

Did you ever notice what happened historically when the remnants of the Library of Alexandria were transferred to Timbuktu? The migration of knowledge from Pharos resulted in Timbuktu becoming one of the greatest gold exchanges in history. The gold follows the migration of the Pharaohs and vice versa.

You will now better understand the tradition that George Washington embraced when he established the lighthouse at Montauk, an act that occurred rather late in his life. Montauk, however, is not only a key spot with regard to the Egyptian mysteries but also to those of Atlantis. It was not only once connected to Egypt but it was a major point of attraction in Atlantean times. The mysteries, however, do not end here. You, my friends, are only at the beginning.

It is thus that the magic of Aiwass, through the blood of Egypt, has served as the enabling factor in world leadership, all couched in hidden symbols of Egyptian occultism which includes the Washington Monument as well. It is for this reason that most of your presidents have carried the bloodline of the Montauk Pharaohs. From Washington onward, each president became a bearer of the duties of Aiwass or the Eye in the Triangle. They are gate-keepers or watchers. Aiwass reigns supreme. While it might seem a daunting task to deal with this fact, do keep in mind that all of this represents a gateway, not a lord to be worshipped. Did you know that *Mikado*, the Japanese word for emperor, means gate-keeper? Once you understand enough to see the key, you can open the door.

So it was that the blood and magic of ancient Khemet was inculcated into the blood of the Welsh Prince Madoc and into the blood of the Montauk Indians. The Latter Day Saints have dutifully kept track of this bloodline, and it has been one of their most cherished secrets. That the Montauk Indians have been declared extinct is only one testament to this bizarre fact. They possess the blood of the gate-keeper.

It is important to remember these things as you negotiate your way through the mysterious path you have chosen. Never lose sight of who is really running your country as opposed to the man behind the curtain. It is a jinn and one named Aiwass. America will always be the land of the Moors, and it cannot be truly negotiated without paying homage to the truth.

I hope, my friends, that you find what I have said helpful, and I wish you nothing but the best in your adventures. Do remember what I said about beginning your journey at the Montauk Lighthouse. It is important.

As one more reminder, the etymology of pharaoh is relevant in regards to the lighthouse. The word *pharaoh* is commonly thought to mean 'great house.' While this is not totally incorrect, it can be misleading. The ancient Egyptian word for 'house' was pa'ar or p'r and this can also be seen in the word *pyre* (meaning fire or light) which is the essence of the word *pyramid*. Tahuti, the builder of the Great Pyramid, was known as the dweller on the threshold (between the two worlds). A light is the same as a fire, and one's dwelling or house was where one kept a fire or light. This can also be seen in the teepees of the plains Indians. The pyramid was not only Tahuti's dwelling but also that of the Pharaoh. The words *pyr* or *pa'ar* equate to *phar* as in *pharaoh*; thus *pharaoh* can be easily construed as 'great light.' The lighthouse at Alexandria, which was lit by fire, represented this great light, but it no longer stands. It has moved to Montauk but, in the tradition of obeah, it is a secret light. Go, my friends, and find the secret and may the world renew itself as a great phoenix.

Yours truly,
Ali Bey

P.S. I forgot to mention something. You might find it relevant, but also quite amusing, that the current curator of the Giza Plateau in Egypt is named Zahi Hawass. His surname is a virtual duplicate of Aiwass. If you adventures take you to Egypt, do keep this in mind. You will be dealing with a real live gatekeeper."

.........BY PETER MOON.........

## AUTHOR'S NOTE

The writing of *Spandau Mystery* interrupted what was to be my next book, *The Montauk Book of the Living*. In the process of writing *Spandau*, I ended up meeting and having different adventures with Artie Crippen, the Montauk Medicine Man. This not only deeply influenced the information in *Spandau*, but it will enable *The Montauk Book of the Living* to be as comprehensive as possible. My meeting with Artie, however, has impelled me to write yet another prequel to *The Montauk Book of the Living*, the working title of which is *Medicine of Montauk*. That book will include the oral history of the Montauks as told through their medicine man. It will include aspects which are touched on in *Spandau* as well.

There are many other books I hope to write as well, but the writing of *Spandau Mystery* has added considerably to the blend. By that, I am referring to the many threads in the story that were left untapped. Originally, I had hoped to include many or most of them in the narrative but the length of the drama that unfolded precluded that.

There are perhaps as many as nine sequels which could be written as a follow-up to *Spandau*. These could include, but are not limited to: the adventures of Gretchen as she travels to South Africa and penetrates the Nazi haven in the Antarctic; the Tibetan connection, especially as it relates to the Russians and The Man with Green Gloves; Karl Wiligut and his influence upon S.S. officer Otto Rahn, the archaeologist who sought, and some say found, the Holy Grail; the full aspect of "Little People" and their connections to various aspects of the story; the Mormons and their connections to the Montauks, Little People and Salt Lake City; the secret history of George Washington, Freemasonry and the Moors; and the final construction of the Washington Monument by Albert Pike and the latter's association with the Vatican, John Wilkes Booth and Abraham Lincoln's assassination.

My newsletter, the *Montauk Pulse*, will give updates on what is coming next and when.

*Peter Moon*
Long Island, 2007

## THE BIGGEST SECRET EVER TOLD

*The Montauk Project: Experiments In Time* chronicles forty years of research starting with the "Philadelphia Experiment" of 1943 when the Navy attempted to make a destroyer escort invisible to radar only to have it teleport out of this reality with accompanying psychological disorders and physical trauma to the crew. Forty years of massive research ensued culminating in bizarre experiments at Montauk Point, New York that actually tapped the powers of creation and manipulated time itself. *The Montauk Project* is a first hand account by Preston Nichols, a technician who worked on the project and has survived threats on his life and attempts to brainwash his memory of what occurred.
160 pages, illustrations, photos and diagrams.........$15.95

## THE ASTONISHING SEQUEL

*Montauk Revisited: Adventures in Synchro- nicity* pursues the mysteries of time so intriguingly brought to light in *The Montauk Project and* unmasks the occult forces behind the science and technology used in the *Montauk Project*. An ornate tapestry is revealed which interweaves the mysterious associations of the Cameron clan with the genesis of American rocketry and the magick of Aleister Crowley and Jack Parsons. *Montauk Revisited* carries forward with the Montauk investigation and unleashes a host of incredible characters and new information that reaches far beyond the scope of the first book.
249 pages, illustrations, photos and diagrams.............$19.95

# THE ULTIMATE PROOF

*Pyramids of Montauk: Explorations In Consciousness* awakens the consciousness of humanity to its ancient history and origins through the discovery of pyramids at Montauk and their placement on sacred Native American ground leading to an unprecedented investigation of the mystery schools of Earth and their connection to Egypt, Atlantis, Mars and the star Sirius. An astonishing sequel to the *Montauk Project* and *Montauk Revisited*, this chapter of the legend propels us far beyond the adventures of the first two books and stirs the quest for future reality and the end of time as we know it.
256 pages, illustrations, photos and diagrams.............$19.95

# THE BLACK SUN

*In* this spectacular addition to the Montauk series, *The Black Sun* continues the intriguing revelations readers have come to expect revealing Montauk's Nazi connection and a vast array of new information. From the German flying saucer program to the SS Tibet mission, we are led on a path that gives us the most insightful look ever into the Third Reich and their ultimate quest: the Ark of the Covenant and the Holy Grail. Going beyond *The Spear of Destiny* and other attempts to unlock the mysterious occultism of the Nazis, Peter Moon peers into the lab of the ancient alchemists in order to explain the secret meaning behind the Egyptian and Tibetan *"Books of the Dead."*
295 pages, illustrations, photos......................................$19.95

# SYNCHRONICITY AND THE SEVENTH SEAL

## by Peter Moon

This is Peter Moon's consummate work on Synchronicity. Beginning with a brief scientific description (for the layman) of the quantum universe and how the quantum observer (the spirit) can or does experience the principle of synchronicity, we are taught that synchronicity is also an expression of the divine or infinite mind. Besides exploring the concept and influences of parallel universes, this book includes numerous personal experiences of the author which not only forges a pathway of how to experience and appreciate synchronicity, but it goes very deep into the magical exploits of intriguing characters who sought to tap the ultimate powers of creation and use them for better or for worse. This not only includes the most in depth analysis and accurate depiction of the Babalon Working in print but also various antics and breakthroughs of the various players and that which influenced them. These characters include the legacies and personas of Jack Parsons, Marjorie Cameron, L. Ron Hubbard and Aleister Crowley. Peter Moon adds exponential intrigue to the mix by telling us of his personal experiences with these people and their wake which leads to even deeper encounters which penetrates the mysterious legacy of John Dee. Eventually, this pursuit of synchronicities leads Peter Moon to a most intriguing and mysterious encounter with Joseph Matheny, an adept who has not only had similar experiences to Peter, but has his own version of a space-time project known as Ong's Hat. Matheny has not only had incredible synchronicities himself, he created one of the highest forms of artificial intelligence known to man, a computer known as the Metamachine which is designed to precipitate and generate synchronicities. These many synchronicities lead to the books climax, a revelation of the true Seventh Seal. The proof is delivered. No theologian nor anyone has even tried to counter the claim.
*Over 400 pages..............................ISBN 0-9678162-7-0* **$29.95**

# THE MONTAUK BOOK OF THE DEAD

## by Peter Moon

**In 1992,** a new genre of literature was born when Peter Moon collaborated with Preston Nichols to author "The Montauk Project: Experiments in Time," the story of a quantum time travel event demonstrably proven to have affected mass consciousness. To everyone's surprise, the quest to find out more about this quantum event resulted in serendipitous experiences of synchronicity that have not only continued to repeat but have thrust the entire investigation to the threshold of where myth and legend meet reality. The pace of this quest has afforded Peter Moon scant time to answer the many questions that have arisen about his enigmatic background — until now.

**The Montauk Book of the Dead** is a tale of the intrigue and power which hover over the most sacred kernel of our existence: the secrets of life and death. It begins with the personal story of Peter Moon and reveals fascinating details of his years aboard L. Ron Hubbard's mystery ship and gives the most candid and inside look ever at one of the most controversial figures in recent history. This includes how, at age 27, L. Ron Hubbard clinically "died" only to discover that he could "remote view." From this state of consciousness, which would later be called "exterior," he was able to access what he termed the answers to all of the questions that had ever puzzled philosophers or the minds of men. Transcribing this into a work entitled **Excalibur**, still under lock and key to this day, he developed one of the most controversial movements in history: Dianetics and Scientology. The truth and import of the above can only be evaluated by the all out war which was waged by governmental forces and spy agencies to obtain the legally construed rights to this work and all of the developments and techniques that ensued from it. This book will teach you about things you have not even thought about and more than you ever thought possible.

*Over 400 pages......................ISBN 978-0-9678162-3-4* ***$29.95***

# A QUANTUM ADVENTURE

### Ong's Hat: The Beginning
### by Joseph Matheny
### with Peter Moon

**ONG'S HAT: THE BEGINNING** is the story of mysterious legends from an obscure location in South Central New Jersey, historically known as Ong's Hat, which has inspired a counterculture revolution in physics. Beginning with a club house atmosphere of physicists from the Institute for Advanced Study and Princeton University, exotic pursuits in the Many-Worlds Interpretation of quantum mechanics paved the way for avantgarde experiments in quantum consciousness. Integrating procedural meditation with biofeedback and brain machine techniques, synchronicity attractors were developed which sought out tangible states of existence that reached beyond the bounds of the Consciousness Authority we know so well on Earth. Allegedly, the experimenters ultimately achieved success with time travel and the accessing of parallel universes. *192 pages, ISBN 0-9678162-2-X*......................$19.95

# THE MONTAUK PULSE ™

Characterized as a "Chronicle of Time," a newsletter by the name of *The Montauk Pulse* went into print in the winter of 1993 to chronicle the events and discoveries regarding the ongoing investigation of the Montauk Project by Preston Nichols and Peter Moon. It has remained in print and been issued quarterly ever since. With a minimum of six pages and a distinct identity of its own, the *Pulse* will often comment on details and history that do not necessarily find their way into books. The *Pulse* is interested in and covers quantum phenomena that is pertinent to the understanding of the predicament of time. Subscribing to *The Pulse* directly contributes to the efforts of the authors in writing more books and chronicling the effort to understand time and all of its components. Past support has been crucial to what has developed thus far. We appreciate your support in helping to unravel various mysteries of Earth-based and non-Earth-based consciousness. It makes a difference............*$15.00 annually*

# SkyBooks ORDER FORM

We wait for ALL checks to clear before shipping. This includes Priority Mail orders. If you want to speed delivery time, please send a U.S. Money Order or use MasterCard or Visa. Those orders will be shipped right away.
Complete this order form and send with payment or credit card information to:
Sky Books, Box 769, Westbury, New York 11590-0104

| Name |
| --- |
| Address |
| City |
| State / Country        Zip |
| Daytime Phone (In case we have a question) (     ) |

☐ This is my first order   ☐ I have ordered before   ☐ This is a new address

Method of Payment:   ☐ Visa   ☐ MasterCard   ☐ Money Order   ☐ Check

#  ___  ___  ___

Expiration Date        Signature

| Title | Qty | Price |
| --- | --- | --- |
| The Montauk Pulse (1 year subscription).................$15.00 | | |
| | | |
| | | |
| | | |
| | | |
| | | |
| | | |
| | | |
| | | |
| | | |
| | | |
| | | |
| Subtotal | | |
| For delivery in NY add 8.625% tax | | |
| Shipping: see chart on the next page | | |
| U.S. only: Priority Mail | | |
| Total | | |

Thank you for your order. We appreciate your business.

# SHIPPING INFORMATION

## United States Shipping

Under $30.00 ........ add $4.00
30.01 — 60.00 ... add $5.00
60.00 — $100.00 add $8.00
$100.01 and over .add $10.00

Allow 30 days for delivery. For U.S. only: Priority Mail—add the following to the regular shipping charge: $4.00 for first item, $1.50 for each additional item.

## Outside U.S. Shipping

Under $30.00 ........ add $10.00
$30.01 — $50.00 .. add $15.00
$50.01—$ 75.00 .. add $20.00
$75.01—$100.00 .. add $25.00
100.01 and over ... add $35.00

These rates are for SURFACE SHIPPING ONLY. Do <u>not</u> add extra funds for air mail. Due to the vastly different costs for each country, we will not ship by air. Only Visa, Mastercard or checks drawn on a U.S. bank in U.S. funds will be accepted. (Eurochecks or Postal Money Orders cannot be accepted.)

For a complimentary listing of
special interdimensional books and videos —
send a $1.06 stamp or one dollar to:
Sky Books, Box 769, Westbury, NY 11590-0104

## *FUTURE BOOKS*

# Medicine of Montauk
### by Peter Moon and Artie Crippen

# The Montauk Book of the Living
### by Peter Moon